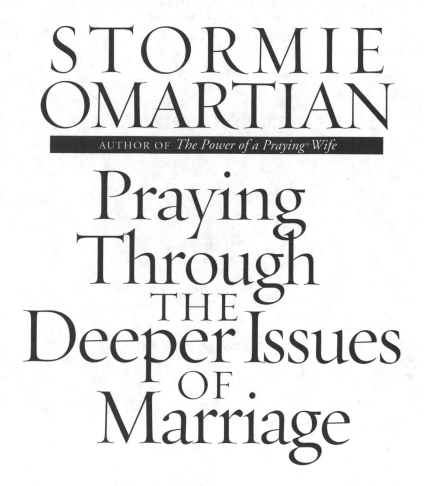

STORMIE OMARTIAN

AUTHOR OF *The Power of a Praying® Wife*

Praying Through THE Deeper Issues OF Marriage

HARVEST HOUSE PUBLISHERS

EUGENE, OREGON

Cover by Koechel Peterson & Associates, Inc., Minneapolis, Minnesota

Cover photo © Fjvsoares / Dreamstime.com

Back cover author photo © Michael Gomez Photography

PRAYING THROUGH THE DEEPER ISSUES OF MARRIAGE
Copyright © 2007 by Stormie Omartian
Published by Harvest House Publishers
Eugene, Oregon 97402
www.harvesthousepublishers.com

Library of Congress Cataloging-in-Publication Data
  Omartian, Stormie.
  Praying through the deeper issues of marriage / Stormie Omartian.
    p. cm.

Hardcover Edition	International Edition
ISBN-13: 978-0-7369-2005-6	ISBN-13: 978-0-7369-2042-1
ISBN-10: 0-7369-2005-6	ISBN-10: 0-7369-2042-0

  1. Married people—Religious life. 2. Marriage—Religious aspects—Christianity. 3. Prayer—Christianity. I. Title.
  BV4596.M3O43 2007
  248.8'44—dc22

2007020531

Printed in the United States of America

07 08 09 10 11 12 13 14 15 / LB-SK / 12 11 10 9 8 7 6 5 4 3 2 1

CONTENTS

*With God's power working in us,
God can do much, much more than
anything we can ask or imagine.*

EPHESIANS 3:20 NCV

What Are the Deeper Issues and How Can I Avoid Them?

———— ✦ ————

You may be thinking, *Who, me? I don't have any issues. I don't see any of the 14 areas of prayer focus listed on the Contents page as being a problem in my marriage. Except…well…maybe one…or two…or more…but they are my husband's (wife's) problem, not mine.*

But please hear me out on this, because I believe that every married person will have to make a decision at some point in their lives on *each one* of these 14 areas as to whether they will *allow* them to *become* issues in their marriage or not. Just because they aren't a problem now doesn't mean they won't be in the future. In fact, these major concerns are traps that are easier to fall into than we might think, as recent statistics prove, suggesting that soon nearly half of all marriages will end in divorce. The common reasons given for these divorces are often found in this list of 14 potential problem areas.

This means that every marriage has a fifty-fifty chance of making it. Of course, there are exceptions. I'm sure there must be some couples who have never had a problem and their marriages have always been perfect. I have never met any of them, but they must be out there. And there are newly married couples for whom the glow has not worn off and reality has not set in, and they have not yet experienced the stresses, losses, and trials of life that can put a strain on any marriage. But this book is for them as well as those who have struggled. In fact, this book is for all of us who are married. Because it is not only about praying *through* struggles to find healing and restoration; it is also about praying to *prevent* these struggles from ever developing into anything serious in the first place.

Thanks to countless letters, emails, phone calls, and contacts on my website, thousands of couples have told me about the problems they are facing in their marriages. Add to that the experiences I've had in my own marriage, and I have what I believe to be the 14 most common problems that lead to divorce. If we can conquer these, we will have divorce-proof marriages. But God has more for us in our marriages than just avoiding divorce. He wants us to be happy and fulfilled in them too. He is not glorified when we are married and miserable. He has a great purpose for each marriage, but His purpose can't be fully realized if the people in them are living in strife.

You would be surprised if you knew how many people there are who *appear* to have perfect marriages and yet are struggling with serious problems. Even the friends and family around them would never suspect they are having difficulties because of their ability to cover them up and present an amazingly strong front. Many people believe they can gut it out and live with the situation, but too often that proves unbearable. This is especially true as people get older and realize that nothing is changing in their marriage and they can't live as they have been for the rest of their lives.

I am thoroughly convinced that all of these problems could be avoided if we would truly understand what God wants for our marriages and how the enemy of our soul will always try to thwart that. And we help him by playing into his hand. But there is a way to hasten the demise of the enemy's plans and see God's plans for our marriages prevail.

If your marriage has already been challenged in any number of ways, the good news is that God has a plan to restore it to the way He intended it to be. And He wants you to partner with Him in order to see that happen. The way you do it is to live God's way and be in prayer every day for your mate and your marriage.

I know this works because my husband and I have at one time or another struggled with most of these issues ourselves. We have had times of communication breakdown between us that were so bad we didn't speak to each other for days, and then we only spoke what was absolutely necessary and nothing that bordered on real communication for months. My husband's anger and my supersensitive reaction to it nearly caused our marriage to be one of the 50 percent that didn't make it. We've had our seasons of unforgiveness, and we've both struggled with negative emotions such as depression, anxiety, and fear that permeated the atmosphere of our home. There have been seasons when we were so occupied with raising children that we completely forgot about us. We've had times of financial difficulty and disagreements over it. We've experienced a hardening of our hearts toward one another, and occasions when we each felt as though we were very low on the other's priority list. We have actually used the "D" word, threatening to get a divorce, even though neither of us really wanted that. I have personally felt at times that all hope was lost and we needed a miracle. And it was true, because outside of the Lord there was no hope. It took a miracle of God to turn things around. I saw God do a miracle by changing our hearts and teaching us to move into the wholeness He has for us.

How Our Past Affects the Present

The reason I was so sensitive to my husband's anger was because I was raised by a mentally ill mother who was angry about everything. She was angry because she thought her father—my grandfather—loved her older and younger sisters more than he loved her. She thought this because when she was 11, *her* mother died suddenly and tragically in childbirth and her father wasn't able to care for his three daughters. My mother had to live with other families, and she felt rejected because of it. This happened during the Depression when times were hard and money was scarce. People were just trying to cope with their own problems and didn't have the time, resources, or knowledge necessary to help a young child cope with hers.

When my mother was 19, she had rheumatic fever, and her mental illness manifested with anger and delusions after that. She became angry at people she thought were following her and trying to kill her. She could seem normal one minute and crazy the next. She was adept at hiding her dark side when she needed to, but she couldn't keep up the facade for long. Her illness always came out, usually when someone powerless and vulnerable was with her.

When my dad married her, he thought she was normal. That is, until they were driving to their honeymoon destination and she made him bypass the hotel where they were supposed to stay because she thought people were following her there to kill her. After driving to and fleeing from two more hotels in the same manner, my dad finally put his foot down. Upon arriving at the fourth hotel, he said, "This is enough. We're staying here." He was in love with her, and it seemed as though he was willing to put up with anything to be married to her.

My mother was beautiful. Everyone said she looked like Vivian Leigh in *Gone with the Wind*. I looked like my dad. In fact, when people would say, "Your mother looks like Vivian Leigh and you look like your dad," I felt hurt. I took it to mean that I resembled a guy instead of a girl. Once I became an adult and my friends had children who looked like their fathers, I realized it didn't mean that at all. So I suffered all those years for nothing. Anyway, I got her good eyes and teeth, and for that I am grateful.

My mother was always angry at my dad because he could never *do* enough, *be* enough, or *give* enough to suit her. And she took all this anger out on me when he was gone. We lived on an isolated ranch in Wyoming, miles from town and the nearest neighbor. My dad was gone a lot out in the fields rounding up and feeding cattle; mending fences; planting, irrigating, and harvesting crops; and working at a logging mill for extra money. Life on a ranch with no one to help is beyond a full-time job. It is many hard and burdensome jobs. When he was gone, my mother kept me locked in a small closet underneath the stairs where the basket of laundry was kept. I was safe in the closet from her physical abuse for a while, but other terrors lurked there. It was pitch-black inside except for a tiny ray of light coming from underneath the door. I always kept my legs pulled up into the basket so that any rats or mice claiming this closet as their home would not be able to touch me. I had once discovered a big snake coiled up in the house and that memory never left me. My dad killed the snake, but meeting that snake's mother in the closet was always an imminent possibility in my mind. I was terrified.

Once we moved from that ranch I was not locked in the closet anymore, but my mother became more and more physically and verbally abusive. I never knew when she would slap me hard across the face. That was her favorite thing to do, and it seemed to give her joy and satisfaction. I feel now that every time she did it, she was getting even with the mother and father who abandoned her, the family she lived with whom she thought didn't want her, and the God who never rescued her from the people she believed were trying to kill her.

By the time I was in my teens I knew she was mentally ill, but I often wondered to myself, *What if she is really telling the truth? What if Frank Sinatra and the pope had actually hired the mob to kill her like she said?* For a while I watched carefully to see if I could identify any of the shadowy figures she said were behind her everywhere she went, but as hard as I tried I never did see even one suspicious thing. When she started using foul language at the people she thought were watching her through the mirrors and TV, I could no longer even give her the benefit of the doubt. Many times when she was out in public—at the grocery store, for example—she would suddenly turn on some innocent person and verbally attack them, saying loudly that she knew what they were up to, she knew they were following her and trying to kill her, and she was going to report this to the police. If I was with her at those times, I quickly walked the other way and pretended I didn't know her. I didn't dare look at the faces of the people she was attacking to see how they were taking it. I can only imagine their fright as she could become quite scary.

As a result of living with her, I grew up with fear, anxiety, depression, hopelessness, loneliness, and a deep sadness in my heart that never went away. I never felt as though I were a part of anything or anyone. I needed acceptance and love, and I looked for both wherever and however I could find them. I tried everything to get rid of the pain I felt inside. I tried Eastern religions and occult practices, always attempting to find some kind of purpose and meaning for my life. I looked for love in all the wrong faces and became more and more depressed with the failure of each relationship.

In my twenties I found great work in television as a singer/dancer/actress, and drugs and alcohol were everywhere. I only took them when I wasn't working because I was too professional to do anything stupid enough to jeopardize my jobs. But a few times I way overdid the drugs and came dangerously close to accidentally killing myself.

When I was 28, my friend Terry, with whom I had been working a lot on recording sessions and television shows, took me to meet her pastor—Pastor Jack Hayford at The Church on the Way in California. He talked to me about Jesus in a way I had never heard before. He told me God had a purpose for my life, but I would never realize that purpose outside of the power of the

Holy Spirit, who would live in me if I received Jesus as my Lord. He gave me three books to take home and read, one of which was the Gospel of John in a small book form, and I read them in the days following our meeting. Terry took me back to see Pastor Jack the following week, and I received the Lord in his office. That's when I began to see the plan God had for my life, and my years of purposelessness finally came to an end.

I had met a young man named Michael Omartian before I became a believer during a week of recording sessions that Terry and I were both singing on. But I was about to get married to another man who I knew was wrong for me, and I also knew that the marriage wouldn't last two years. But I was in desperate shape and wanted to feel what it was like to belong somewhere to someone, so I went ahead and married him. As it turned out, it felt like hell because it was the wrong place with the wrong person.

Amazingly, I saw Michael Omartian again in church a couple years later after that first marriage had ended. We started attending church together and dated about a year before we were married. During that time I prayed and prayed for God to show me if Michael was the one I should marry, and every time I did that I felt the peace of God assuring me that this was His will. I kept releasing Michael to the Lord, saying, "God, take him out of my life and close the door if we are not to be together." And I would have let him go if God had showed me to do so because I was well aware of how I had ruined my life doing things my own way. I wasn't going to trust my judgment now; I wanted only what God wanted. By the time we did get married, I was convinced it was the right thing to do. Because of that certainty, when Michael and I had problems in the years to come, I always remembered the assurance from God that we were supposed to be together.

The Problems Started Right Away

The greatest problem I saw in our marriage was my husband's anger. It was explosive, unpredictable, and always directed at me. Because of my past I was way too sensitive and fragile to take it or deal with it. At first I thought it was all my fault. I thought, *I must be a terrible person to make him so angry at me all the time.* I was trying the best I could, but it wasn't enough. I was already too broken and hurting to be able to stand up to it, or better yet to understand where he was coming from.

After we were married less than a year, I went through major deliverance from fear, depression, and anxiety with the help of a gifted pastor's wife named Mary Anne, who prayed for me. And that helped tremendously. Also, my husband and I went to Christian marriage counselors, and I began to see that Michael's anger was *his* problem, not mine. In fact, one of the marriage counselors we went to at the time said to me, "Michael would have this anger no matter whom he was married to. If he had married someone else, he would have directed his anger at her."

That knowledge helped me to not feel like a failure, but I still couldn't get on top of how beat up I felt when he would attack me with angry words. It was as though my mother were slapping me in the face all over again. It made me feel the same way—small and without value. His anger was like a snake hidden from sight, always coiled and ready to strike when I least expected it. It would become a deep issue that nearly destroyed our marriage.

For a long time I was mad at God for letting me marry someone who was like my mother in any way. I saw no signs whatsoever of Michael's anger before we were married, and I questioned why it was never revealed to me. I did see him battle with depression and feelings of failure, but I had those issues too, and I thought I could help him through them. I thought we would be there for each other. I mistakenly believed that because God had called us to be together that there wouldn't be any problems when we got married.

In Michael's defense, I believe now that his anger came from having dyslexia back in the days when people didn't know what that was. His mother told me she was very hard on him because he struggled so much in school and she thought he was being rebellious. Having been blessed with a dyslexic child myself, I now understand the frustration of the person who has it and the deep feelings of failure they have because they can't learn the same way everyone else does. I also understand it from a parent's perspective. Before the problem is diagnosed, you can't figure out why your child isn't doing as well as they should be doing in school. You know how bright the child is, how creative and gifted, and how amazing their memory is, but when it comes to reading they seem to shut off. They appear rebellious because it seems that they are refusing to do the work, but the truth is they can't. So while I definitely sympathize with what Michael's mother went through, I also felt sorry for Michael. He suffered with tremendously overwhelming feelings of failure and depression because of it.

I believe now that's where his anger came from. He was angry over the frustration of being a creative dyslexic in a rigid and uncreative educational system. He was angry at his mother for often being angry at him for something he couldn't do anything about. And he took his anger out on me.

I'm going to tell you more of our story later in the book, but I want to reveal to you now that it has a good ending. Our marriage has gone through many tough times, but we have been married for more than 34 years. My husband and I have changed a lot for the better, and I will be sharing with you how that happened. I'm not saying we are perfect. Far from it. But we are living proof that if you *want* to, you can change. And if you hang in there and keep praying, you can see things turn around. So if you want to protect your marriage from the things that can destroy it, or you long to restore the damage that has already been done, read on and see how to do it. You can find the success you desire in your marriage if you do things God's way and refuse to give up.

You Can Change and So Can He (She)

We are told over and over, "Don't even try to change your husband (wife) because he (she) will never change." Hearing those dire predictions repeatedly can make you feel hopeless. If your marriage is miserable because of something intolerable your spouse does, and you're told he (she) will never change, then what hope do you have for your future together? Here are five important truths about that from God's perspective.

1. The truth is, everyone needs to change. God says so. In fact, it's His will for our lives that we change because He wants each one of us to become more like Him. And that is a never-ending project, for we all fall far short of the glory of God (Romans 3:21-23). We will always need to submit to Him and not think so highly of ourselves that we feel we don't need to change. God is in the business of changing people. That's why, through our prayers and the power of the Holy Spirit, there is always hope for change.

2. The truth is, every person can change. *You* can change. And *your spouse* can change. Don't let anyone tell you otherwise. It's not that a person *can't* change. It's that they don't *want* to. Or they don't want to make the effort to do anything differently than they always have. Or they don't care to seek God about what changes He would like to see worked in them. Or they are so totally happy with themselves that they don't think they need to change. Never mind that everyone around them does.

People usually don't change because:

1. They aren't aware they need to.
2. They don't believe they have to.
3. They don't want to.
4. They don't know how to.
5. They don't feel they are able to.

3. The truth is, being married creates the perfect opportunity for change. When you are married, you find out how much you need to improve yourself. It is prideful and selfish for anyone to get married and think they are so perfect they don't need to change in any way. Each one of us always needs to change in many ways, some more than others, but God will start with the one who is willing. And the good news is, this is where His blessings will be directed first as well. Remember that both you and your husband (wife) *can* be changed. God is waiting for you to invite Him to do that. Marriage always inspires change.

4. The truth is, people cannot make someone else change. Never is that more true than in a marriage. A wife can't change her husband. A husband can't change his wife. But *God* can change both. We have to learn that it's not *our* job to change our spouse, anyway. It's the work of the Holy Spirit. No amount of criticizing and nagging will accomplish it, no matter how hard we try. God made each of us in *His* image, and He doesn't want us to try and make our spouse over into *our own* image. Our job is to accept our spouse as he (she) is and pray for the Lord to make the necessary changes in him (her). Meanwhile, as He is working on your spouse's heart, God will also be working in yours. In the process of praying for *him* (*her*), God will change *you*.

5. The truth is, only God can work changes in us that last. Only God can transform us. We just have to be willing to say, "Lord, I recognize that I am far from perfect, and I realize I need to be changed in order to become more like You. I know I can't change myself in any lasting way, but You can. Lord, change me into the person You want me to be and show me what I need to do. I praise You and thank You for the transformation You are working in me."

Only God can:

1. Make someone aware they *need* to change.
2. Help someone see they *have* to change.
3. Encourage someone to *want* to change.
4. Show someone *how* to change.
5. Enable someone to *make* a change.

What Are "Issues," Exactly?

Every marriage has issues. Every marriage has difficult times of negotiating and compromising that, if not handled carefully, can allow a wedge to get in between the husband and wife. If not repaired, this division can grow with each new unresolved problem and eventually become a *great divide*. Issues that are allowed to grow deep can completely break a marriage apart. And it can happen so stealthily that you don't even see it coming until one day you wake up and wonder how you let it get this far. And then you don't know what to do to stop the divide from widening. You don't see how you can ever bring it all back together again because the damage seems irreparable. But in the Lord nothing is irreparable. And every division can be eliminated. It just takes knowing what you're dealing with.

First of all, it helps to understand exactly what the issues are. Knowing the definition of "issues" makes resolving them seem more reasonable and attainable. It keeps us from being overwhelmed by the emotions and reactions they bring up. An *issue* is *a point that is disputed*. It is *a matter that has to be decided*. It is *a question that has to be answered* in a way that is acceptable to both parties. Having an *issue* means you have *entered into a disagreement or a conflict* over something. It is *a particular point that you do not agree upon*.

To take issue with your spouse means to have a difference of opinion with him (her). It means the two of you are at variance over something, and it's causing you to enter into arguments, disagreements, or conflicts over it. For example, if a husband drinks alcohol from time to time and his wife doesn't think it's the right thing to do, then this is something they don't fully agree on. They have a difference of opinion. They have a point that needs to be decided. If the wife confronts her husband about this and asks him to stop and he continues to drink anyway, knowing that his wife does not approve of it, then this problem has not been decided in a way that is acceptable to both of them, and so it becomes an issue. It makes the wife feel that her husband doesn't care enough about her to stop doing something that deeply bothers her. It becomes a point of contention that can turn into a deal breaker with regard to their marriage.

The wife can do one of four things:

1. She can negotiate. She can resolve the issue with some kind of compromise, such as agreeing that he can have a glass of wine with dinner. But this compromise may not be enough to satisfy her if any kind of drinking is against her religious beliefs.

2. She can choose to be silent and not press the issue. However, she may become resentful over time, especially if his drinking begins to affect his performance, such as his ability to walk, talk, drive, work, or be a kind, decent, and productive human being.

3. She can enter into conflict with him. This means having unpleasant disagreements, arguments, or strife, especially if he did things while drinking that made her feel threatened, such as jeopardizing her physical safety, mental stability, or sense of emotional well-being. Or, if he caused her to see her entire life going down the drain and their future being threatened because of it.

4. She can pray for him. She can pray that his eyes will be opened to God's will and perspective, and that God will do whatever it takes to bring about necessary changes in his life.

I'm not picking on the husband here. It's the same when the wife is doing something—or *not* doing something—and the husband objects. It doesn't matter what the issues are; they have to be resolved in a way that is acceptable to *both* husband and wife. If they are not, these disagreements will become deeper and deeper. Every issue in a marriage must be confronted because they usually don't go away on their own without one or both people making a great effort. But there is a powerful way to deal with the issues of marriage that will not only keep them from becoming deeper, but will heal and eliminate them completely.

It Takes Three to Agree

In order for a marriage to not only survive, but also to be fulfilling and successful, there needs to be three parties involved: the husband, the wife, and God. The reason marriages have issues in the first place is because every married couple is made up of two *imperfect people*. One imperfect human plus another imperfect human equals one *imperfect marriage*. However, if you add the presence of a *perfect God* into this imperfect mix of two imperfect people, you then have unlimited possibilities for growing closer to the perfection God intended for the marriage relationship. Whether that happens or not is determined by how frequently and fervently God is invited to reign in the hearts of both the husband and wife. It has to do with being willing to have three agree.

You and your spouse can agree about something, but it can still be an issue if *God* doesn't agree with it. For example, if your spouse wants you to view a film that has sexually explicit scenes in it and you agree to it, this is a compromise you have *both* chosen, but it doesn't agree with *God's Word*. Therefore, *God doesn't agree* with it. The two of you may be fine with it, but it offends God and violates His laws. If it is a point of contention with God, it will always be an issue in your lives together. It will inhibit all that God wants to do in each of you and in your marriage. You may agree on something together, but if it doesn't agree with God, it will open the door for problems that will undermine your marriage.

There are consequences for violating any law of God—whether ignorantly or knowingly. Some people think that God's laws don't apply to them, but that doesn't make the consequences for violating them any less destructive. They may believe they are innocent of any violation, but God doesn't see it that way. It's like the law of gravity. You can jump out a tenth-story window and deny the law of gravity all the way down, but the consequences are still going to be the same when you hit the ground. God's laws are for our benefit. Life works better for us when we live by them.

SIXTEEN WAYS TO DESTROY YOUR MARRIAGE

1. Stop communicating openly and honestly.
2. Be consistently angry, selfish, rude, and abusive.
3. Refuse to forgive your spouse for any offense, no matter how small.

4. Stay depressed and negative as much as possible.

5. Convince your spouse that your children are far more important to you than he (she) is.

6. Be consistently lazy and refuse to do much around the house or on your job.

7. Spend money foolishly and continually run up great debt.

8. Give place to addictions or annoying habits and defend your right to have them.

9. Don't care about what your spouse needs sexually as long as you get what you want.

10. Habitually look at explicit films, magazines, or advertising and compare your husband (wife) to the glorified images you see there, and especially mention others whom you find more attractive.

11. Allow your heart to grow hard toward your husband (wife) and refuse to ever say "I'm sorry," "Forgive me," or "I forgive you."

12. Make something other than God and your spouse your top priority.

13. Threaten to get a divorce every time something comes up between you and your spouse that needs to be worked out.

14. Have an affair or entertain an obsession of the heart over someone other than your husband (wife).

15. Move out of the home and don't try to reconcile your differences.

16. Give up and refuse to believe that God is a God of miracles who can restore love and hope.

It Can Happen to Anyone

Each of the above 16 ways to destroy a marriage can start as something small and turn into something big overnight, even in the best of relationships. You may have an idyllic marriage with the most perfect of mates and you may be close to perfection yourself, but so were Adam and Eve, and look what happened to them. I know a number of women—and men as well—who thought they had it all together in their marriage and didn't need to ask God to change their heart so they could be a better marriage partner. They didn't learn to intercede for their spouse. Sadly, they are all divorced now. In each case, their spouse left them. They neglected to take the necessary steps to prevent it, and they refused to do what was required to repair the damage.

Don't buy into the dangerous belief that you are immune to such problems in your marriage. Too many people have thought that and ended in divorce court. Or equally as bad, they have allowed their marriage to be filled with so much strife and unforgiveness that it became miserable, lifeless, and dead. They lost sight of the purpose God had for them in being married in the first place. And make no mistake, He does have a great purpose for your marriage.

Today there is an epidemic of despair, hopelessness, and pain because of marriages in crisis. There is no greater torment, outside of the death of a loved one, than that which is suffered when a marriage relationship has broken down. The sense of failure, guilt, sadness, and heartbreak over a divorce is unbearable. And staying in a miserable marriage is intolerable. Either choice is heartbreaking.

However, just like the *problem* can happen to *anyone,* so can the *solution* to it. I'm not going to tell you that the solution I have written about in this book is easy, but it's *doable.* And not just for the deeply spiritual and highly disciplined. It's doable for *everyone.* If *I* can do it, *you* can do it. *The reason it's doable* is because it is God's way and He will help you accomplish it if your heart is willing. *The reason it's not easy,* however, is because of this one thing—*the condition of our own heart has to be right,* and changing that can often seem impossible. It's hard to take our blinders off when we've grown so used to them that we don't even know they are there. Deeper issues develop in the heart first, so that is where we have to go to find the root of the problem, and that is where the healing begins.

God Has Given You Authority

God is sovereign. And He has sovereignly declared that He will not work independently of us in our lives. He's not going to just fix things for us without any input on our part. He wants to work through anyone who will move in the authority He has given us in prayer. Without us praying, He *won't* do it. Without His help and power, we *can't* do it.

Let's get some basic facts straight. If you believe Jesus Christ is the Son of God and you have invited Him into your life to rule there, then you are a child of God. That makes you the son or daughter of a King. You were born again into royalty. And you are destined to reign over the forces of evil. God has "delivered us from the power of darkness and conveyed us into the kingdom of the Son of His love" (Colossians 1:13).

Knowing Jesus and being God's child is where our authority in prayer begins. Praying is putting our authority into action. Satan has the power to destroy us, but we have been given authority over him. "Behold, I give you the authority to trample on *serpents* and *scorpions, and over all the power of the enemy,* and nothing shall by any means hurt you" (Luke 10:19, emphasis added).

As I mentioned earlier, I was raised in the wild lands of Wyoming, and I have had way more experience with snakes than I ever wanted. When I think of how many times I came close to rattlesnakes coiled and ready to strike—I have been just inches away a few times—it's a miracle I have never been bitten by one. Snakes slither silently in, and you don't realize they are there until suddenly you are upon them and they startle you. Scorpions are known for their sudden, painful, and venomous sting. If you would think of all the threats to your marriage as being like snakes and scorpions, it will help you to see their potential for pain and destruction. Whether it is something dangerous that sneaks silently into your marriage unnoticed at first, or something small but deadly that rises up and stabs you when you least expect it, leaving you wounded and poisoned, God will help you to face the enemy with courage. He will work His power through you so you can exercise your authority over the enemy through prayer in Jesus' name.

God has given us *free choice* concerning who we will allow to have authority in our lives. Will we respect God's authority, or will we give it to Satan? When we choose Jesus, He gives us authority over all situations in our lives. But if we don't submit to Him in obedience to His ways, in reverence for who He is and what He accomplished on the cross, we will not be able to move in the authority He paid for with His life. The only way to move into all God has for us is to be totally submitted to the authority of Jesus in our lives. We have *authority* over the enemy because of what Jesus did on the cross. When we learn to use our authority over the enemy in Jesus' name, incredible things happen in our lives and in our marriages.

In a powerful book about the authority we have in prayer, Dutch Sheets writes, "...strictly speaking, authority and power are not the same. Power is the 'strength or force' needed to rule; authority is the 'right' to do so. They are governmental twins and must operate in tandem; authority without power to enforce it is meaningless; power exercised without authority—the right to use that power—is usurpation and is morally wrong."* God not only gives us His *power* in prayer, He gives us *authority* as well.

Taking Authority over Your World

The best place to start taking authority over your world and your life is by praying regularly for your husband (wife) and for your marriage. Your prayers for your husband (wife) have great power in the spirit realm. The same enemy of your soul who wants to see *you* destroyed also wants to see *your marriage* destroyed. If you don't realize that, you will end up thinking that your spouse is the enemy and your fight is with him (her). While it's true he (she) may be *acting* like the devil sometimes, he (she) is not the enemy. Jesus won the victory over death and hell, so if you are living in hell in your marriage relationship, you have not yet moved into the victory God has for you.

Whenever you find yourself in a tough situation in your life or in your marriage, take authority over it with prayer in Jesus' name. Then praise God for the victory He has already won on your behalf. Thank Him that He has a way out of any situation, even when it appears completely hopeless.

When you pray with God-given authority, it releases the power of God to work in both of your lives. You can't necessarily change the strong will of your spouse, but when you pray for him (her), you invite God to create an atmosphere in the spirit realm around him (her) that helps him (her) to better see the truth.

Becoming More Than a Conqueror

God never said we wouldn't have problems. He said we *will*. We can count on it. And when you are married you will not only have *your* problems;

---

* Dutch Sheets, *Authority in Prayer: Praying with Power and Purpose* (Bloomington, MN: Bethany House Publishers, 2006), p. 20.

you will have your spouse's problems as well. But the good news is that Jesus overcame those problems for us. When we align ourselves with Him in prayer and obedience, He will help us to either rise above our problems or walk through them successfully. He will give you the power to be more than a conqueror (Romans 8:37).

You may be wondering, *How can you be more than a conqueror? Either you conquer or you don't.* But even when one country conquers another, it can still be dealing with constant strife and problems in that conquered country. (You can probably think of at least one example in your lifetime where that has happened in the world.) In reality, to be able to conquer a country *without* strife or problems would take a miracle. In our lives, Jesus has done that miracle. He has already conquered death and hell and has secured the victory over the enemy without strife for us. We have to learn to walk in that victory.

God has a destiny for you and your husband (wife), not only as individuals but also as a couple. Every chapter in this book deals with a trap the enemy has set for you to fall into so that your marriage can be destroyed and you won't reach that destiny. The enemy of your soul and your marriage is also the enemy of your purpose, both individually and together as a couple. Jesus enables you to be more than a conqueror in your life and your marriage. You can not only conquer the territory God has for you, but you can also experience the miracle of peace in the process.

Learning to Pray with Power

I don't want to just talk to you *about* praying for yourself, your husband (wife), and your marriage, I want to teach you *how* to pray in power. I want to inspire you with great hope that things can change. I'm not talking about being religious, saying "church" words, speaking "Christianese," or quoting "catchy phrases" without any power accompanying them. I am talking about praying in a way that will bring results.

I can tell you how to swim, I can describe the water, and I can teach you all the correct moves, but at some point you are going to have to get in the water. Once you get into the stream of God's Spirit flowing through you as you pray, you are going to find yourself not only staying afloat, but also rising to the top of each wave of life that would normally overwhelm you.

One of God's greatest promises says that "all things work together for good to those who love God, to those who are the called according to His purpose" (Romans 8:28). But if you read the verses *before* that promise, you will see that the Bible is talking about prayer. In other words, all things work together for good if we are *praying.* Things are not promised to work out for good automatically. If there have been things in your life you feel did not work out for good, it's possible that somewhere, sometime, the people who should have been praying for you or your situation weren't.

You have the power to control your own destiny. You can choose heaven or hell as your eternal home. You can choose to give God control of your life and let Him move you into the purpose for which He created you. You can choose either to give up on your marriage or stay and fight for it in prayer.

What Jesus accomplished at the cross seems baffling and foolish to someone who has never been born again and had their spiritual blinders removed, but to us who believe, it is the greatest manifestation of God's power. "The message of the cross is foolishness to those who are perishing, but to us who are being saved it is the power of God" (1 Corinthians 1:18). When you invite Jesus into your life, that same power that resurrected Him will manifest and resurrect all the dead areas of your life—including your marriage.

God knows we need that. He knows we can't come up with a foolproof plan that will keep our marriages together. We are way too selfish and blind. We lack wisdom and the spirit of self-sacrifice. "The LORD knows the thoughts of man, that they are futile" (Psalm 94:11). He wants *us* to realize that too. He wants *us* to understand that we can't do it without Him. He wants us to believe that He is greater than any hurricane, flood, or tsunami of circumstances and emotions that would threaten to wash over your relationship.

God is even greater than your husband's anger or your wife's lack of interest in sex. He is greater than your wife's depression or your husband's inability to communicate. He is greater than your unforgiveness or your husband's (wife's) hardness of heart. God is powerful enough to help you get out of debt and free of addictions. He is stronger than your bad habits and weak willpower. He made you to be victorious over all that and more, but you cannot proceed "having a form of godliness but denying its power"

(2 Timothy 3:5). You have to run to the cross with gratefulness for His sacrifice on your behalf and acknowledge God's power in your life.

God had a plan for your life before you were even born. He says it is He "who has saved us and *called us with a holy calling,* not according to our works, but *according to His own purpose* and grace which was given to us in Christ Jesus before time began" (2 Timothy 1:9, emphasis added). He called you for a purpose, but He still gives you a choice. You can choose *His* destiny for your life, or you can make your own. Let me give you a tip about this that will save you a lot of time and effort: The life *you try* to make happen will never be as good as the one you *let God* make happen.

What if I Am the Only One Praying?

Your prayers for your marriage have power, even when you are the only one praying. That's because the two of you are one in the eyes of God, and what one does affects the other—either for good or for bad. Of course, the power is even greater when the two of you pray together, but I don't want to belabor that point. If you have a husband (wife) who will pray with you, consider yourself blessed. Most people don't have that.

What if you are the only person in the marriage who is a believer? Or only you are really living God's way? Or only you are willing to submit to God's perfecting process? Or are willing to work on the relationship? What if you understand the enemy's attack on your marriage and your spouse doesn't get it? Can *your* prayers alone save the marriage? I believe they can. In fact, I have heard of miracles in that regard. Don't allow anything other than God to rule in your marriage when you can take authority over it—even by yourself—and expect to see answers to your prayers.

Every marriage has two hearts that need to be changed, issues that need to be dealt with, and two completely different perspectives. In order for two different individuals to truly become one, they have to align themselves with God and each other. You have to be willing to let God transform you into the person He created you to be. Of course, if your husband or wife is sold out to their own selfish desires and determined to rebel against the ways of God, or be abusive enough to destroy the relationship, there is only so much you can do. But if your spouse has any desire at all to preserve the marriage, your prayers can pave the way for God to do miracles.

The good news is that God will still bless *your* life, even if your spouse has to go through some things until he (she) gets it. The problem is that what happens to your spouse happens to you. Everything he (she) does affects you in some way. But when you pray, God can rescue you from any situation—even your spouse's mistakes or sins. You can even be rescued from any negative aspect of your marriage while God works through your prayers to restore it.

Seek Godly Counsel When You Need It

There may be times in your marriage when it seems as though your prayers are not being heard. Or you feel so upset that you can't pray. Or you are at an impasse and unable to get beyond the great disconnect between you and your spouse. Or there is so much hurt and strife between you that you can't even talk. That's when you need the help of a good, godly marriage counselor. And you may need more than one in a lifetime of being married because "in a multitude of counselors there is safety" (Proverbs 24:6).

Keep in mind that any deeper issue can threaten a marriage seriously enough to cause a divorce. That's why I strongly suggest that if even one of the issues addressed in this book is already negatively affecting your marriage to the point where you or your spouse are miserable or are contemplating divorce because of it, find a godly and wise counselor who is willing to work with you both in order to save the marriage. And I say "godly" because not all "Christian counselors" necessarily give godly advice.

My husband and I once sent a Christian couple who are close friends of ours to a Christian counselor we had seen ourselves. This counselor had given us godly counsel at an impasse in our marriage and it helped us tremendously. However, when we sent this couple to him years later, he told them that their problem was so serious that they should get divorced. When the couple told us what happened, we were shocked and greatly disappointed. Fortunately, this couple was committed to staying married and didn't take this counselor's advice. They ended up going to our pastor instead and he helped them recover. This was more than 15 years ago, and their marriage is still going strong to this day. There are many great Christian counselors out there. Ask God to lead you to the right one and keep praying the prayers in this book.

I am aware that the expense of counseling can make you think about it carefully, but the cost of divorce is far greater in the long run. If you absolutely cannot afford even two or three sessions with a professional counselor, ask at your church if there is a person or a couple who are gifted in Christian marriage counseling and who are knowledgeable, mature, trustworthy believers who know that divorce is not the best answer to the deeper issues of marriage and who would be willing to help you save your relationship.

Can Prayer Keep These Things from Happening?

Of course, it would be best to pray about the deeper issues of marriage before any of them ever develop. Or better yet would be to pray about them *before* you walk down the aisle. However, even though it would be wonderful to have all these things resolved *before* you get married, I believe it is actually impossible. That's because you and your spouse have never before lived together as man and wife. And this is true even if you have lived together before marriage. No man or woman truly understands their own limits and capabilities before they have made that public declaration and have entered into this legally binding lifetime commitment. When you do that, you are forced to deal with issues in yourself and in your spouse because they deeply affect your lives together.

We all put our best foot forward when we are dating, but it's impossible to do that every day for the rest of our lives. Everyone has good days and bad days, weaknesses and strengths, times of patience and times of not so much. Everyone has moments when they let words slip out of their mouth that shouldn't have been spoken, and times they should have said or done something and didn't. But marriage provides a base in which you can give one another the security to come face-to-face with who you really are and have the freedom to be set free to heal and grow. That's why praying in advance of these things happening doesn't mean that difficult things won't ever happen, but if something does, you will be able to survive these times successfully, knowing God is using them to perfect both of you.

Remember the Good Times

Where I live in Tennessee, the fall season is exquisite. When the colors change, they are breathtaking shades of red, purple, orange, fuchsia, yellow, and one color that is a combination of coral and magenta that is so beautiful it defies description. It's similar to the most astounding sunset you've ever seen. Sometimes when I am driving in this colorful season, I want to pull over to the side of the road and just breathe in the hues. Standing in the midst of them gives me life.

It is the memory of those beautiful colors of fall that get me through the winter. When everything is dark and gray and stark, I think back to those fall colors and know I will see them again.

That's the way it is in a marriage too. It is the memory of the good times—the colorful and happy times—that can get you through the tough times—the dark and gray seasons. You remember what it *can* be, and that spurs you to not give up. Good memories encourage you to hang on and keep praying.

That being said, there is a surprising beauty about the winter too. It's stark nakedness. It's crisp monotones of black and gray and white. The leaves are off the trees, and the season exposes what is really there. You can see everything that the leaves were covering up before. You notice the bare bones of the supporting structure. That's the way it is in a marriage as well. The tough times expose what you are really made of—what's strong and what is weak. What is good and what isn't. They help you see what's really there. If you go through a season of difficulty and look at it from a perspective of growing deeper, of changing in the ways God wants you to change, of working things out and coming to new conclusions, of new and better compromises between you and your spouse, and of refusing to compromise with the laws of God, then you can always find beauty in the season you're in.

God Has More for You Than You Can Imagine

The thing you have to remember is that God has more for you than you can imagine. I know this is hard to comprehend because we can imagine some amazing things. We can dream big. But even considering your greatest dream for yourself, what God has for you is far greater. The Bible says: "Eye has not seen, nor ear heard, nor have entered into the heart of man the things which God has prepared for those who love Him" (1 Corinthians 2:9). It's true as a married couple too. You may have trouble imagining your marriage being better than your greatest dream for it, but it can be. The reason I know this is true is because it is God's will for your life. It's what He wants for you. I have seen God do miracles in my own marriage and in the lives of countless married couples I have prayed with and heard from over the years. I'm not saying our marriage is perfect, but it's a lot better than I thought it could ever be at this point. And I know it's because of the power of God working through our prayers.

The Cold Hard Facts

Now, you need to be sitting down for this. This may be the part where you throw the book across the room and say, "I'm not doing that," just as some of you did when you read the first chapter of my book *The Power of a Praying Wife,* where I told wives that you have to stop praying the "Change him, Lord" prayer for your husband and start praying "Change me, Lord" instead. Don't blame me for that. It was definitely not my idea. I liked the "Change him, Lord" prayer. Never mind that it wasn't getting answered. Most of us liked that prayer because we didn't think *we* were the ones who needed changing. But God says we *all* need to be changed, and He will start with whoever is *willing* to be changed. So, if you don't like this next part, take it up with God. This is *His* idea, not mine. But at least hear me out on this because it works. Prayer gets answered this way. And what I have learned is that you will have to accept this truth at some point in your life anyway, so you might as well do it now.

Okay. Here it is. Brace yourself.

The bottom line in saving, improving, and enriching your marriage is that you have to *be willing to have a repentant heart.*

Wait! Don't throw the book. I know what you're thinking. You're thinking, *My husband (wife) is the one who really needs to repent, so why should I have to do it? Besides, I'm a good person. I haven't murdered anyone or robbed a bank. Why do I need to repent?* But God says we *all* need to. That's because we all fall far short of what God wants for us in the way we think, act, and live our lives. And for the most part we don't understand the true meaning of having a repentant heart. It doesn't mean you have necessarily done something blatantly bad, although it *can* mean that. Rather, it means you are willing to let God show you where you have not done things perfectly and then respond by prostrating yourself before Him and asking for His forgiveness.

We have to get to the point in our marriage where we live with a repentant heart all the time. A heart that says *I am willing to see my errors, and no matter how I have been offended by the things my spouse has done, I will clean house on my own soul. I will pray to have eyes to see the truth about myself before I pray the same for my husband (wife).*

How often does God want to do amazing things in our lives and our marriages, but because we don't pray with a repentant heart, those things don't happen? God said of Israel that *they* would determine whether He could *bless* them or whether they would receive *curses* instead (Deuteronomy 28, emphasis added). He was ready to bless them, but they didn't listen. Instead, they arrogantly went their own way and chased after idols. We, likewise, determine whether we will have blessings or misery in our marriage by whether we will listen to God or chase after what feels good. Whether we will self-righteously think we don't ever need to repent of anything because we see worse sins in our spouse, or we will bite the bullet and repent of every bad thought or action as we humbly come before God in prayer.

I just heard on the news that more and more married couples are choosing to continue living together after they divorce and lead separate lives. Their reason is that "it's cheaper that way." But I have an idea. Why not do what it takes to stay together and actually learn to love and enjoy one another? It can be done with hearts that are *repentant enough* to be *willing* to let God *change them.* Even if you are the only one with a willing heart, your humble prayers can pave the way for God to do miracles in you and in your marriage relationship. Are you ready to get started?

1

If COMMUNICATION BREAKS DOWN

The most difficult thing about a marriage is that there are *two* people in it. And we all know that the problem is usually with the other person. If we were just trying to work things out by ourselves, we could certainly do a good job of it, but we have to fit our dreams, desires, hopes, abilities, mind-sets, assumptions, needs, and habits in with those of our spouse. And that takes three things: Communication, communication, and communication.

Verbally, emotionally, and physically.

The foundation of a good marriage that will last a lifetime has to be built by communication. It is the way intimacy is established. Anytime communication is shut off, intimacy suffers greatly. And a marriage without intimacy is dying. You and your spouse must each be able to have a sense of closeness in your marriage—an assurance you are on the same team. Without good communication, you won't have that.

The closest relationship you will ever have is with your spouse because you share everything. Not being able to communicate with him (her)—or he (she) not being able to communicate with you—paves the way for an intolerable existence. Not knowing what your spouse is thinking or feeling makes building a life together impossible. If neither of you know what the other's internal plans and visions are for the future, how can you move into it together?

How can you show your commitment to the relationship if you never share that with your spouse? How do you get the sense that you are always going to be there for each other if you don't talk? If you don't express your fears and inner turmoil, how can you receive the encouragement you need? If there isn't good verbal communication, then there isn't an emotional connection, and that means there won't be good physical intimacy, either. That part of your life together will then become an act without feeling or passion. If *one* of you believes that the communication is not good in your relationship, then some changes have to be made.

Time for a Change

Have you ever felt as though your life is stuck in one place? That you cannot move beyond where you are? Things can become that way in a marriage too. You can get into a rut. You can feel stuck in a relationship that isn't growing, isn't getting better, and isn't going anywhere. And only one of you—or perhaps neither of you—is willing to change anything in order to make it better.

God is a God of change. Although *He* is unchanging—*He* is the same yesterday, today, and forever—He doesn't want *us* to be like that. That's because *He* doesn't *need* to change. *We do. He* is *perfect. We're not.* He wants us to always be changing because He desires that we become more and more like Him. If we are resistant to being changed, then we are resistant to God because God is all about changing *us.*

If one or both people in a marriage are resistant to the changing, trans-forming, and perfecting work of the Holy Spirit, then there are certain to be bad habits that develop. Our flesh is like that—it's always headed toward the destructive. The longer these bad habits go on, the more entrenched they become. But the good news is that any stronghold of bad habits can be broken in an instant by the power of God, no matter how long they have been there. Even bad habits with regard to communication in your marriage can be completely eliminated. Anyone can learn to communicate better if they are willing to make the effort.

Marriage is not something you enter into to see what you can get *out* of it. It's something you ask yourself every day what you can put *into* it. Marriage is a covenant relationship, which means it is supposed to be a commitment until death parts us. Unfortunately, too often the *marriage* dies before the *people* in them do. *Getting* married is just the very beginning of your relationship. *Being* married frees you to feel secure enough to let your true self show—for better or for worse—so you can see where you need God's healing and transformation. *Staying* married depends on you both being able to communicate with one another.

The only way you can keep growing together and not apart is by good communication. What other way can love and respect be shown? How else can you really be on the same team? What would happen in a football game if the quarterback never communicated with the rest of the team? It would be a disaster. They would never reach their goal. They would never experience victory. It's the same in a marriage. That's why it is entirely selfish and destructive to refuse to communicate with your spouse for whatever reason.

Right from the Start

From the beginning God had the marriage relationship in mind. Even though Adam was able to communicate with God every day, God saw that this wasn't enough. God said, "It is not good that man should be alone; I will make him a helper comparable to him" (Genesis 2:18). He could have created another man so Adam would have a golfing buddy, but He didn't. He created a woman who was "comparable to him." That means she wasn't merely an airhead with a great body. She *complemented* him. She *helped* him. And he needed her *companionship* and *support*. He needed someone to *communicate* with him on his level. If Adam could have done it all by himself, he wouldn't have needed Eve.

God made Eve from the rib He took out of Adam (Genesis 2:21-22). That means a man will always have something missing without his wife. She completes him. And, likewise, a woman has a natural sense of belonging at a man's side as his support. I've known a number of single men and women for years who are now in their sixties and have never married, and no matter how many friends they had in their life, they still suffered with bouts of severe loneliness. And this only increased with age. I know there are exceptions to that, such as the men and women who have devoted their lives to God's service and because of His grace didn't suffer with that kind of loneliness. But most single people *do* struggle with it. Right from the start God recognized a man's and a woman's deep need to commune with one another.

I took a survey of women before I wrote *The Power of a Praying Husband,* and one of the most important things women wanted was that their husbands would talk to them more. This is a very big issue in a marriage. You may have been married 30 years to a poor communicator—or you may be one yourself—but God can change both of you. We *all* can learn to communicate better.

I know a couple who spend more time in silence than they do talking. They argue so much when they talk that they have chosen to not communicate at all. This is an unnatural way to live. If you have that kind of situation, you are not fulfilling the plan God has for your marriage. Communication is more about *serving God's will* than it is your own. It's more about doing *what's right* than it is deciding *who's right.* If you want to glorify God in your marriage, pray that the two of you will have good communication. That takes two hearts caring enough about one another to refuse to be selfish.

If your husband (wife) doesn't want to change right now, then be glad that God can change *you first* while you pray for the Holy Spirit to work on *him* (*her*). God can help *you* to not be so easily hurt by your spouse's poor communication skills. The Lord can give *you* such joy and excitement about *your* life in Him that you don't feel rejected when your husband (wife) is silent. If *you* are the one who has trouble communicating, ask God to give you a heart for your spouse that desires to express your love and thoughts openly.

You and your spouse became one in God's eyes the day you were married (Ephesians 5:31), but there is still a process of becoming one in your everyday lives together from then on. The day-to-day living out of this concept of total unity doesn't just happen; it takes time and effort. *Both* husband and wife have to compromise in order to do it. When one person stops putting forth any effort to talk things out or make the marriage better, it becomes a nightmare for the other. If only one is communicating and the other is not, the marriage is headed for serious problems. One person trying to carry the entire weight of a marriage relationship will work for only so long.

The Reason I Know How Important Communication Is

If you're like me and have already experienced divorce, you know the horrible pain of it and don't want to ever go through it again. You also know that when you are contemplating a divorce, you make a list in your mind of all the things that will change, and you ask yourself, *Is it worth it? Do the gains balance out the losses?* If communication is bad—or if the only communication is negative—you end up thinking you don't have much to lose and everything to gain.

When I was married the first time, before I became a believer, there was no communication in our relationship at all. Not only were we not on the same page, we weren't even in the same book. I came to the point where I felt as though I were living in hell, and I was ready to give up anything in order to feel hope, relief, and some degree of peace again. I wanted out so badly that I walked away from everything, taking only the possessions I brought into the marriage in the first place, even though I worked for two years to support him while he stayed home and watched TV. I didn't want to live another day in that slow death, and I saw no way whatsoever that life could ever be any different.

In his culture, men did not lift a finger to help around the house—or anywhere else, for that matter. Nor did they work, apparently. I found that I could not physically work 10- to 12-hour days and then come home to do *all* the cooking and *all* the cleaning because that was what he demanded. He daily evaluated my performance and recited the ways I had not lived up to the standards of his mother. He wanted me to be her and I just couldn't. He spent hours every day at her house while I worked, and he would still be there when I came home at night. It was like living alone again, except not as much fun. And I wasn't strong enough to take the constant criticism without any encouragement or sense of being loved. In his defense, he was probably trying to make me into the wife he wanted, and I was not a whole enough person at that time to be able to be all that.

He wasn't a believer, and he became extremely angry when he found out I had become one. After we had been married less than a year, I started going to church by myself every Sunday, which he thought was a waste of time when I could be cleaning or working another job to support him. One Sunday afternoon I came home from church feeling especially uplifted in my spirit, and I tried to talk to him about the Lord. He became irate and told me in a loud and threatening voice that I was forbidden to ever speak the name of Jesus in *his* house again and never as long as I was with *him*. It was the final straw that broke the back of my thinly spined marriage. I had been hanging on to the edge of a cliff by a delicate branch and had finally found hope and a reason to live, and now he was going to chop off the branch. It was like cutting off the air I breathed.

Soon after that I decided to do what he demanded and never speak the name of Jesus in *his* house or in *his* presence again. That meant, of course, I had to leave his house and his presence. After I left him I felt free to not only breathe, but to speak the name of Jesus whenever I wanted. It was liberating.

When I got married again, it was different. The most important difference being that my second husband, Michael, was a believer. We went to church together. We prayed together. We went to Christian marriage counselors together. So there was always hope for change in both of us. And I believed that any problems we had could be easily fixed.

However, we each came into the marriage with deep insecurities. He felt like a failure because he couldn't live up to his mother's expectations. I felt like a failure because my mentally ill mother had no expectations of me whatsoever. When she told me repeatedly that I was worthless and would never amount to anything, I had no reason to doubt her, even though I desperately looked for one. So my husband was *angry* and depressed. I was *anxious* and depressed. We were two damaged people, and hurting each other was easy. Although we communicated well in the beginning, there would be lapses where he would lash out in anger and I thought he was being cruel, so I would withdraw out of hurt, causing him to believe I didn't care. Communication became more and more difficult as time went on, and it was miserable.

When our marriage came to the ultimate crisis point after years like this, I wanted to leave. But in prayer about it one day, the Lord showed me that if I would pray for my husband every day the way God wanted me to, He would use me as an instrument of healing and deliverance for our marriage. I said yes to that and learned to pray the way the Lord was showing me. As I did, I began to see changes—especially in our communication. It wasn't an overnight transformation. It was more like a day by day moving into the territory God had for us to conquer and not giving up when there were times of setback.

The suffering that happens in an unhappy marriage is horrendous because there is no escape. Unless you get a divorce and dissolve the relationship completely, you are stuck there and have to work it out. If your spouse isn't willing to do anything to make it better, it is a nightmare. That's why praying about having good communication is so important. Yes, it's very good to be reading the Word of God and attending church where there is good Bible teaching, but I've seen too many marriages in the church end in divorce. I've even seen too many people who were great Bible teachers leave their husbands or wives. I've also seen marriages between people who never go to church or read the Bible last a lifetime. So there has to be more to saving a marriage than any kind of pat answer like "read the Word and stay in church." Even though I believe these two things are a must, you still have to do more. You have to pray and pray. And you have to pray specifically about your communication, because without that your marriage doesn't have a chance. I want to share specifically some ways I learned to pray about our communication that made a difference in our relationship.

Pray That You Can Just Be Nice

How many marriages could be saved if both the husband and wife would just be nice to one another? It's called common decency. The Bible says, "Love edifies" (1 Corinthians 8:1). That means love builds up and makes stronger. Love doesn't speak mean spirited and sarcastic words that tear down. *What* we say and the *manner* in which we say it can either communicate love or total disregard. Loveless words of criticism destroy a marriage relationship, so we have to ask ourselves if the satisfaction derived from saying them is really worth the hurt and destruction they cause. God doesn't think so. He says that real love "does not behave rudely, does not seek its own, is not provoked, thinks no evil" (1 Corinthians 13:5). There is no reason to treat your spouse badly. If you want to improve your marriage, just being nice is a good place to start.

When a person is not treated well by their spouse, it keeps them from feeling safe enough to share their deepest thoughts and emotions, and this shuts off an important part of their relationship. If you have already fallen into bad habits of critical and insensitive speech toward your spouse, repent of that now and ask God to change your heart. If your husband (wife) frequently directs negative and critical speech toward *you*, pray for an awakening in him (her). Pray that the grave consequences of such careless words will be revealed to his (her) understanding. I know it may seem pointless to do anything if *you* are the only one making the effort and your spouse seems to be doing nothing, but I have found that when *you* do the right thing, even when your spouse doesn't, God blesses *you*. And that makes a big difference.

Have you seen couples who are married but seem like strangers? I used to know a couple who must have memorized the old saying, "If you can't say something nice, then don't say anything" because they never said anything. At least not to each other. Theirs was a lifeless marriage. When one spouse is emotionally distant or noncommunicative, it forces the other to have to endure all struggles alone. When there is no compatibility, there is no one with whom to share life. And when some people realize that they cannot rely on their spouse to come through with friendship and emotional support, it becomes too easy to turn to another person who will. If you can't be nice, you can't be friends, and your marriage will be an endurance test.

Friends enjoy being with one another. They don't act like strangers. They don't say words to bring the other down and destroy any hope or joy. If you and your husband (wife) have not been good in the friendship department, ask God to help you change your ways. If you have been friends all along, ask God to show you how to be better friends than you have ever been in the past.

God says our words have power. If "death and life are in the power of the tongue," then we must choose our words carefully (Proverbs 18:21). Pray that God will help you and your spouse speak words to each other that are kind, loving, positive, good, uplifting, encouraging, and life-giving. Ask God to be in charge of your marriage, and tell Him you will do whatever it takes to see that it becomes all it was intended to be. Even if it means being nice when you don't feel like it.

Pray That You Will Always Be Truthful and Honest

A marriage absolutely must be based on trust. If you can't trust each other, then whom can you trust? That's why lying to your spouse is one of the worst things you can do to damage your relationship. The Bible says clearly, "Do not lie to one another, since you have put off the old man with his deeds" (Colossians 3:9). Every lie has dangerous and far-reaching consequences. "A false witness will not go unpunished, and he who speaks lies will not escape" (Proverbs 19:5). The worst consequence is that lying distances you from God. "He who tells lies shall not continue in my presence" (Psalm 101:7). Lying also distances you from one another and stops the flow of good things God has for you personally.

In a marriage, it's important to be both *truthful* and *honest*. And there is a difference between the two. When you tell a lie, you are not truthful, but it is possible to tell the truth and still not be honest. That happens when you are not forthcoming with the *whole* truth. You may not have actually told a lie, but you didn't reveal everything you needed to reveal. Now, you don't need to reveal every single thing to every person you see, because then no one would want to be around you. But you do need to be forthcoming with your spouse, because he (she) will be with you for the rest of your life.

You know if you have told a lie or not, but sometimes you can inadvertently be less than honest about your true feelings because you don't know how to express them fully. You are not entirely honest if you haven't shared your feelings and thoughts. *A person who never communicates with their spouse cannot be completely honest because total honesty requires good communication.* Of course, it's not good to be expressing every thought you have every moment you have one even with your spouse, because then he (she) won't want to be around you either. But God will give you discernment about that too, if you ask Him for it.

Here are some things to remember about being honest:

1. Be honest about how you feel regarding the things your spouse does. You have to express your feelings when something seriously bothers you about your spouse's actions. If you are not honest with him (her) about this, nothing will ever change. Then bitterness and anger will build up in your heart and lead to resentment and unforgiveness. You not only have to know *what* to say, but *when* to say it. And God will always be the best judge of that. So anytime you need to say something important to your husband (wife) that may be hard to hear, ask God to show you the right time to say it. Ask Him to prepare your spouse's heart to receive it and give you the perfect words to say so you can speak "the truth in love" (Ephesians 4:15). The Bible says that there is "a time to keep silence, and a time to speak" (Ecclesiastes 3:7). Ask God to help you know the difference between the two.

2. Be honest about the way you see things. It's important for each of you to share your thoughts, plans, fears, concerns, hopes, and dreams for the future. You have to get these things out of your heart and into the open. Job said, "I will speak, that I may find relief" (Job 32:20). And that's exactly what you will find too. If your husband (wife) is the kind of person with whom it's difficult to communicate, ask God to break down that barrier in his (her) heart. Outside of going to a counselor who will be able to help you both open up and talk, you need a move of the Holy Spirit to do that, so pray for one. A husband and wife are constantly adjusting to each other in their marriage because no two people *are* the same or *stay* the same. (Even though at times it may seem as though nothing ever changes.) But they can never adjust properly to each other if they don't know what adjustments to make. If you are not honest with your spouse about these things, you can easily make wrong assumptions and incorrect adjustments.

3. Be honest about your past. When I first realized that Michael and I were getting serious, I knew I couldn't go any further in my relationship with him without being completely forthcoming about my past. But before I told him everything, I prayed that God would prepare his heart to receive it and give me the right words and time to say it.

He already knew about my mother, even though he didn't fully comprehend the seriousness of her mental illness until after we were married and we went to visit my parents for a weekend. But there were other things I had to tell him, and I didn't know whether he would totally reject me because of them. But he was completely accepting of what I told him and said it didn't change his mind about me at all. It was a great relief to get it out in the open and off my shoulders.

I've known other people who had secrets from their past that they never revealed to their spouse until well after they were married, and this late revelation shook the level of trust that had been established early on. Being totally honest about your past helps you to live more successfully in the present. It helps you to better move into the future God has for you. You don't want to always be looking over your shoulder to see if something is coming back to haunt you. The sooner you are forthcoming, the better.

4. Be honest about everything you are doing. I know a man who is constantly lying to his wife about the things he does. They don't have a close relationship, and his dishonesty could very well lead to a divorce in the future. Every lie breaks down trust. And when a husband or wife loses trust, the foundation of their marriage crumbles. Of course, trust can be restored again when the one who is lying confesses and truly repents. If you have to lie about what you are doing, then your priorities are completely out of order. You are not putting God first and your husband (wife) second above all else.

Ten Things That Are True About Telling the Truth

1. *Truth is what you must choose to think about.* "Finally, brethren, whatever things are true...meditate on these things" (Philippians 4:8).

2. *Truth is a decision you make about the words you speak.* "My mouth will speak truth; wickedness is an abomination to my lips" (Proverbs 8:7).

3. *Truth is the way you choose to walk.* "I have chosen the way of truth; Your judgments I have laid before me" (Psalm 119:30).

4. *Truth liberates you.* "You shall know the truth, and the truth shall make you free" (John 8:32).

5. *Truth protects you.* "Stand therefore, having girded your waist with truth, having put on the breastplate of righteousness" (Ephesians 6:14).

6. *Truth purifies your soul.* "Since you have purified your souls in obeying the truth through the Spirit in sincere love of the brethren, love one another fervently with a pure heart" (1 Peter 1:22).

7. *Truth pleases God.* "I have no greater joy than to hear that my children walk in truth" (3 John 1:4).

8. *Truth can be branded in your heart.* "Let not mercy and truth forsake you; bind them around your neck, write them on the tablet of your heart" (Proverbs 3:3).

9. *Truth brings you into God's light.* "He who does the truth comes to the light, that his deeds may be clearly seen, that they have been done in God" (John 3:21).

10. *Truth in your heart invites a greater sense of God's presence when you pray.* "The LORD is near to all who call upon Him, to all who call upon Him in truth" (Psalm 145:18).

Pray That God's Love Will Be Poured into Your Heart

The best way to have good communication with your spouse is to first be in good communication with God. If it's true that "out of the abundance of the heart the mouth speaks" (Matthew 12:34), then you have to ask God to fill your heart abundantly with His love every day so that the words you speak are loving. The Bible says that "no man can tame the tongue. It is an unruly evil, full of deadly poison" (James 3:8). Left to ourselves, we will naturally say hurtful and destructive words. The Bible also says, "The preparations of the heart belong to man, but the answer of the tongue is from the LORD" (Proverbs 16:1). We can prepare our heart by being in the presence of God in prayer, in worship, and by reading His Word.

When truth is hard to hear in a marriage, ask God for a greater portion of His love with which to communicate it. Whenever you speak from a bad attitude or a loveless heart, it cuts off your spouse's ability to hear what you're saying. Ask God to give you wisdom to say the right things the right way. "The heart of the wise teaches his mouth, and adds learning to his lips" (Proverbs 16:23). When you make an effort to speak words that communicate love, it pays off. It pleases God, and there is always great reward in that.

Don't let animosity swell up and become a flood pouring over your relationship. Dam up arguments with honest communication and loving words. "The beginning of strife is like releasing water; therefore stop contention before a quarrel starts" (Proverbs 17:14). Ask God to make your heart so filled with His love that your words will be like healing waters of encouragement and restoration instead of an open floodgate that produces serious water damage.

Pray That You Can Understand the Signs

We have a little white long-haired Chihuahua. He is actually my daughter's dog, but she wasn't able to take him with her when she moved out because of her work and travel schedule. I guess that makes him our grand-dog. His name is Wrigley, but Michael and I call him "The Great I Want." That's because unless he is sleeping, Wrigley always wants something. Wrigley communicates his wants by sitting up on his hind legs and putting his paws together as though he is praying, and he waves them up and down while relentlessly squeaking. He can balance that way for longer than you ever dreamed possible. You can ignore the sitting up and the praying hands, but there is no way you are going to ignore the squeaking. It will drive you crazy. The only way to get him to stop is to ask him simple questions about all the things he usually wants and see how many times his paws go up and down. Because he always wants *everything,* his paws will go up and down at least one or two times for anything you say. There are key words we have to speak, such as "Outside?" "Dinner?" "Hold you?" "Bed?" "Blanket?" "Bone?" "Biscuit?" "Toy?" "Walk?" "Ride?" He understands all of these perfectly.

Do you want to go *outside?* Do you want *dinner?* Do you want me to *hold you?* Do you want a *biscuit?* Do you want your *bone?* Do you want to go for a *ride?* Actually, we've learned not to say "ride" unless we are committed to taking him on one. Because no matter how much he needs to go "outside" or how hungry he is for "dinner," a "ride" takes precedent over everything. And once you said the "R" word, if you didn't follow through you would be squeaked to death.

When you ask Wrigley these questions, you have to be very discerning as to how many times his praying paws go up and down. One time for "bone," two times for "dinner," two times for "hold you." And so on through the entire cycle because all his wants are relative. The word that gets the greatest up and down movement of the praying paws indicates what he wants most. The only word he doesn't respond to is "bath." I tried throwing that word in a couple times, and Wrigley was frozen in silence with a look on his face that said *Don't see me. Don't see me.* One time when he desperately had to go outside, he waved his paws at least six times in the space of two seconds and we knew it was an emergency.

The thing is, the expression on Wrigley's face never changes when he is doing his praying paws, so you cannot tell by looking at his face what he wants. And his squeaks all have the same intensity. It's the subtle signals in his body language that you have to take into consideration in order to discern what it is he is after.

The point in all this is that sometimes we have to look very carefully at the body language of our spouse in order to figure out what he (she) wants and what is going on inside him (her). We have to ask the right questions and be able to discern his (her) reaction to them. We have to read between the lines. Ask God to enable you to recognize the vital signs in your husband (wife). Ask God to help *you* communicate so clearly that your husband (wife) doesn't have to search for helpful signs in your body language.

Pray That You Will Enjoy Doing Things Together

What do you and your husband (wife) like to do together? If you can think of something, that's good. But if you are struggling to think of even one thing, then this is a problem for your relationship. In order to have good communication you must have things you enjoy doing together, even if it's something as simple as sitting together watching the sunset or reading books or taking walks or going out to eat. If you work together, you still need something to do together outside of work.

My husband and I tried golfing together for a short period of time. We tried tennis too. But my husband's goal was to win at all costs and mine was to just have fun. I didn't like risking my life trying to have fun. So we gave that up.

At this stage in our lives, due to a miraculous answer to my husband's prayers, we both like football. (Watching, not playing.) He bought me a book called *Football for Dummies,* took me to games, and was willing to explain the same thing over and over and over until I got it. Not an easy task for an impatient type A, but this was important to him and so he persevered. And it paid off because I love the game. Now we watch football games together on TV and attend them in person when our team is in town. If you knew how much I used to think that this was the biggest waste of time, you would realize how miraculous this is. Michael and I had *both* been praying that we would have something we like to do together. And *he* won. I still have to shop alone.

Pray That You Will Grow Closer with Each New Stage of Life

There are many stages of life and marriage, and you need to pray that you and your spouse will grow together through them instead of apart. You don't want to wake up one morning and find that you're in bed with a stranger and realize that he (she) is the person you married. Sometimes situations change. Perhaps your spouse was originally the main wage earner in the family, but then for one reason or another, *you* became the main wage earner. Or when children arrived on the scene, the perfect husband didn't turn out to be the perfect father. Or what used to be the perfect wife suddenly becomes the perfect mother *instead*. Or the children leave home. Or they come *back home* after they have finally left home. Or there are job changes, health changes, or financial changes. All these things can affect communication or cause serious miscommunication.

The proof of love for your spouse is the willingness to make changes as your lives progress together. Ask God to enable you both to always be sensitive to what is going on in the other in each stage of life, and to make any adjustments necessary in how you communicate. That way you'll continue to grow together.

Pray That You Will Honor One Another

Don't you hate it when you are with another couple and one of them says something critical, demeaning, or dishonoring about the other? Nothing causes people to feel more uncomfortable than a husband or wife making unkind jabs at one another in front of them. And it can force *you* into the awkward position of having to take sides in the matter, which you really can't because no one knows the inner workings of someone else's marriage. Sometimes the one who appears to be the charming and wonderful person is actually the offending person who is nice to everyone but their spouse. And the spouse who appears bitter or nasty has actually been pushed to the edge of what she (he) can take.

Husbands are especially exhorted to give honor to their wives, and the consequence of failing to do so is not having their prayers answered. "Husbands, likewise, dwell with them with understanding, giving *honor* to the wife, as to the weaker vessel, and as being heirs together of the grace of life, *that your prayers may not be hindered*" (1 Peter 3:7, emphasis added). This consequence is about as serious as it can get and should not be taken lightly.

Husbands are also admonished to *love* their wives, and wives are to *respect* their husbands and *submit* to them (Ephesians 5:22-33). For wives, godly submission is something you willingly do. It's not something your husband forces you to do. That's slavery. Submission is communicated in a godly way by showing respect to your husband. But a wife finds submitting to her husband far *easier* if he is submitted to God, which is the way God wants it. She finds it *harder* to do if he is not submitted to God or if he has disrespected her in any way. Ask God to help you and your husband (wife) to unfailingly show honor, respect, appreciation, and love to one another—*especially* in front of other people.

TEN THINGS TO REMEMBER ABOUT THE WORDS YOU SPEAK

1. ***Choose your words carefully.*** "Let no corrupt word proceed out of your mouth, but what is good for necessary edification, that it may impart grace to the hearers" (Ephesians 4:29).

2. ***Gentle words have more power than harsh words.*** "A gentle tongue breaks a bone" (Proverbs 25:15).

3. ***You have to think before you speak.*** "The heart of the righteous studies how to answer, but the mouth of the wicked pours forth evil" (Proverbs 15:28).

4. ***Don't talk too much.*** "In the multitude of words sin is not lacking, but he who restrains his lips is wise" (Proverbs 10:19).

5. ***Your words can cause you to stumble.*** "We all stumble in many things. If anyone does not stumble in word, he is a perfect man, able also to bridle the whole body" (James 3:2).

6. ***Kind words are life-giving.*** "Pleasant words are like a honeycomb, sweetness to the soul and health to the bones" (Proverbs 16:24).

7. ***Your words can bring about great destruction.*** "The tongue is a little member and boasts great things. See how great a forest a little fire kindles!" (James 3:5).

8. ***If you want a good life, watch what you say.*** "He who would love life and see good days, let him refrain his tongue from evil, and his lips from speaking deceit" (1 Peter 3:10).

9. ***Your words can be inspired by the enemy.*** "The tongue is a fire, a world of iniquity. The tongue is so set among our members that it defiles the whole body, and sets on fire the course of nature; and it is set on fire by hell" (James 3:6).

10. ***Your unkind words hurt you more than they hurt your spouse.*** "By your words you will be justified, and by your words you will be condemned" (Matthew 12:37).

Pray That You Both Will Have Ears to Hear

A big part of communicating is learning to listen. That means not doing all the talking. It means asking God to give you ears to hear and a heart that is willing to receive what your spouse is saying. Often you can "bear one another's burdens, and so fulfill the law of Christ" by simply *listening* to your spouse talk about what his (her) burdens are (Galatians 6:2). If you are married to someone who is too self-absorbed to listen, or refuses to listen because it might give the appearance of not being in control, or doesn't value what you have to say, pray that God will give him (her) ears to hear. Believe me, there is a greater impact when God convicts someone of not listening than there is when *you* try to do it.

Sometimes we *think* we know what the other person is saying, but God says not to answer too soon before you fully listen. "He who answers a matter before he hears it, it is folly and shame to him" (Proverbs 18:13). Listening means not talking while the other talks. How can you "rejoice with those who rejoice, and weep with those who weep" if you don't listen well enough to know if they're weeping or rejoicing? (Romans 12:15). If it seems your spouse never listens to you—or if your husband (wife) is always saying that *you* don't listen to him (her)—ask God to give you both a heart to hear. He loves answering that prayer.

Pray That the Enemy's Plan to Disrupt Communication Will Not Succeed

Always keep in mind that the enemy of your soul is also the enemy of your marriage, and therefore the enemy of your communication. Have you ever had something come between you and your spouse just when everything seems to be going well and break down the lines of communication so that you suddenly find yourselves completely missing each other? Suddenly there will be confusion or an argument or a distortion of what is being said, and you can't understand the reason for it. Disrupting the lines of communication between a husband and wife is one of the enemy's most common tactics. This can happen in even the best of marriages and in subtle ways so you think it's you. Ask God to keep you both aware of the enemy's hand trying to stir up strife and misunderstandings between you. Don't allow it to happen. If you see that it already has, declare that because *God* is *for* you, no one can be against you—not even the two of you.

Prayers for My Marriage

Prayer for Protection

LORD, I INVITE YOUR PRESENCE to dwell in our marriage. I pray that You would protect my husband (wife) and me from any kind of breakdown of communication. Enable us to always share our thoughts and feelings and refuse to be people who don't talk. Teach us to trust each other enough to share our deepest hopes, dreams, fears, and struggles with one another. Help us to spend time communicating with *You* every day so that our communication with each other will always be good. Teach us how to openly express love for one another, and keep us from any laziness or selfishness that would cause us to neglect to do that. Help us to refuse to speak words that tear down, but only words that build up (Ephesians 4:29).

Deliver us from any temptation to lie to each other about anything or deal falsely with one another (Leviticus 19:11). Help us to be totally honest and open about everything. Teach us to speak with truth, wisdom, instruction, and understanding. We don't want to be "always learning and never able to come to the knowledge of the truth" (2 Timothy 3:7).

Teach us to listen to one another and recognize the signs in each other that give us greater understanding. Help us find things we enjoy doing together so that we will grow closer and not apart. Enable us to be able to communicate love, appreciation, and honor to each other at all times. Teach us to recognize the enemy's plan to steal, rob, and destroy our marriage. Enable us to understand his methods and see his attempts to stir up strife and miscommunication between us. Help us to take instant authority over any attack he brings against us—especially in the area of communication. Help us to settle all matters of disagreement between us in a loving, compromising, and considerate manner. Enable us to always be in unity with You and with each other. In Jesus' name I pray.

Prayer for Breakthrough in Me

LORD, I INVITE YOUR PRESENCE to dwell in me and change me where

I need to be changed. Reveal any times where I have not said the right words or communicated the right things to my husband (wife) and I will confess it as sin, for I know I fall far short of Your glory (Romans 3:23). Teach me how to communicate openly and honestly so I will speak excellent, right, and truthful words (Proverbs 8:6-9). I know I cannot live in Your presence if I don't speak the truth in my heart (Psalm 15:1-3). Take away any deceit in my heart and any perversity in my mind so that evil will be far from me (Proverbs 17:20).

I pray that Your love will be so much in my heart that it comes out in everything I say. Give me the right words for every situation. Help me to remember to show appreciation to my husband (wife) for the good things he (she) does. Open my eyes if I am not seeing all of them. Give me ears to really hear what my husband (wife) is saying so that I can bear some of his (her) burdens by simply listening. Make me quick to hear and slow to speak (James 1:19). Give me the wisdom to have a good sense of timing.

Lord, You are greater than anything I face and stronger than all that opposes me and our marriage. Thank You that You have given me authority over the enemy. I pray I will always recognize his hand in our lives so that I will not allow any of his evil intentions to disrupt us. I pray that "my mouth shall speak wisdom, and the meditation of my heart shall give understanding" (Psalm 49:3). I thank You in advance for the answers to my prayers. In Jesus' name I pray.

Prayer for Breakthrough in My Husband (Wife)

Lord, I thank You for my husband (wife) and pray that You would open his (her) heart to all that You have for him (her) and for our marriage together. Help him (her) to know You better, to understand Your ways, and to see things from Your perspective. Help him (her) to view the two of us the way You do. Make changes in him (her) that need to be made so that nothing will hinder him (her) from fulfilling the purpose and destiny You have for his (her) life and our lives together.

Lord, fill my husband's (wife's) heart with Your love so that it overflows in the words he (she) speaks. Help him (her) to understand the consequences for any careless or hurtful words. Help us both to be more discerning about what wounds the heart of the other. Speak through us so that our words to each other will be *Your* words. Help us to be instruments of Your peace and grace every time we speak to each other. Convict my husband's (wife's) heart of times he (she) has said words that have hurt me and did not glorify You. Enable him (her) to speak words of life and not death, words that build up and not tear down. Increase his (her) knowledge of Your ways so that he (she) will refuse to speak negatively. Help him (her) to communicate openly, and not allow a cold silence to exist between us.

Lord, help my husband (wife) to be honest about everything. Convict his (her) heart about any lies he (she) has told me or anyone else, and break down any thought in him (her) that lying is acceptable, or that there are different versions of the truth. Strengthen him (her) to resist the father of all lies and refuse to fall into any temptation to lie (John 8:44). Help him (her) to stop all deceit (1 Peter 2:1). May he (she) refuse to be snared by his (her) own words (Proverbs 6:2). May there be no division between us, because we are of the same mind and have the same good judgment (1 Corinthians 1:10). Where he (she) has not communicated well in the past, help him (her) to do so now. Thank You that You are our rock and our Redeemer, and You can redeem all things (Psalm 78:35). In Jesus' name I pray.

Truth to Stand On

Let the words of my mouth and the meditation of my heart
be acceptable in Your sight, O Lord, my strength and my Redeemer.

Psalm 19:14

Though I speak with the tongues of men and of angels, but have not love,
I have become sounding brass or a clanging cymbal.

1 Corinthians 13:1-3

We all stumble in many things. If anyone does not stumble in word,
he is a perfect man, able also to bridle the whole body.

James 3:2

Husbands ought to love their own wives as their own bodies;
he who loves his wife loves himself...
and let the wife see that she respects her husband.

Ephesians 5:28,33

Wives, submit to your own husbands, as to the Lord...Husbands love
your wives, just as Christ also loved the church and gave Himself for her.

Ephesians 5:22,25

2

If ANGER, RUDENESS, *or* ABUSE POISONS YOUR RELATIONSHIP

―――⤳⤶―――

Arguments happen in every marriage. Every one of us can get angry sometimes. But it's possible to argue without venting anger at one another. It's possible to express anger in a civilized and godly manner and not attack your spouse or children. If you frequently see anger rising up in either you or your spouse, it's a sign of trouble ahead. Anger always turns off communication, so if one or both of you can't get control of your anger, then the distance between you is bound to grow. The quickest way to put a halt to all meaningful and constructive communication in your marriage is to direct your anger toward your spouse. Do it enough times and it will not only damage your spouse's soul, but also *yours* as well.

The anger I am talking about in this chapter is not expressed in an infrequent heated argument or a rare spirited disagreement. It is something that resides deep within a person that seems to have a life of its own. It festers and churns and always maintains a readiness to surge and strike at any moment, for any reason. And the degree of manifestation of the anger is way out of proportion to the offense. Some little thing can trigger it, and suddenly rage will come forth when least expected over what seems to be a nonissue. Anger looks for a reason and a way to attack and hurt, and there seems to be great satisfaction in it because this is what anger lives to do. There appears to be little if any recognition in the angry person of what their anger does to those toward whom it is directed. In the angry person's mind anger is always justified because he (she) deserves to be angry for whatever reason.

A person's frequent anger can be explained, but it is never justified. I am not talking about an incident happening that would make anyone angry. I am talking about someone who has an angry spirit inside of them that they give place to because it gives them the opportunity to be in control and get their way. It forces their spouse and children to walk on eggshells because they are always afraid that it is going to erupt again. This is no way to live—especially not in a marriage, where there is no escape.

One of the most common complaints I hear from women struggling in their marriages is a problem with anger in their husbands. I occasionally hear it from men as a complaint about their wives, but it seems that more women suffer because of their husband's anger. I have never seen any good come from one spouse venting their anger on the other, but I have seen a whole lot of devastation. That's why God has plenty to say about anger in His Word.

How to Inherit the Wind

The Bible says that "he who troubles his own house will inherit the wind" (Proverbs 11:29). That means a person who constantly stirs up strife in his own family will never find all the success and blessing the Lord has for him. It means even when that person does get anything, it will blow through his fingers like the wind and he won't be able to hold on to it.

Anything you do that upsets your spouse and children troubles your house. Using anger to control your spouse troubles your house. Raising your voice in explosive, loud, demeaning words troubles your house. Being rude and abusive troubles your house. While anger hurts the person it is directed toward, there are serious consequences for the angry person as well.

The anger I am talking about can drive a person to go beyond what is acceptable behavior. That kind of anger directed at your spouse is always selfish, and it will cause deep resentment. No one wants to be ruled by someone's anger—especially not from a spouse. Every angry outburst directed at a family member kills something in that person. It will eventually kill love, erode hope, and destroy the relationship.

We can be angry about something that happened. Anger's good when it's in response to a violation of human rights, social injustice, or irreverence for the things of God. It is not good when communicating with your husband (wife). We can have temporary anger toward someone we think is an offender, but we cannot sin in the process. The Bible says, " 'Be angry, and do not sin': do not let the sun go down on your wrath, nor give place to the devil" (Ephesians 4:26-27). That means no attacking or hurting.

When angry words and actions beat up the soul of a family member, even if their body is untouched, it destroys their sense of who God made them to be. It hurts them in a grievous way and sucks love out of their heart. The Bible says, "Put off all these: anger, wrath, malice, blasphemy, filthy language out of your mouth" (Colossians 3:8). Pray that neither you nor your spouse will ever trouble your family with anger.

When Your Love Fails, God's Won't

The first commandment says that the *most important thing* you can do is *love God.* The second commandment says that the *next most important thing* you can do is *love others* as you love yourself (Matthew 22:37-39). And the *most important person* to love above all others is your *spouse.*

A husband is supposed to love his wife (Ephesians 5:25), and a wife her husband (Titus 2:4). Loving your spouse is one of the ways you love and serve the Lord. God wants you as a married couple to love each other the way He loves you. But who can love the way Jesus loves *us?* He laid down His life for us. Who can love like that every day? When you get up every morning. When you see each other after a hard day. When one or both of you are definitely not at your best. *The only way you can truly love each other as God intended and Jesus demonstrated is to be filled afresh with the Holy Spirit every day.* Selfless love, which is a fruit of the Spirit, comes by having the Spirit of love poured in you.

Christ demonstrated His love for the church by sacrificing Himself for her. (The "church" in the Bible refers to all of us who are believers in Jesus, not to a building.) He didn't get angry and yell at the church or be mean to the church or criticize and put down the church. He loved the church and gave Himself for her. This is the kind of love God wants you to have for your spouse. But this kind of love cannot be conjured up in the flesh. It takes the enablement of the Holy Spirit and the infilling of your heart with His love.

No matter what happens in your life or your marriage, the Holy Spirit will always fill your heart afresh with God's love if you ask Him to. Or, if you spend time in God's presence in prayer, praise and worship, and in His Word, you will be infused with His love. When you love because Jesus commanded you to and the Holy Spirit has filled your heart with God's love, it's far different than trying to conjure up a feeling of love in the flesh when you don't feel like it. By being filled with God's love—which is far greater than human love—you will have the ability to love your husband (wife) the way God wants you to, no matter what is happening.

Feelings of love in a marriage can rise and fall and come and go. Human love ebbs and flows. It changes because of emotions, circumstances, and seasons. The love God wants us to have for our spouse is something that stays steady. It is a constant stream that pours from heaven into the human soul and overflows to those around them. But we can't love that way without *His* help. That's why we have to stay connected to the Lord and tap into that love every day by spending time with *Him*. The only way you can always be patient, kind, loving, and *not easily angered* is if you are plugged into God. The only way for God's love to consistently flow out of you toward your spouse is to be filled to overflowing with it.

God's love is the fountainhead from which a good marriage flows. *Loving your husband or wife is the most important thing you can do next to loving God, because you have to become like God to do it.* The love of God will keep you from being selfish, demanding, critical, angry, rude, or abusive. When God's love is in your heart, you will want to be patient and kind, and you won't want to insist on having your own way. You will be happy to say you're sorry, and you won't care about keeping a record of wrongs. In the flesh this is not possible, but with God it is.

If you want to stay in love with your spouse, stay in love with the Lord first. That flow of love found in Christ can touch you wherever you are and create an atmosphere of love, peace, and harmony within you that will overflow into your relationship with your husband (wife).

God Cares About the Way You Treat Your Spouse

It matters to God how you treat your spouse, and you will be called to account for it. Knowing that should make us all watch what we do and say. Knowing that should also help us to be more forgiving.

The way I reacted to my husband's anger was to withdraw from him. But that meant that while Michael would get all of his anger out of *his* system, it would still be stuck in *mine*. Eventually, when I was finally able to see the ultimate consequences for not treating your spouse with love and kindness, I began to feel sorrier for him than I did for myself. I saw that as long as I repented of any unforgiveness I had, I would be free. There would be consequences only in *his* life, not *mine*. I prayed for him to see the truth about his anger—how it displeased the Lord—and how he would bear the consequences for it. Even though it hurt me every time he was angry, I still loved him enough to not want to see him suffer because of it.

If you are married to someone who is often angry and takes his (her) anger out on you, know that this kind of behavior is hurting him (her) more than it is you. It may hurt you now, but it will hurt him (her) for a lifetime if it does not stop. It will shut off the blessings God wants to bring into his (her) life. He (she) will have delayed his (her) destiny because of anger. "Do not let your mouth cause your flesh to sin, nor say before the messenger of God that it was an error. Why should God be angry at your excuse and destroy the work of your hands?" (Ecclesiastes 5:6). Pray for your husband (wife) to be free of anger.

Anger Is a Work of the Flesh

It's not that you can never get angry at one another. But if it happens in a hurtful way, there must be genuine repentance on the angry person's part—that means having the intention of never doing that again—and there must be complete forgiveness from the spouse to whom the anger was directed. If those two things do not happen, the damage from that anger will be as if a hole was shot through the fabric of your relationship. Enough holes like that, and they will weaken the relationship so badly that only a miracle of God can keep it from ripping apart. We can only escape the consequences of our anger—which is sin—by the forgiveness of God and the power of the Holy Spirit.

An angry person *can* get free of his own anger because God sent His Son, Jesus, to save us from the consequences of our sins (Romans 8:2). When we receive Jesus, the Holy Spirit enables us to "not walk according to the flesh, but according to the Spirit" (Romans 8:4). In other words, because of the Holy Spirit in us, we have the power to reject all works of the flesh. But we have to *want* that, because if we don't, we will set our desires on constant fleshly gratification.

There is never a time when anger directed at your spouse will please God. It will always be fleshly minded and God hates it. "To be carnally minded is death, but to be spiritually minded is life and peace. Because the carnal mind is enmity against God; for it is not subject to the law of God, nor indeed can be. So then, those who are in the flesh cannot please God" (Romans 8:6-8). No one who has any sense of who God is wants to be in the position of not pleasing Him.

When you are giving place to a *sin,* you invite the spirit associated with it to have a *place* in your *life.* For example, if you tell enough lies, you invite a lying spirit to operate in your life. Then you start lying even when you have no reason to, and lying becomes a habit you can't break. In the same way, if you allow yourself to frequently give place to feelings of anger at your spouse or your children, you will end up with an angry spirit that can surface and attack at any time. When you don't control your anger, anger will control *you.* Only the power of the Holy Spirit can set you free from a spirit of anger. But you cannot be set free from something you don't even recognize that you have invited into your life.

Everyone gets angry sometimes. Some people get angry *all* the time. Those people have an angry spirit. They can't hold their anger in. A person who has an angry spirit always has it bubbling just under the surface waiting for some perceived imperfection in someone or some situation to summon it forth. It can explode in a moment of weakness on those around them. To be able to communicate without anger takes someone who can control his own spirit and is not controlled by their flesh. It takes a person of mercy instead of a person of wrath. "The merciful man does good for his own soul, but he who is cruel troubles his own flesh" (Proverbs 11:17).

If we live according to our flesh—that is giving the flesh what it wants when it wants it—we reap death. The death of our relationships and the death of the future God wants us to move into. If we want to see our marriages live, we have to put to death the constant gratifying of our flesh. And that's what giving place to anger is. If we want to see our purpose and future be fulfilled, we have to live according to the Spirit and not the flesh. "If you live according to the flesh you will die; but if by the Spirit you put to death the deeds of the body, you will live. For as many as are led by the

Spirit of God, these are sons of God" (Romans 8:13-14). We don't have to be a slave to our flesh by giving place to anger. When we are led by God's Spirit, we are truly children of God, and we will inherit the blessings God has for us.

SEVEN THINGS THAT ARE TRUE ABOUT ANGER

1. ***You are able to stop being angry.*** "Cease from anger, and forsake wrath; do not fret—it only causes harm" (Psalm 37:8).

2. ***Anger stirs up strife and causes you to sin.*** "An angry man stirs up strife, and a furious man abounds in transgression" (Proverbs 29:22).

3. ***Taking control of anger makes you stronger.*** "He who is slow to anger is better than the mighty, and he who rules his spirit than he who takes a city" (Proverbs 16:32).

4. ***It is to your benefit to let some things go instead of getting angry.*** "The discretion of a man makes him slow to anger, and his glory is to overlook a transgression" (Proverbs 19:11).

5. ***Only fools are quick to get angry.*** "Do not hasten in your spirit to be angry, for anger rests in the bosom of fools" (Ecclesiastes 7:9).

6. ***Angry people are never good to be around.*** "Make no friendship with an angry man, and with a furious man do not go" (Proverbs 22:24).

7. ***Angry words inspire more anger.*** "A soft answer turns away wrath, but a harsh word stirs up anger" (Proverbs 15:1).

If You Are the One Who Has an Anger Problem

There is an epidemic of anger in marriages today. If anger is expressed frequently without repentance and forgiveness, it erodes all that has been established in the relationship and builds a wall between the husband and wife that will eventually become insurmountable. Anger has consequences, and they are never more apparent than in a marriage.

If you are the one with anger, you can make an intelligent decision to not be ruled by it. The hurt you inflict on the soul of someone God has given you to love will bring consequences you won't want to experience. Stop directing anger at your spouse and start directing it at the enemy of your soul and your marriage. No matter what happens in your life, don't respond to it in anger. Take it to God first. See where it's coming from. Ask God if displaying your anger will be glorifying to Him.

As with all negative emotions, anger begins in the mind. What you do and say comes out of what takes root in your mind. So fill your mind with the right things.

> Summing it all up, friends, I'd say you'll do best by filling your minds and meditating on things true, noble, reputable, authentic, compelling, gracious—the best, not the worst; the beautiful, not the ugly; things to praise, not things to curse. Put into practice what you learned from me, what you heard and saw and realized. Do that, and God, who makes everything work together, will work you into His most excellent harmonies (Philippians 4:8-9 MSG).

Don't let anger control you. Control *it* instead. When you let anger control you, you constantly blame your spouse for the things that upset you. Anger makes you blind to the feelings of other people. It causes you to hurt people you love. When you are angry you can't see anything except your own feelings. That's why most angry people have no clue as to how hurtful their anger is and what it's doing to their spouse and children.

If your husband (wife) makes you angry, ask God to reveal to you if this is something He wants you to be angry about. If not, ask Him to take it away. If so, ask Him to give you a calm spirit, the right words, and perfect timing so you can confront your spouse in a godly way about what has angered you. Then, with the leading of the Holy Spirit, calmly express your feelings without attacking your husband (wife). Write out your feelings *first* so you can delete any words you might regret.

Try to remember that both of you are on the same side and have a common enemy, so be angry at the enemy. Don't ever take revenge. It will only make you sick. Let *God* punish the offender if it's necessary. God says, "Vengeance is Mine" and He means it (Deuteronomy 32:35). Lashing out at your spouse with the desire to hurt will only punish you.

If Your Spouse Is the One with the Anger Problem

Common courtesy is required in a marriage. Why should a person be polite, considerate, and kind to everyone else, and rude, inconsiderate, and mean to the family they are supposed to love? If your spouse treats a stranger with more courtesy than he (she) does you, then he (she) is committing a sin that will grieve the Holy Spirit. This is not a good position to be in. If you are the one being treated that way, know that God does not want you to deal with your spouse's angry spirit. If you have been hurt and deeply wounded as a result of your spouse's anger, turn to God to save, heal, and deliver you and give you peace.

Most people with an anger problem don't see themselves as angry; they see themselves as right. They feel completely justified in what they say and do because they think they have a right to be angry. And the more self-centered they are, the more they feed off their own anger.

If there is an anger problem in your spouse, take it to God immediately. Ask Him to give you His perspective on it. If it is minor and a rare occurrence and you should just overlook it, ask God to help you do so. If it is a problem, ask God to show you how to confront it. Letting any issue go unresolved is dangerous—this is especially true of anger. Pray for your husband (wife) to be completely free of it. One of the greatest things you can give your spouse is your commitment to pray for him (her). Your prayers are a gift that will help him (her) get his (her) anger under control. "A gift in secret pacifies anger" (Proverbs 21:14).

When Anger Becomes Abuse

If a person gives *place* to anger and goes with it wherever it takes them, and if they say and do whatever feels good at the moment as they release that anger toward their spouse, it is abuse. There is a difference between simply getting angry about something, and letting anger become a weapon that crushes a person's heart, beats down their spirit, or hurts their physical body. Someone who will allow their anger to go that far has a mental and emotional disorder and needs professional help. In order to be free of that kind of anger disorder and the abuse that comes as a result of it, they also need the power of the Holy Spirit to cleanse their heart and deliver them from this selfish work of the flesh.

Abusive people love their anger to the point of actually looking for ways to be angry. Anger empowers them and fuels the fire they love to fan into flame. It gives them what they perceive as control. But actually, anger illustrates their utter lack of control. Lashing out and yelling at someone God has given you to love is sin. Abuse is sin.

Any words spoken in explosive anger can be abusive. A loudly raised voice and poor choice of words can cut like a knife into a person's soul. Angry outbursts are loveless and full of the desire to hurt. The verbal abuser doesn't try to see it from the perspective of the person they are abusing. They don't care to know how badly their anger makes the recipient of their anger feel because all they care about is how *they* feel themselves. If there have been times when your spouse's angry outbursts have killed something in you, that's abuse. Or if there are times when your own angry words have destroyed something in your spouse or your children, that is abuse. Abuse destroys lives.

You are in a battle for your marriage, but the battle is not with your spouse. If he (she) is the one firing the shots at you and you are being forced to defend or protect yourself, give the situation *your* best shot in prayer. Ask God to deliver your husband (wife) from the evil spirit troubling him (her) (1 Samuel 16:14-23). Ask God to give you the ability to stay calm in the midst of the battle. Ask Him to help you to resist striking back.

All that being said, I am definitely not saying to stop defending or protecting yourself if you are in harm's way. *I'm not telling any wife to stay in her marriage if her mental or physical health is in danger, and especially not if her life is being threatened in any way whatsoever.* Abuse of any kind goes against all that God is and all that He has for you. No one is required to take it. If you are afraid of what your spouse might do to harm you or your children, make plans to get free. Find a place to go and people to help you move out. I have known of too many people who waited too long and suffered devastating consequences. Don't be one of those statistics.

If your husband is physically abusing you, call a domestic violence hotline. You will usually find it listed under "Community Services" or "Emergency Services" at the beginning of your phone book. They understand the situation and can help you make the right decisions as to what to do about it. If you need to leave home for your own safety or the safety of your children, they will help you do that. Even if you don't end up leaving, it is good to have a plan. You need a safe place to go, a way to get there, someone to help, money you can have access to, and the legal papers and possessions you need to take with you.

Physical abuse doesn't go away on its own. It only gets worse. If you don't want to help yourself, then think about helping your husband by leaving and not returning until he gets help and is cured. Being destroyed by someone who has an emotional disorder such as uncontrolled anger is not the kind of self-sacrifice or martyrdom God is looking for. Don't enable your husband to suffer the consequences of his own sin of abuse. Help him get the healing needed to become a whole person.

There is no excuse for abuse. It is never justified. A man who physically or emotionally abuses his wife is emotionally sick and has a serious problem. Of all emotional disorders, anger can be by far the most destructive. It is more destructive than depression, anxiety, or fear because it is usually directed at the spouse in some abusive and destructive way. Don't fool around with this; it's too dangerous. He needs professional help and fast. A man who beats his wife and children in any way should be removed from them completely. Even if the abuse is only verbal, it is still extremely damaging. Scars happen internally as well as externally. Anger and abuse is the problem of the person who has it and not the fault of the one abused. No possible action or words of yours deserve violent, angry outbursts. Do not blame yourself.

You are not saved by your husband (wife) or your marriage. You are saved by Jesus Christ. While I am not advocating divorce, you should still know that you will not lose your salvation if you end up getting divorced. In an abusive situation, you may lose your life if you don't.

Seek Good Christian Counseling

If you or your spouse has an anger problem, even if it has not progressed to abuse, seek counseling together as soon as possible. If nothing else, you may need a referee. If your spouse refuses to go, seek it for yourself. Don't ignore signs that suggest something is broken and needs to be fixed. Find a good Christian counselor who does not believe "the abused person asked for it," or that "you have to stay in an abusive relationship because God said to submit to your husband." Both of these views are not only unbelievably out of touch with reality, but are cruel, wrong, and ungodly. Find a counselor who truly knows God's ways and values your individual lives as God does.

SEVEN THINGS THAT ARE TRUE ABOUT BEING A FOOL

1. *A fool thinks he is always right.* "The way of a fool is right in his own eyes, but he who heeds counsel is wise" (Proverbs 12:15).

2. *A fool cares only about himself.* "A fool has no delight in understanding, but in expressing his own heart" (Proverbs 18:2).

3. *A fool finds it easy to quarrel.* "It is honorable for a man to stop striving, since any fool can start a quarrel" (Proverbs 20:3).

4. *A fool trusts himself completely.* "He who trusts in his own heart is a fool, but whoever walks wisely will be delivered" (Proverbs 28:26).

5. *A fool vents all his feelings.* "A fool vents all his feelings, but a wise man holds them back" (Proverbs 29:11).

6. *A fool's words will do him harm.* "The words of a wise man's mouth are gracious, but the lips of a fool shall swallow him up" (Ecclesiastes 10:12).

7. *A fool destroys himself.* "Fools are undone by their big mouths; their souls are crushed by their words" (Proverbs 18:7 MSG).

If You Love Your Calling, Then Love Your Spouse

You and your husband (wife) are called together, and neither of you will completely accomplish the great purpose God has for you without the other. God made man and woman in His image. God's image is expressed in *both* male and female, and when you become one with your spouse spiritually, you begin to experience a measure of God's image in you that you wouldn't experience as fully without your mate.

The fact that you are designed to serve God together doesn't mean you have to be attached at the hip. You don't have to go every place together and do everything together. In fact, you can be separated as far as being on opposite sides of the world and still complement each other. You are still individuals with gifts and talents unique only to you, but God will combine those talents to bring out the best in each of you, and you will be an important part of each other's calling. God designed the two of you to complete each other. But your personality differences—especially if you are opposites—will either be the greatest blessing of your life or the greatest battle of your life, depending on whether you live in the Spirit or in the flesh. If you recognize that you are called together, it will help you appreciate each other's gifts, talents, abilities, and strengths, and you will know that directing anger toward your spouse is inappropriate.

PRAYERS FOR MY MARRIAGE

Prayer for Protection

DEAR LORD, HELP MY HUSBAND (WIFE) and me to be "slaves of righteousness" so we will always do the right thing and not allow anger to control our lives in any way (Romans 6:19). Keep us from ever using anger as a weapon to hurt one another so that it doesn't drive a wedge between us. Fill our hearts full of Your love and peace so there is no room for anger. Teach us to pray about everything and make all of our needs known to You, knowing that when we do You have promised in Your Word to give us Your peace (Philippians 4:6-7).

Lord, enable us to always see the best in one another and not the worst. Teach us to find things to praise about each other and not complain about, so that we can be brought into harmony with You and each other in our marriage (Philippians 4:8-9). Help us to always "pursue the things which make for peace" and the things by which we may edify one another (Romans 14:19). Enable us to exhibit the fruit of the Spirit—"love, joy, peace, longsuffering, kindness, goodness, faithfulness, gentleness, self-control"—and not a harvest of the flesh (Galatians 5:22-23). Take all anger from us and teach us to love each other from pure hearts and a good conscience (1 Timothy 1:5-6). In Jesus' name I pray.

Prayer for Breakthrough in Me

LORD, HELP ME TO DWELL ON the good and the positive in my life and in my husband (wife). I know that it is You who "looks deep inside people and searches through their thoughts" (Proverbs 20:27 NCV). Search the inner depths of my heart and expose anything that is not of You so I can be set free of it.

Lord, where I have directed anger toward my husband (wife) or held anger inside of me, I confess that as sin and ask You to forgive me and take all anger away. Heal any wounds that I have inflicted in him (her) with my words. Help me to speak good words and healing to my husband (wife), for I know that pleases You (Proverbs 15:23). Where I have shown anger toward any other family member,

I confess it to You as sin. Bring Your restoration to every situation where it is needed.

Thank You, Lord, that You will redeem my soul in peace from the battle that is against me (Psalm 55:18). I believe that You, the God of peace, "will crush Satan" under my feet shortly (Romans 16:20). Help me to live righteously because I know there is a connection between obedience to Your ways and peace (Psalm 85:10). Help me to "depart from evil and do good; seek peace and pursue it" (Psalm 34:14). Thank You that You will take away all anger in me and keep me in perfect peace, because my mind is fixed on You (Isaiah 26:3). In Jesus' name I pray.

Prayer for Breakthrough in My Husband (Wife)

LORD, I DON'T WANT TO ever feel that "my soul has dwelt too long with one who hates peace" (Psalm 120:6). Deliver me from anger in my husband (wife). Your Word says, "A wholesome tongue is a tree of life, but perverseness in it breaks the spirit" (Proverbs 15:4). Where I have ever felt that an angry spirit in my husband (wife) has hurt me or broken my spirit, I pray You would heal those wounds and take away any unforgiveness I have because of it.

I pray You would set my husband (wife) free from anger. Help him (her) to recognize a spirit of anger rising up in him (her) and reject it completely. Strengthen him (her) to be able to control his (her) mind and emotions and help him (her) to remember that "we do not wrestle against flesh and blood, but against principalities, against powers," and the rulers of darkness and wickedness (Ephesians 6:12). Teach him (her) to be slow to anger the way You are (James 1:19). Help him (her) to understand that anger never produces spiritual fruit (James 1:20). I pray that all anger in my husband (wife) will be evaporated by the power of the Holy Spirit, and that he (she) will have a strong desire to reject his (her) carnal side and become spiritually minded. Let there be no reason to fear his (her) anger and what he (she) might do. Help me trust that "I will both lie down in peace and sleep; for You alone, O LORD, make me dwell in safety" (Psalm 4:8).

I pray now that You, the God of all hope, will fill my husband (wife) with faith and hope by the power of the Holy Spirit (Romans

15:13). I pray You would lift up Your countenance upon him (her) and give him (her) Your peace (Numbers 6:26). I pray You would direct his (her) heart "into the love of God and into the patience of Christ" (2 Thessalonians 3:5). Help him (her) to flee anger and pursue righteousness, godliness, faith, love, patience, and gentleness (1 Timothy 6:11). In Jesus' name I pray.

TRUTH TO STAND ON

Be angry, and do not sin.
Meditate within your heart on your bed, and be still.

PSALM 4:4

So then, my beloved brethren,
let every man be swift to hear, slow to speak, slow to wrath;
for the wrath of man does not produce the righteousness of God.

JAMES 1:19-20

Beloved, let us love one another, for love is of God;
and everyone who loves is born of God and knows God…
In this is love, not that we loved God,
but that He loved us and sent His Son
to be the propitiation for our sins.
Beloved, if God so loved us,
we also ought to love one another.

1 JOHN 4:7,10-11

Above all things have fervent love for one another,
for love will cover a multitude of sins.

1 PETER 4:8

If you abide in Me, and My words abide in you,
you will ask what you desire, and it shall be done for you.

JOHN 15:7

3

If FORGIVENESS DOESN'T COME EASY

You know the feeling. You've already said "I forgive you" to your spouse. You've confessed your unforgiveness to the Lord and asked Him to cleanse your heart and set you free of it. But you still have that feeling. That feeling of not being able to let it go completely. You're trying to be forgiving, but you just cannot seem to do a thorough job of it. Unforgiveness is still there!

This happens when you have to forgive your spouse for the same things over and over again, and it gets harder instead of easier as time goes on. Layers of offenses have accumulated, and therefore layers of forgiveness are needed. We have to realize that in our lives—and especially in our marriages—forgiveness is ongoing; sometimes daily. We always need the *willingness* to forgive ready in our heart. And only a heart humbled by the forgiveness of God has the ability to completely forgive time and again.

You have to forgive your spouse the way Jesus has forgiven you (Ephesians 4:32). Jesus forgave you completely. No looking back. No remembering. It means not keeping a list of the ways you have been wronged. It means refusing to carry bitterness and resentment about anything. It means not allowing yourself to be an injustice collector who keeps one foot in the past, always brooding over what happened there. It means living each day free of bad memories and looking to the future with hope. True forgiveness means completely letting go of an offense and refusing to hold it against the offender. That kind of forgiveness is impossible without the Lord. We need God helping us to forgive every day.

In the beginning of your relationship, forgiving your spouse comes easy. But when you have to be forgiving time and again, you wonder if perhaps you are encouraging him (her) by *appearing* to condone his (her) actions. Sometimes you may be hesitant to forgive because you're afraid that in doing so you are setting yourself up for the same thing to happen again. But there is a clear line between enabling and forgiving. In other words, you can still confront your spouse about changing his (her) ways, and you pray for that to happen, but if he (she) doesn't do it, you refuse to let it eat at you and make you bitter. Forgiving does not mean you are giving the offender a free pass to commit the offense again and again. It does not mean you are inviting abuse or giving that person a license to walk all over you or continue to hurt you. It doesn't make you a doormat. *Forgiveness doesn't make the other person right; it makes you free.*

Ask God to Show You

Forgiveness is a decision we make, and we *know* if we made it or not. We don't accidentally forgive someone without realizing it. But it is possible to *not forgive* without realizing it. We think we've let it go when we haven't.

Mary Anne—the Christian counselor I had seen—had me confess my unforgiveness toward my mother. Months later she called me into her office and told me she felt I had unforgiveness toward my dad as well. I didn't think that was right, but she said to ask God about it anyway.

On my way home from her office I said, "Lord, do I have any unforgiveness in me toward my dad?"

I fully expected God to say, "Definitely not, My good and faithful servant." But instantly I was struck through the heart by the truth. God impressed upon me that I had truly not forgiven my father.

My father? I thought. *Why would I need to forgive him?*

In that moment I saw all the unforgiveness I had toward my dad for all those years of not protecting me from my mother. And he was the only one who could. He was never abusive to me, so I didn't think there was any reason to forgive him. But when my eyes were opened to the truth, I saw how my father had never rescued me from my mother's insanity, and I had held this against him without even realizing it.

I broke down and sobbed so hard I had to pull my car over to the side of the freeway. I confessed my unforgiveness toward my dad and asked God to forgive me. When I did that, I felt a release in my spirit that I had never felt before. Looking back now, I believe that if I had not *asked* God to reveal any unforgiveness in my heart, I doubt if I could have ever seen this on my own. We can't always see our unforgiving attitudes when we have them, but God will show us the truth if we will just ask Him to.

The Choice Is Yours

Forgiveness is a choice you have to make every day. You choose to *live* in forgiveness. And never is that more true than when you are married. Besides *loving* your husband (wife), the next most important thing you can do in your marriage is *forgive* him (her).

Even in the best of marriages, forgiveness is always necessary. For two completely different humans to live together in harmony, there are bound to be disappointments, misunderstandings, and hurts. We have to continually be "bearing with one another, and forgiving one another" (Colossians 3:13). We can't wait until our spouse deserves it or asks for it. Not forgiving is a killer. It kills your relationships. It kills your health. And it kills your joy. It also upsets your close walk with God.

When Jesus was asked by His disciples if we need to forgive others as many as *seven times,* He said that *seventy times seven* was more like it (Matthew 18:21-22). I did the math and that's 490 times. The point is, we need to forgive as often as necessary. You might be living with someone you have to forgive 490 times a day, but you will still have to forgive as often as it takes for your heart to be free.

In the prayer that Jesus taught us to pray, He said to *ask* God to forgive us, just as we *give* forgiveness to *others*. "Forgive us our debts, as we forgive our debtors" (Matthew 6:12). That means if we ask God for forgiveness for things we've done, while at the same time refusing to forgive our spouse, then we are not going to enjoy the full benefits of God's forgiveness to us. In other words, if we don't release others by forgiving them, we ourselves will not find the release we need to move on in our lives. Not forgiving will always hold us back. We will be attached to invisible unforgiveness ties, and though we may try hard, we won't be able to move beyond where we are to where we're supposed to be.

When you have been emotionally devastated by something your husband (wife) has said or done—or something he (she) did *not* say or do—sometimes the hurt is so great that you feel you can't get over it enough to forgive. The unforgiveness and bitterness can become so deeply rooted that it takes a major work of God to make you even *want* to forgive. When that happens, ask God to help you. Say, "God, help me to want to forgive my husband (wife). Help me to forgive him (her) completely." You have to do this "lest any root of bitterness springing up cause trouble, and by this many become defiled" (Hebrews 12:15). Bitterness is hard to get rid of, and it does the most damage to *you*.

Not only is it important to forgive your spouse, but it is also important to your marriage for you to forgive everyone else in your life. If you have any unforgiveness toward a family member, neighbor, friend, acquaintance, or coworker, it will take its toll on you personally. It will cause you to become bitter, and it will show on your face and be revealed in your voice when you speak. It will come out in your body in the form of sickness, disease, or disability of some sort. Our bodies, minds, and souls were not designed to live in unforgiveness. It destroys us from the inside out. It is a poison for which there is no antidote except total forgiveness. And it will affect your marriage whether you realize it or not, because unforgiveness comes out in your personality and people sense it, even if they don't know what it is.

Decide in Advance

I have learned that the best way to live is to decide in *advance* to be a person who forgives. It takes the pressure off because you don't have to try to make that decision every time something bad happens and you're reeling from disappointment, hurt, or your own anger.

Once I was finally convinced that not forgiving destroys you and forgiveness sets you free, I decided to be a forgiving person all the time. Once I made that decision, of course I was put to the test. The next time my husband became angry, instead of reacting to him in my normal negative way, I caught myself and remembered that I had made the decision to forgive him even for the future times when he gets that way. I already knew that I had not done anything deserving of this anger to my knowledge, so instead of withdrawing in hurt the way I usually would have, I pressed him for why he was angry and upset. As it turned out, it was something that had happened at work. When he told me about it, I could totally understand why he felt the way he did. I would have been upset too. What I did not understand was why he felt it was right to take it out on me. He later recognized it was wrong and apologized.

After I completely forgave my mother for the abuse I suffered at her hands, I wanted so much to go back to that time when she was an 11-year-old girl who lost her mother and was deprived of her father. I wished I could have comforted her and done something to take away the pain. Even though I knew she was with the Lord now, I wept for the devastating tragedies she had suffered.

I asked the Lord, "What good are these tears now that she's gone and nothing can be done?" I felt impressed that God wanted me to use this grief to help people understand that every person has a story in their past that has made them who they are. And only God knows the whole story. Every angry and cruel person has had some kind of mistreatment, pain, and tragedy in their past—sometimes a hurt so deep they can't even express or understand it—and they sometimes do terrible things to the very people they are supposed to love because of it. Their need to express it outweighs their sense of decency and compassion. It's as if a spirit of revenge takes over for them, and they vent their pain and frustration through their anger without even considering what it does to the heart and soul of the person on the receiving end. No matter how cruel or mean a person has been to you, releasing them with your forgiveness frees *you*. It releases you from them so you can move on without that bad memory keeping you stuck in the past.

After I was truly freed from the powerful effects of my husband's anger by deciding *in advance* of it ever happening again that I was going to forgive him, I felt sad for Michael when he became angry. I knew he was cutting off what God wanted to bring into his life and that he would be the loser because of it. I felt sorry for the little boy who was made to feel like a failure for something he didn't understand and couldn't help. I regret that I wasn't healed, whole, and mature enough sooner so I would not have taken his anger so personally. Even though it was directed at me, it had a history back before I even knew him. Only after God had worked complete forgiveness in my heart was I able to see all that.

You Are Being Followed

Because God is a God of mercy and His mercy endures forever, you can trust that He will have mercy on you (1 Chronicles 17:13). Therefore you can show mercy to your spouse by forgiving whenever he (she) does or says something that hurts or disturbs you.

David said, "Surely goodness and mercy shall follow me all the days of my life; and I will dwell in the house of the LORD forever" (Psalm 23:6). That means if goodness and mercy are following you, they are covering your back. When you see goodness and mercy in your rearview mirror, it makes it easier for you to show goodness and mercy to your spouse. Jesus said, "Blessed are the merciful, for they shall obtain mercy" (Matthew 5:7). If you want to continue to have mercy from God, you have to give it to others. The way you show mercy toward your spouse is by forgiving him (her) at all times.

God's mercy is far-reaching. "As the heavens are high above the earth, so great is His mercy toward those who fear Him; as far as the east is from the west, so far has He removed our transgressions from us" (Psalm 103:11-12). That is about as far-reaching as it gets. We will always have trouble extending that much mercy without the enablement of God. In other words, if on our own we can't find the mercy in us to be able to forgive completely, God will help us if we ask Him to. There are times when something in us wants to punish, get even, or hurt back instead of being merciful and forgiving. But when we do that we get locked up inside, just as if we are in a physical prison. Forgiveness is the only key to unlock that prison door and get free. And it starts with having a heart of mercy.

SEVEN THINGS THAT ARE TRUE ABOUT GOD'S MERCY

1. **God's mercy is great.** "Great is Your mercy toward me, and You have delivered my soul from the depths of Sheol" (Psalm 86:13).

2. **When you have mercy the way He does, you find life.** "He who follows righteousness and mercy finds life, righteousness and honor" (Proverbs 21:21).

3. **God's mercy is abundant toward you.** "The LORD is merciful

and gracious, slow to anger, and abounding in mercy" (Psalm 103:8).

4. ***Forgiveness is an act of mercy.*** "I desire mercy and not sacrifice, and the knowledge of God more than burnt offerings" (Hosea 6:6).

5. ***God's mercy covers all your concerns.*** "The LORD will perfect that which concerns me; Your mercy, O LORD, endures forever; do not forsake the works of Your hands" (Psalm 138:8).

6. ***When you don't have mercy, you are not shown mercy.*** "Judgment is without mercy to the one who has shown no mercy. Mercy triumphs over judgment" (James 2:13).

7. ***God's mercy never ends.*** "The LORD is good; His mercy is everlasting, and His truth endures to all generations" (Psalm 100:5).

Because God is merciful, He doesn't remember your sins once He forgives them. "I, even I, am He who blots out your transgressions for My own sake; and I will not remember your sins" (Isaiah 43:25). If you are having trouble forgiving your husband (wife), be honest with God about it. Job cried out honestly to God in his pain saying, "I will not restrain my mouth; I will speak in the anguish of my spirit; I will complain in the bitterness of my soul" (Job 7:11). We have a God who understands our pain when we pour it out to Him.

If you feel you can't forgive, ask God to penetrate your unforgiveness with His love. When we have to do the impossible, God says that the way it happens is "not by might nor by power, but by My Spirit" (Zechariah 4:6). This means that certain things will not be accomplished by human strength, but only by the power of God. The Holy Spirit will enable us to forgive even the unforgivable.

First Things First

The first thing the disciples did after they received the Holy Spirit was to forgive others (John 20:21-23). It is also the first thing we need to do as we come before God each day. Say, "Lord, show me where I have unforgiveness, and I will confess it to You as sin so I can be free from it." If you already know that you have unforgiveness in your heart, say, "Lord, take the burden of unforgiveness off my shoulders and help me to let go of it completely so I can walk free."

What's even harder is that God asks us to *bless* those who hurt us (Matthew 5:43-44). Sometimes it feels as though not killing them should be enough. But God wants more than restraint. He wants us to actually want good things for them. He want us to show mercy to someone who we think doesn't deserve it, just as He showed mercy to us when *we* didn't deserve it. The thing is, forgiving your spouse does not depend on him (her) asking you for forgiveness or showing any repentance. If we wait for that, we could wait a lifetime for something that may never happen.

Of all the horrible things that were done to Joseph, he was amazingly forgiving. He was sold into slavery by his jealous brothers, but he still found favor wherever he went. He ended up in prison falsely accused, but was eventually appointed second in command to Pharaoh. Through it all, Joseph knew that what others intended for evil, God was using for good. He eventually said that very thing to his brothers who had betrayed him (Genesis 50:20). When we have that kind of amazing willingness to forgive, God will use our very act of forgiveness to turn things around in our marriage. He can even restore a marriage that is dying if the people in it extend total forgiveness.

SEVEN THINGS THAT ARE TRUE ABOUT FORGIVING

1. ***Forgiving brings blessings to you.*** "Finally, all of you be of one mind, having compassion for one another; love as brothers, be tenderhearted, be courteous; not returning evil for evil or reviling for reviling, but on the contrary blessing, knowing that you were called to this, that you may inherit a blessing" (1 Peter 3:8-9).

2. ***Forgiving others paves the way for you to be forgiven.*** "Judge not, and you shall not be judged. Condemn not, and you shall not be condemned. Forgive, and you will be forgiven" (Luke 6:37).

3. ***Forgiving allows you to forget and move forward.*** "One thing I do, forgetting those things which are behind and reaching

forward to those things which are ahead, I press toward the goal for the prize of the upward call of God in Christ Jesus" (Philippians 3:13-14).

4. ***Forgiving frees you to worship God with your whole heart.*** "Therefore if you bring your gift to the altar, and there remember that your brother has something against you, leave your gift there before the altar, and go your way. First be reconciled to your brother, and then come and offer your gift" (Matthew 5:23-24).

5. ***Forgiving proves that you are kind and tenderhearted.*** "And be kind to one another, tenderhearted, forgiving one another, just as God in Christ forgave you" (Ephesians 4:32).

6. ***Forgiving makes you Christlike.*** "Even as Christ forgave you, so you must also do" (Colossians 3:13).

7. ***Forgiving is the way you pursue peace and keep from becoming bitter.*** "Pursue peace with all people, and holiness, without which no one will see the Lord: looking carefully lest anyone fall short of the grace of God; lest any root of bitterness springing up cause trouble, and by this many become defiled" (Hebrews 12:14-15).

When You Need to Forgive God

Blaming God for something is not the best position to take. Remember, He is the one with the lightning. It's better to talk to Him and tell Him honestly how you feel. Say, "Lord, I confess I am angry at You for requiring me to be married to someone who hurts me so much." Or, "Lord, I don't understand why he (she) is never required to change and I *am*." Or, "Lord, why doesn't my husband (wife) have any financial wisdom and why do I have to suffer for it?" Or, "Lord, why did You let me marry someone with an alcohol problem just like my dad had? Haven't I suffered enough?" Or, "Lord, why do I have to be the responsible one and he (she) can just float through life like a child?" God understands those feelings and He can take the honesty. You're not telling Him anything He doesn't already know. He is just waiting for you to share it with Him so He can set you free.

The best way to break down that unforgiveness toward God is to confess it and thank Him for His forgiveness toward you. In fact, whenever you feel unforgiveness toward anyone trying to grip your heart like a vise, lift up praise to God until you feel that thing break in your soul. It will transform your heart.

What Happens When We Don't Forgive?

Not forgiving interferes with the effectiveness of your prayer life (Mark 11:25). That means your prayers don't get answered. That means you can't experience the full benefits of God's forgiveness if you are not forgiving others—especially your spouse. That means God puts your blessings on hold and waits until you take care of that unfinished business.

Not forgiving evaporates your joy. When you don't forgive, it brings up a barrier to the joy God has for you. *No one is ever truly happy if they have unforgiveness in their heart.*

Not forgiving weakens your body. It eats away at you and eventually takes over and destroys your life from the inside. It makes you physically sick as well as spiritually crippled. When you forgive you release it into God's hand and healing comes for your body as well as your soul.

Not forgiving opens the door for the enemy to work in your life. We have to forgive "lest Satan should take advantage of us" (2 Corinthians 2:11). We invite the enemy in if we harbor unforgiveness. And when you treat your spouse as if he (she) is the enemy—or your spouse acts as if *you* are—you align yourselves with your true enemy and his plans for your future.

Not forgiving pollutes your soul. The Bible says, "Does a spring send forth fresh water and bitter from the same opening?" (James 3:11). If you have unforgiveness, the water in your soul will become bitter.

SEVEN MORE THINGS TO REMEMBER ABOUT NOT FORGIVING

1. *Not forgiving will torture you.* " 'Should you not also have had compassion on your fellow servant, just as I had pity on you?' And his master was angry, and delivered him to the torturers until he should pay all that was due to him. So My heavenly Father also will do to you if each of you, from his heart, does not forgive his brother his trespasses" (Matthew 18:33-35).

2. ***Not forgiving causes you to entertain thoughts of revenge.*** "Do not say, 'I will do to him just as he has done to me; I will render to the man according to his work'" (Proverbs 24:29).

3. ***Not forgiving means you won't be forgiven by God.*** "But if you do not forgive men their trespasses, neither will your Father forgive your trespasses" (Matthew 6:15).

4. ***Not forgiving delays the answers to your prayers.*** "Whenever you stand praying, if you have anything against anyone, forgive him, that your Father in heaven may also forgive you your trespasses" (Mark 11:25).

5. ***Not forgiving means you see the failures of others, but not your own.*** "Why do you look at the speck in your brother's eye, but do not consider the plank in your own eye? Or how can you say to your brother, 'Let me remove the speck from your eye'; and look, a plank is in your own eye? Hypocrite! First remove the plank from your own eye, and then you will see clearly to remove the speck from your brother's eye" (Matthew 7:3-5).

6. ***Not forgiving means you are walking in darkness.*** "He who hates his brother is in darkness and walks in darkness, and does not know where he is going, because the darkness has blinded his eyes" (1 John 2:11).

7. ***Not forgiving means you are not pursuing what is best for your marriage.*** "See that no one renders evil for evil to anyone, but always pursue what is good both for yourselves and for all" (1 Thessalonians 5:15).

The Bottom Line

The bottom line is that forgiveness has to do with *repentance* and *love*. You have to *love* your spouse enough to *forgive* him (her) *and let it go*. And you have to *confess* your attitude of unforgiveness as a sin against God and *repent* of it. You have to be deeply sorry before the Lord that you were unforgiving because you know it displeases Him. You have to choose to forgive because you want to live God's way, because it's the right thing to do, and because it's the best thing for you. When you don't forgive, you feel separated from

God and you can't move ahead into the life God has for you. The truth is, *you* cannot be changed, *your husband (wife)* cannot be changed, and your *marriage* cannot be changed as long as you give place to unforgiveness in your heart.

I know that the last thing you may feel like doing is praying for your spouse if he (she) has hurt you, but that is what God wants you to do. In the process He will heal your pain because He is the God who "heals the brokenhearted and binds up their wounds" (Psalm 147:3). God will help you forgive so completely that you really don't think about those hurtful things anymore. As you pray, God will give you His heart of love. *You always grow to love the person you pray for.* Try it; you'll see. God wants you to live "not returning evil for evil or reviling for reviling, but on the contrary blessing, knowing that you were called to this, that you may inherit a blessing" (1 Peter 3:9). God isn't calling you to forgive so He can rub your nose in what offended or hurt you. He is asking you to forgive because when you do, you will inherit all that He has for you.

God does not violate a person's will who is determined to have a rebellious heart that refuses to take advice, seek counsel, or be open to the Lord's working in his (her) life. But your prayers for your spouse will still be rewarded with healing, release, strength, peace, and blessing for *you* when you pray for him (her), even if he (she) is not responding at the time. The Lord who loves *you* will "comfort *your* [heart] and establish *you* in every good word and work" (2 Thessalonians 2:17, emphasis added).

Forgiveness is not an option in our lives; it is a mandate. It is God's will for us every day. It doesn't depend on whether the person we must forgive is *repentant,* or *deserving* of it. It depends entirely on *us.* It is between *us* and *God.* We do it for the Lord, ultimately. Don't give up on forgiveness because you think you're just going to have to be doing it over and over again. Forgive because it is God's way and great good will come out of it. David said, "I would have lost heart, unless I had believed that I would see the goodness of the LORD in the land of the living" (Psalm 27:13). He wanted God's presence in his life enough to do whatever it took. I believe you want that too. Forgiving your husband (wife) is the best place to start.

PRAYERS FOR MY MARRIAGE

Prayer for Protection

LORD, I PRAY THAT YOU would help my husband (wife) and me to always be completely forgiving of one another. Help us to be humble enough to ask for forgiveness when we need to. And give us a heart to forgive freely—whether the other asks for it or not. Help us both to "grow in the grace and knowledge of our Lord and Savior Jesus Christ" (2 Peter 3:18), so that we will become forgiving like You are. Help us to forgive so that we will be forgiven (Luke 6:37).

Protect us from ourselves, Lord, so that we will not let our own flesh dictate whether we should hang on to offenses or let them go. Help us to love one another the way You love us, so that letting go of offenses will be easy. Help us to be merciful to one another, because we have Your goodness and mercy following us as You promised in Your Word (Psalm 23:6). Thank You that when we love each other Your way, You will bless us and show us Your favor by surrounding us like a protective shield (Psalm 5:12).

Lord, I know Your Word says that "if we say that we have no sin, we deceive ourselves, and the truth is not in us" (1 John 1:8). Help us to be undeceived about our own sins. Help us to live in truth and not be arrogant enough to think we have no sin in us. Help us to be quick to confess our sins to You and to one another. In Jesus' name I pray.

Prayer for Breakthrough in Me

THANK YOU, LORD, THAT I CAN DO *all* things through Christ who strengthens me, and therefore I have the strength to forgive my husband (wife) for anything that has hurt or disappointed me. Thank You that You are the God of forgiveness. Thank You for Your mercy and grace to me. Thank You that You have released me from any stronghold of unforgiveness. Take away any feelings in me that cause me to think I need to pay back hurt for hurt. I "strive to have a conscience without offense" toward You or my husband (wife) (Acts 24:16). Where I need to be forgiven, help me to apologize and receive forgiveness from my husband (wife).

Where there are places in me that harbor unforgiveness that I am not even aware of, please reveal those to me so I can confess them to You. I know that "You, Lord, are good, and ready to forgive, and abundant in mercy to all those who call upon You" (Psalm 86:5). I call upon You this day and ask You to forgive me for any unforgiveness I have toward anyone, especially my husband (wife). I know that You, Lord, are the only one who knows the whole story, so I refuse to be the judge of all that happens in my husband (wife). You are the one "who will both bring to light the hidden things of darkness and reveal the counsels of the [heart]" (1 Corinthians 4:5). Break any entrenched unforgiveness in me by the power of Your Spirit. Help me to love the way You do, so I can release all unforgiveness and be cleansed from all unrighteousness. In Jesus' name I pray.

Prayer for Breakthrough in My Husband (Wife)

LORD, I LIFT MY HUSBAND (WIFE) to You in prayer and ask You to help him (her) let go of any unforgiveness that he (she) harbors. I don't want him (her) to hang on to it and limit what You want to do in his (her) life. Help him (her) to forgive me for anything I have done—or *not* done—that was displeasing to him (her). I pray that You, "the God of patience and comfort," will grant to my husband (wife) the ability to be "like-minded" toward me so that we together may glorify You with a single-minded voice of unity (Romans 15:5-6). Give him (her) a heart of mercy toward me so that he (she) can truly let go of anything I have said or done that has hurt him (her).

You have said, Lord, that if we *don't* forgive people for their sins against us, You *won't* forgive us for *ours* (Matthew 6:14-15). Help my husband (wife) to become aware of anyone he (she) needs to forgive and enable him (her) to forgive that person completely, so that he (she) can move into the wholeness and restoration You have for him (her). Take away all thoughts of revenge or payback and make him (her) to be a forgiving person. In Jesus' name I pray.

TRUTH TO STAND ON

Whenever you stand praying, if you have anything
against anyone, forgive him that your Father in heaven may
also forgive you your trespasses.

MARK 11:25

Confess your trespasses to one another, and pray for one another,
that you may be healed. The effective, fervent prayer
of a righteous man avails much.

JAMES 5:16

Why do you judge your brother?
Or why do you show contempt for your brother?
For we shall all stand before the judgment seat of Christ.

ROMANS 14:10

If there is any consolation in Christ, if any comfort of love,
if any fellowship of the Spirit, if any affection and mercy,
fulfill my joy by being like-minded, having the same love,
being of one accord, of one mind.

PHILIPPIANS 2:1-2

Be submissive to one another, and be clothed with humility,
for God resists the proud, but gives grace to the humble.

1 PETER 5:5

4

If DEPRESSION or NEGATIVE EMOTIONS SPOIL the ATMOSPHERE

I think my depression started in the closet. That tiny dark space underneath the stairs in my parents' tiny old ranch house that had no running water, no bathroom, no electricity, and no heat in the bitter freezing Wyoming winters, except what came from an old coal-burning stove in the kitchen and a small stone fireplace in the living room. Upstairs, the two small bedrooms were always freezing, and it took forever till the sheets warmed up. Seeds of anxiety, sadness, fear, loneliness, and rejection were planted there like weeds that would grow deeper and more rampant every year of my early life until they would eventually suffocate all hope within me.

As far back as I can remember, I had that depressed feeling. I didn't know I was experiencing depression at the time; I thought it was just me. *This is the way I am,* I thought as I grew up. *I am a frightened, hopeless, lonely, hurting, anxious, and depressed person, and there is nothing I can do about it. No one can help me, nor does anyone want to, nor will anyone ever want to, or even be able to.*

I am not talking here about a chemical imbalance, although I probably had one. Terror, dread, sadness, and stress have a way of depleting your mind, body, and soul until you not only have a physical imbalance, but a spiritual and emotional one as well. And that's enough to depress anyone. I had gone to doctors and tried different medicines, but nothing ever worked for me. This was a deep wounding of the soul for which there is no cure outside of the power of God.

It wasn't until I received the Lord and began to learn of the wholeness He has for each of us that I became more aware that depressed, anxious, and afraid wasn't the way He made us to be. Depression, fear, and anxiety were not His will for my life. His promise for me was peace—if I would pray fervently and be thankful and worshipful of Him. "Be anxious for nothing, but in everything by prayer and supplication, with thanksgiving, let your requests be made known to God; and the peace of God, which surpasses all understanding, will guard your hearts and minds through Christ Jesus" (Philippians 4:6-7). That meant because of Jesus, I had a way out of anxiety, depression, and fear if I would learn to pray about everything. Every situation, condition, and relationship in my life would respond to prayer. Because of the power of God working through prayer, I eventually found deliverance and healing from all the negative emotions that crippled me. Sometimes just my own prayers alone were enough, but often the faith-filled prayers of others, praying *with* and *for* me, paved the way for miracles.

In my case, I went to our church for help at the suggestion of my husband. We had been married a few months, and I still couldn't shake the grip of depression, fear, and anxiety I was under. The first time I saw Mary Anne, the pastor's wife and counselor I mentioned earlier, I noticed she had the most beautiful eyes that sparkled like the ocean when the sun dances on the waves. I had heard she was especially gifted in the knowledge of God's Word and the understanding of the power of prayer, so when she asked me to fast and pray for three days—which was no easy feat for someone such as I, who had gone to bed hungry many nights as a child—I was willing to do it.

I went back to that same counseling office the following week after not having anything to eat or drink but water for three days, carrying a list Mary Anne had asked me to make of all the sins I could remember committing in my life. I was grateful when she didn't want to read it, but asked that I would present the list before God and confess it all at once. I also had to confess my unforgiveness toward my mother and renounce all my occult involvement. Even though I had completely stopped any practice or involvement with the occult when I received the Lord, I had never gone before the Lord and renounced those practices.

Once I confessed and renounced all that, Mary Anne and another pastor's wife prayed for me, and I literally felt the depression lift off of me. I am not exaggerating this. In fact, I am understating it so it won't be hard for you to believe. But I felt the depression lift off from me as though it were a heavy, wet, dark blanket. And the best part about the story is that it never came back. I am not saying I never felt depression again. There are many depressing things that happen in life. But I was never gripped or controlled by it again. I could always go to God in prayer and He would take it away.

This is not to say that if you are taking medication prescribed by a doctor for depression or anxiety that you are to suddenly stop taking it. To the contrary, this can be dangerous. That also doesn't necessarily sentence you to a lifetime of medication, either. I believe you can find wholeness without medicine. But there is no sin in taking prescribed medicine if you need it. Taking medicine doesn't make you any less holy than someone else who doesn't take anything. In a world spinning faster, with pressures increasing and the rigors of life becoming more monumental every day, it is no wonder we have gotten ourselves out of balance. Every *body* is different. Every *mind* and *soul* are different. Everyone's past is different, and each person's *reaction* to their past is different. Some of us are born depleted; some of us develop an imbalance later. It doesn't matter. What does matter is that you look to God as your healer and pray for healing. God will heal you in His way and time, and you can keep taking your medicine until that happens. You'll know when to stop, and a doctor can help you wean off of it if that's what you're supposed to do. If not, keep taking your medicine and praise God that it's working.

Whether you are taking medicine or not is entirely between you and God and your doctor. But I would tell you that medicine alone will never be enough. The only total cure for depression I have ever found is the love of God and His power working on your behalf to break all oppression on your life. And the love of God gives us hope. "Now hope does not disappoint, because the love of God has been poured out in our hearts by the Holy Spirit who was given to us" (Romans 5:5).

When the Problem Is Depression

It's normal to feel depressed about the things that happen in life from time to time. The loss of a job, a loved one, finances, or possessions. The experience of failure, disappointment, sickness, or accidents. But when you stay depressed, then it becomes a problem. You were not made to live in depression. Depression every day is not God's will for your life. When every day seems dark and gray and without joy or light, then it becomes a grip of hell in your life and must be broken.

When I received the Lord, I began to finally see a light at the end of the long dark tunnel of my life, but I still had depression. I was born again into the kingdom of God because I received Jesus and I know something happened to me that day, but I still had depression. I felt hope for the first time in my life, but I still lived under a heavy blanket of depression. Not everyone is instantly freed of every bondage the minute they receive the Lord. I have no doubt they can be, and I have no doubt that some are, but this is not most people's experience. There are way too many depressed Christians for this to be true. There are people who adamantly believe that if you are a true Christian you will never have depression. May I politely suggest that the people who are saying this are people who have never been depressed? They have been blinded by their own arrogance and legalism to the plight of others.

I have also heard it suggested that in light of the following verses, if we are really walking in the light then we wouldn't have to go through the darkness of depression. "God is light and in Him is no darkness at all. If we say that we have fellowship with Him, and walk in darkness, we lie and do not practice the truth" (1 John 1:5-6). They are saying that these verses bring into question our born-again status. Can we really be saved if we have depression? As one who has been depressed while being a born-again believer, this attitude makes me mad. Let me get something straight in case anyone has ever suggested that to you. *Yes, you can be born again and depressed at the same time!*

The verses above have to do with the *decision* to walk in fellowship with darkness. Being depressed does not mean you are *choosing* to walk in depression. Depression is something that you can have *on* you once you are a believer, but not *in* you. It can't possess you. It doesn't own you. The Holy Spirit is in you, not depression. Depression is not you. It may be on you like an oppression of the enemy designed to steal your joy and rob you of life, but you are not your depression. You can still have the light of the Lord *within* you and yet have the darkness of oppression settle *on* you and invade your life like an enemy encroaching on the territory of your being.

How Depression Feels

In case you have never been depressed yourself, let me describe it for you. It may help you to better understand your spouse if he (she) ever gets depressed. Job described what seemed like depression as "a land as dark as darkness itself, as the shadow of death, without any order, where even the light is like darkness" (Job 10:22). When you are depressed, even good things can't be enjoyed because they are tainted by that dark oppression. He said, "When I looked for good, evil came to me; and when I waited for light, then came darkness" (Job 30:26). In other words, it seems as though no matter what you do, it never gets better.

Perhaps no one ever struggled with depression more openly or wrote about it more clearly than King David. He knew depression well. Listen to what he said about the way he felt and see if this sounds like depression to you. "My life is spent with grief, and my years with sighing; my strength fails because of my iniquity, and my bones waste away" (Psalm 31:10). "Turn Yourself to me, and have mercy on me, for I am desolate and afflicted. The troubles of my heart have enlarged; bring me out of my distresses! Look on my affliction and my pain, and forgive all my sins" (Psalm 25:16-18). "Consider and hear me, O LORD my God; enlighten my eyes, lest I sleep the sleep of death" (Psalm 13:3). "Why are you cast down, O my soul? And why are you disquieted within me? Hope in God, for I shall yet praise Him for the help of His countenance" (Psalm 42:5). I especially appreciate the phrase "cast down" referring to a heavily burdened soul. That's exactly what it feels like—you have fallen in a pit far from hope.

David's solution to all this was to look up and put his hope in God. Sometimes we can feel as though God has abandoned us when we sink in depression and our prayers are not being answered. As a result, we feel separated from Him. But God has *not* abandoned us. He will comfort us when we turn to Him. Paul said, "God, who comforts the downcast, comforted us" (2 Corinthians 7:6).

David said, "I said in my haste, 'I am cut off from before Your eyes,'" but he also said, "*Nevertheless You heard the voice of my supplications when I cried out to You"* (Psalm 31:22, emphasis added). David knew deep despair and depression, but he also knew his hope was in God.

David said, "The pangs of death surrounded me, and the floods of ungodliness made me afraid. The sorrows of Sheol surrounded me; the snares of death confronted me" (Psalm 18:4-5). But he *also* said, *"You have delivered my soul from death, my eyes from tears, and my feet from falling"* (Psalm 116:8, emphasis added).

In the midst of David's sorrow he said, *"Yea, though I walk through the valley of the shadow of death, I will fear no evil; for You are with me; Your rod and Your staff, they comfort me"* (Psalm 23:4, emphasis added). *"Indeed, the darkness shall not hide from You, but the night shines as the day; the darkness and the light are both alike to You"* (Psalm 139:12, emphasis added). God can see plainly into the darkness that hangs over you. He sees the truth about you and your situation, and He wants you to see it too. That means "there is no darkness nor shadow of death where the workers of iniquity may hide themselves" (Job 34:22). That's because we have authority over all the power of the enemy.

When you feel as David did—"My spirit is overwhelmed within me; my heart within me is distressed" (Psalm 143:4), then say as David did, *"Hear me when I call, O God of my righteousness! You have relieved me in my distress; have mercy on me, and hear my prayer"* (Psalm 4:1, emphasis added).

This is the way depression feels to me. You feel distant from other people as if you are in another realm when you are around them. You are not on the same plane they are. You can be in the same room with them, but you feel as though there is a wall separating you from them, so you don't really make contact. It feels as if they are fading from you, as if the darkness around *you* is swallowing *them* up. When you speak, it's almost like an out of body experience. It's as if you are outside your body listening to yourself speak, but you are not really connecting to the other person. There is a barrier to their connecting with you. And it is your own depression. It is described in Psalms, saying, "Loved one and friend You have put far from me, and my acquaintances into darkness" (Psalm 88:18).

When you are depressed, it's hard to do anything, even the basic necessities for life. It takes all your energy just being depressed. You're tired all the time because fighting anxiety, fear, and depression is exhausting. You lose interest in activities and doing things that you would normally do. You are pessimistic about most things and you feel hopeless about everything else. You feel hopeless because there seems to be no way to rise above your predicament. When you don't believe your miserable situation will ever change, you can't see a reason to live. You wonder, *Why try?* At its worst, depression can make you feel suicidal, which means you see death as the only way out.

You feel as though you can't do anything that involves the future, even as close as the next day, so you live moment to moment. You are unable to think ahead and prepare in advance. You can't think clearly about things, and you find it hard to get anything done, so it's extremely difficult to keep your home straight or your closet clean. You have a difficult time planning anything because you will never feel good about what you are planning. You see no point to it. Depression can overshadow your ability to make solid and rational decisions. People may tell you to snap out of it, but you are powerless to do so on your own strength. That's why telling your spouse to "get over it" will only make them feel more hopeless.

We can also get depressed from being overextended, exhausted, malnourished, or sick. There is nothing more depressing than being sick or in pain. And any kind of loss can make us depressed too, such as the loss of a job, a person, a relationship, an ability, or a body part. The ultimate example of suffering loss was Job. He lost everything and said, "My heart is in turmoil and cannot rest; days of affliction confront me" (Job 30:27). Habits of the mind can keep us depressed because we are always focusing on a negative side of something or someone. Feeling helpless in the face of some threat or trauma makes us depressed.

When you are depressed, you have a strong need for physical touch and verbal affirmation, but this is the time when you find it hardest to communicate that need. It's difficult to communicate your need for love when you feel unlovable, unworthy, and unable to respond, but love is what you need most.

Don't ever feel that suffering from depression has separated you from God. It hasn't. The enemy wants you to believe that God is far from you and that's why you have to live in the darkness of depression. But God refers to the treasures of darkness saying, "I will give you the treasures of darkness and hidden riches of secret places, that you may know that I, the LORD, who call you by your name, am the God of Israel" (Isaiah 45:3). When you go through the dark times of depression, it forces you to walk closer to God. And that is a good thing. I have been there, and I have found that the treasure we find in darkness is *Him*. It's the promise of God's presence in the midst of our darkness. That means we don't have to be afraid of the dark, because His light will come into our darkness and He will reveal Himself to us.

TEN THINGS YOU NEED TO KNOW ABOUT DEPRESSION

1. *God is with you in it.* "Fear not, for I am with you; be not dismayed, for I am your God. I will strengthen you, yes, I will help you, I will uphold you with My righteous right hand" (Isaiah 41:10).

2. *Even though you are in a struggle, you will not be destroyed.* "We are hard-pressed on every side, yet not crushed; we are perplexed, but not in despair" (2 Corinthians 4:8).

3. *God hears when you call to Him about it.* "In my distress I called upon the LORD, and cried out to my God; He heard my voice from His temple, and my cry came before Him, even to His ears" (Psalm 18:6).

4. *The Lord will be a light to you at all times.* "The people who walked in darkness have seen a great light; those who dwelt in the land of the shadow of death, upon them a light has shined" (Isaiah 9:2).

5. *God will bring you out of darkness.* "For You are my lamp, O LORD; the LORD shall enlighten my darkness" (2 Samuel 22:29).

6. *God wants you to trust in Him through it.* "Who among you fears the LORD? Who obeys the voice of His Servant? Who walks in darkness and has no light? Let him trust in the name of the LORD and rely upon his God" (Isaiah 50:10).

7. *Jesus understands your sorrow.* Jesus was "despised and rejected by men, a Man of sorrows and acquainted with grief" (Isaiah 53:3).

8. *God's presence will save you.* "In all their affliction He was

afflicted, and the Angel of His Presence saved them; in His love and in His pity He redeemed them; and He bore them and carried them all the days of old" (Isaiah 63:9).

9. ***You need to keep praying about it.*** "Attend to my cry, for I am brought very low; deliver me from my persecutors, for they are stronger than I" (Psalm 142:6).

10. ***Jesus has more for you than living with depression.*** Jesus said, "The thief does not come except to steal, and to kill, and to destroy. I have come that they may have life, and that they may have it more abundantly" (John 10:10).

Rejection, Anxiety, Fear, Loneliness, and Other Negative Emotions

Feelings of rejection are often caused by something traumatic that has happened in the past—especially in childhood. Those of us who have been through difficult things in childhood often have a hard time sharing those things because they make you different. And you don't want to be different in any way when you're young. If you have had trouble accepting yourself or feeling accepted, you don't want to open the door of possibility for other people to reject you too. You have a constant internal life going on inside you that you don't share with others because you don't want to appear stupid, inferior, or rejectable.

I suffered with deep feelings of rejection because my mother told me from the time I was very young that I was worthless and no good and would never amount to anything. Because I believed her, the constant feeling of never being worth anything—always feeling unloved and uncared for—made me a magnet for every negative emotion there is.

Anxiety is a feeling of intense worry or fear that something bad is about to happen. You have a constant torturous uneasiness about the outcome of most events or situations. In the extreme, you feel anxious even when you are not sure why. At its worst, anxiety leads to panic attacks, which can grip you so strongly that you feel as though you are going to have a heart attack, stop breathing, and die.

When I was working as a singer, dancer, and actress on TV in my early twenties, I would have panic attacks so bad that I would go into the ladies' room and lock myself in a bathroom stall so I could double up against the door and hang on for dear life. If no one else was there I would cry. If someone was in the room, I would just hold my breath, try to gain control, and make myself breathe in and out. Although I didn't have a relationship with God then, I still said, "God, help me." In my mind I wasn't actually asking this distant being to take the anxiety away because I thought it was warranted since I was such a failure. And I continually feared that people were going to find out what a failure I was. All I was asking of God was that He would keep me from dying. I truly thought at the time that this was the most God could do. I thought that depressed, anxious, fearful, suicidal, and hopeless was just the way I was, and I didn't think He could make me into something I wasn't. What more could God possibly do than keep me alive?

Anxiety like this is usually unwarranted or greatly overblown in the face of the truth. When you are chronically uneasy because you think something bad is going to happen, you have no peace and it is uncomfortable to be around you. Jesus said not to have an anxious mind (Luke 12:29). Proverbs 12:25 says, "Anxiety in the heart of man causes depression, but a good word makes it glad." *The good word from God is that you don't have to be anxious about anything you can pray about.*

Fear is not something that comes from God. "God has not given us a spirit of fear, but of power and of love and of a sound mind" (2 Timothy 1:7). If we lay claim to the *love* God has for us, the *power* He has for us, and the *sound mind* He has for us, there will be no room for a spirit of fear. We don't invite a spirit of fear every time we are afraid, only when fear becomes a controlling factor in our lives. It's good to be afraid of danger when it is warranted. It's what will keep you from walking out into traffic or alone in a deserted place at night. But it's not good to have fear as a way of life.

The only kind of fear God wants us to have is to fear Him (1 Peter 2:17). That doesn't mean we are afraid of Him, but that we are afraid of what life would be like *without* Him. And the fear He is talking about is a deep reverence for Him and who He is. Don't live with fear when God says He has love, power, and a sound mind instead. Claim what God has for you.

Loneliness is painful. It causes an ache in your heart that can be unbearable. But you don't have to live with that when God is waiting to be close to you if you will draw close to Him. I used to live in the pain of loneliness even after I was married. One day, in an especially painful time of loneliness, God spoke to my heart that whenever I felt lonely I was to come to Him and He would take it away. I did that right then and the loneliness disappeared completely. Now I recognize any feelings of loneliness—which are rare for me now—as a signal that I need to be with God. Let it be that kind of sign to you as well. Jesus said, "Whatever you ask the Father in My name He will give you. Until now you have asked nothing in My name. Ask, and you will receive, that your joy may be full" (John 16:22-24). Ask God to set you free from loneliness and all other negative emotions.

TWELVE THINGS TO REMEMBER IN THE FACE OF NEGATIVE EMOTIONS

1. ***God knows what you are going through.*** "O LORD, You have searched me and known me. You know my sitting down and my rising up; You understand my thought afar off. You comprehend my path and my lying down, and are acquainted with all my ways. For there is not a word on my tongue, but behold, O LORD, You know it altogether" (Psalm 139:1-4).

2. ***God is there for you in your darkest hour.*** "Unto the upright there arises light in the darkness; He is gracious, and full of compassion, and righteous" (Psalm 112:4).

3. ***You don't have to live with the darkness of negative emotions.*** "I have come as a light into the world, that whoever believes in Me should not abide in darkness" (John 12:46).

4. ***God will rescue you when you cry out to Him.*** "They cried out to the LORD in their trouble, and He saved them out of their distresses" (Psalm 107:13).

5. ***You don't have to be afraid.*** "The LORD is my light and my salvation; whom shall I fear? The LORD is the strength of my life; of whom shall I be afraid?" (Psalm 27:1).

6. ***God will break through all bondage.*** "He brought them out of darkness and the shadow of death, and broke their chains in pieces" (Psalm 107:14).

7. *Even if you fall again, you will rise up yet another time.* "Do not rejoice over me, my enemy; when I fall, I will arise; when I sit in darkness, the LORD will be a light to me" (Micah 7:8).

8. *You have the power to cast off darkness and put on light.* "The night is far spent, the day is at hand. Therefore let us cast off the works of darkness, and let us put on the armor of light" (Romans 13:12).

9. *God keeps His eyes on you when you keep your eyes on Him.* "Behold, the eye of the LORD is on those who fear Him, on those who hope in His mercy, to deliver their soul from death, and to keep them alive in famine. Our soul waits for the LORD; He is our help and our shield. For our heart shall rejoice in Him, because we have trusted in His holy name. Let Your mercy, O LORD, be upon us, just as we hope in You" (Psalm 33:18-22).

10. *God will deliver you.* "He has delivered us from the power of darkness and conveyed us into the kingdom of the Son of His love" (Colossians 1:13).

11. *He will continue to deliver you until you are completely free.* "Yes, we had the sentence of death in ourselves, that we should not trust in ourselves but in God who raises the dead, who delivered us from so great a death, and does deliver us; in whom we trust that He will still deliver us" (2 Corinthians 1:9-10).

12. *God will comfort you.* "Sing, O heavens! Be joyful, O earth! And break out in singing, O mountains! For the LORD has comforted His people, and will have mercy on His afflicted" (Isaiah 49:13).

If the Problem Is with Your Spouse

While it is certainly no fun being depressed, it is definitely no fun being around someone who is depressed all the time, either. Life is hard enough on your own without having to deal with someone else's problems. But when you are married, your spouse's problems become yours as well. In my case, my husband and I both suffered from depression and anxiety in the beginning. However, I found healing for it in that first year we were married. Michael struggled with it longer.

A spouse who is controlled by depression, anxiety, or fear is very self-focused. He (she) is forced to think about himself (herself) most of the time, and therefore has little resource left to give to others—especially his (her) spouse. That's why your husband's (wife's) depression can make your life miserable too. And it will definitely affect your children, because they won't understand what it is and will think there is something wrong with them.

Often after a person gets married, all the weaknesses, negative emotions, and emotional disorders they have surface one by one. Those things can't be hidden for long in the closeness of a marriage. If you see that happening in you or your spouse, don't be afraid. God wants to set you both free from all that, and often these things don't come out until you are in a safe place. A marriage is a safe place—or at least it is supposed to be. It means that you are now with someone who loves you enough to commit to you. If there is anything wrong with you, God is not going to let you hang on to it. He won't allow you to continue with depression, anxiety, fear, bitterness, anger, or loneliness. It will be exposed because marriage shines a spotlight on those kinds of things and there is no place to hide. Who you are will be revealed. And God doesn't want you hiding anyway. He wants you free. When things surface in you or in your husband (wife), be willing to face what is exposed without fear. It is not the end of the good times; it is the beginning of the best times. Be willing to do what it takes to get free and become whole.

When your spouse is depressed, you end up not talking about things that need to be talked about. You avoid the depressed person because you don't know if what you say is going to make things worse. They appear weak to you because they don't have the ability to do things they need to do, which forces you to be the strong one and the decision maker. You can't go to them as a safe place where you can let down and share your thoughts, hopes, dreams, and fears because all they can focus on is getting through the day. Anxiety can be paralyzing, just as depression is, because if you believe that disaster is one step away from you, you won't want to take a step in any direction at all. Dreams for the future are put aside. The future is only tomorrow.

It will be much easier for you to deal with your spouse's depression if you don't see him (her) as a *depressed person* who can't seem to get over it.

See him (her), instead, as a *person God wants to heal*. If your spouse is on medication for depression, don't tell him (her) to get off of it. This could have serous ramifications and he (she) could end up feeling like a failure if it's necessary to resume taking it. As I said earlier, there is no failure in having to take medicine prescribed by a doctor. Some people take it all their lives, and if they are believers I am certain they are still going to heaven and are not walking in darkness. In fact, one of the best things you can do for your spouse is help him (her) find the right doctor who will prescribe the best medicine.

You may feel as though you don't know what to do to help your depressed husband (wife), but one thing you can always do is pray. And it will always make a big difference. You can also show your love and support. That means a lot to a depressed person. Assure your husband (wife) that depression is only temporary and there is an end to it. "Weeping may endure for a night, but joy comes in the morning" (Psalm 30:5).

How to Get Out of Depression and Other Negative Emotions

No matter what negative emotion it is, if it grips you and controls your life, you have to do whatever it takes to break the hold it has in you.

First of all, read God's Word every day. Read as much as you can. Speak it out loud. Find an appropriate verse and say it over and over until it is engraved upon your heart and you believe it. Say, "Thank you Lord, that Your word is a lamp to my feet and a light to my path" (Psalm 119:105). "Thank You for the sound mind You have given me."

Determine to take charge of your mind. Refuse to allow your emotions to rule you. Instead, you rule over them. Don't allow negative thoughts to dictate how you act, what you say or don't say, or what you do or don't do. Think about the good and positive things about your life.

Seek good Christian counseling. If negative emotions are a gripping problem for you and they don't respond to prayer as I have suggested here, there are good medical doctors, psychiatrists, and psychologists who can help you. Don't try to deal with your situation alone.

Pray without ceasing. Always have a dialogue going with God, but don't do all the talking. Listen too. God says you are to give the burden of your soul entirely to Him. If you pray instead of allowing negative emotions to control you, you can have the kind of peace in your heart that is beyond comprehension.

Praise and worship God. This is one of the most powerful things you can do. In fact, every time you begin to feel any negative emotion, worship God right where you are and you will feel that thing lift off of you. The wells of salvation are deep. There is so much that Jesus has saved you from. Draw spiritual water from those wells every day and you will find joy (Isaiah 12:3).

SEVEN THINGS DEPRESSION AND NEGATIVE EMOTIONS ARE NOT

1. They are not inevitable.
2. They are not a life sentence for you.
3. They are not a sign of failure.
4. They are not God's judgment on you.
5. They are not a license to withdraw from your spouse.
6. They are not an opportunity to be rude or mean to your spouse.
7. They are not a tool you use to control your spouse.

I believe God sometimes allows depression and other negative emotions in the lives of even strong believers because it forces us to draw closer to Him in order to walk through it. And He is glorified when we are set free of it. So cry out to God in your need for His love, peace, joy, and power, knowing that He longs to share Himself with you. Say, "Thank You, God, that You make us 'exceedingly glad with Your presence'" (Psalm 21:6).

Negative emotions are not something you have to live with. In fact, you must do whatever is necessary to get rid of them. They not only hurt you, they hurt your spouse and children as well. God has given you a way out of them through the power of prayer, praise, His Word, His presence, and His love. Bask in all that until you are free. And don't lose hope. Be confident of this, that "He who has begun a good work in you will complete it until the day of Jesus Christ" (Philippians 1:6). God won't give up on you, so don't give up on yourself or your spouse.

PRAYERS FOR MY MARRIAGE

Prayer for Protection

LORD, I THANK YOU THAT You show us the paths of life and "in Your presence is fullness of joy; at Your right hand are pleasures forevermore" (Psalm 16:11). Thank You that when we delight ourselves in You, You will cause us "to ride on the high hills of the earth" (Isaiah 58:14). I pray that You will keep my husband (wife) and me from all negative emotions. Help us to see that we never have to live with any of them. Where we have allowed anything such as depression, anxiety, fear, rejection, or loneliness to influence our lives, deliver us out of all that and keep it far from us.

I pray that even though we may go through times where we are hard-pressed on every side, we will not be crushed, nor will we be in despair (2 Corinthians 4:8). We will rejoice in Your Word and the comfort of Your presence. We will not forget that You have the power to set us free.

Your commandments are right and they make our hearts rejoice (Psalm 19:8). We were once in darkness, but now we are in Your light. Help us to always "walk as children of the light" (Ephesians 5:8). I pray we will always look to You and put our hope and expectations in You (Psalm 62:5). In Jesus' name I pray.

Prayer for Breakthrough in Me

LORD, I PRAY THAT YOU would "search me, O God, and know my heart; try me, and know my anxieties" (Psalm 139:23). Wherever I have allowed negative emotions to control me, deliver me forever from them. Show me things in my life that have been passed down in my family—attitudes, fears, prejudices, and even depression—and break these strongholds completely. Keep me from falling into habits of the heart that are learned responses to life. Lord, I pray for healing and deliverance from any depression, anxiety, fear, rejection, loneliness, or any other negative emotion that would seek to find permanent residence in my heart. You are the lamp of my soul, Lord, and I thank

You that You "will enlighten my darkness" (Psalm 18:28). Thank You that You will give me rest from my sorrow and fear (Isaiah 14:3).

Lord, take away all sadness or despair. Heal the hurt in my heart. Give me a garment of praise at all times and take away the spirit of heaviness. Make me to be a tree of strength. Plant me and feed me in Your Word so that Your glory will be revealed in me. Rebuild the places in me that have been damaged or ruined in the past. Lord, I pray that You would "send out Your light and Your truth! Let them lead me; let them bring me to Your holy hill and to Your tabernacle" (Psalm 43:3). May Your light in my life completely evaporate any black clouds around me so that they cannot keep me from sensing Your presence in my life. In Jesus' name I pray.

Prayer for Breakthrough in My Husband (Wife)

Lord, I lift my husband (wife) up to You and ask that You would set him (her) free from depression, anxiety, fear, rejection, loneliness, or any other negative emotions that grips him (her). Thank You for Your promise to bring out Your "people with joy" and Your "chosen ones with gladness" (Psalm 105:43). Thank You that because of You, Jesus, "darkness is passing away, and the true light is already shining" in his (her) life (1 John 2:8). Help him (her) to keep his (her) eyes on You and take refuge in You knowing that You will not leave his (her) soul destitute (Psalm 141:8). Have mercy on him (her) and be his (her) helper! (Psalm 30:10). Anoint him (her) with Your "oil of gladness" (Psalm 45:7). Restore to him (her) the joy of Your salvation, and uphold him (her) "by Your generous Spirit" (Psalm 51:12). Set him (her) free from anything that holds him (her) other than You.

I say to my husband (wife) now, as You, Lord, said to Your people in Your Word, "Be strong and of good courage; do not be afraid, nor be dismayed, for the Lord your God is with you wherever you go" (Joshua 1:9). The Lord *loves* you and has given you *hope* and *grace,* and will *comfort* your heart and *establish* you in all things (2 Thessalonians 2:16-17). In Jesus' name I pray.

Truth to Stand On

We do not wrestle against flesh and blood,
but against principalities, against powers,
against the rulers of the darkness of this age,
against spiritual hosts of wickedness in the heavenly places.

Ephesians 6:12

He has delivered us from the power of darkness and conveyed
us into the kingdom of the Son of His love.

Colossians 1:13

He has sent Me to heal the brokenhearted…
to give them beauty for ashes, the oil of joy for mourning,
the garment of praise for the spirit of heaviness;
that they may be called trees of righteousness,
the planting of the Lord, that He may be glorified.

Isaiah 61:1,3

There is no fear in love; but perfect love casts out fear,
because fear involves torment.
But he who fears has not been made perfect in love.

1 John 4:18

You are my hiding place; You shall
preserve me from trouble; You shall
surround me with songs of deliverance.

Psalm 32:7

5

If CHILDREN START *to* DOMINATE YOUR LIVES

———⌒∽⌒———

Nothing will change a marriage faster and more dramatically than the birth of a child. When children come along, the demands on you are far greater than anyone can really prepare you for. You no longer have time to focus entirely on each other because now you must focus on your child. That means there is a lot less time to be alone. One of you can't work as much, so there is less money. Or if you both try to keep working, you become exhausted. You realize you have to sacrifice all selfish pleasure in order to devote yourself to becoming a good parent. And all that can be overwhelming. But the good news is that all this forces you to grow up, establish firm priorities, and learn to take care of yourself because you can't afford to be sick.

It's important when the size of your family increases that you not lose sight of the fact that one day it will again just be the two of you. I know it's hard to think that far ahead when the children occupy all your time and attention now. In fact, it's easy to let children dominate your lives. And it can happen without you even realizing it. After all, in the beginning your child can't do one thing without you. Your husband (wife) can presumably take care of himself (herself). Your spouse can feed, bathe, and dress himself (herself). Your baby can't do anything without help. So right away, out of necessity, children come between the two of you because of the amount of time you need to devote to them. But that doesn't have to be bad. If the two of you share the load, it will bond you more closely together. Some parents become so focused on parenting that they think of nothing else, not even their spouse. While God wants us to love and care for our children to the best of our ability, He doesn't want us to make idols out of them. There is a fine line between the caring nurture that gives your children the best chance in life, and the other extreme of letting them become an obsession to the point that it jeopardizes your marriage. Allowing your spouse to feel neglected, overlooked, unimportant, unnecessary, or irrelevant doesn't help your marriage stay strong. And having your marriage fall apart doesn't help your children. We all need wisdom and revelation from God in order to find that balance.

Many conflicts can arise between a husband and wife over the raising of their children that are serious enough to lead to divorce. These conflicts may not happen in the busy infancy or toddler states, but rather later on in the complicated teenage years when more is at stake. I have found that the best way to raise your children and take the pressure off of you is to pray for them every step of the way. In my first book in the Power of a Praying series, *The Power of a Praying Parent,* I gave 30 ways to pray for your child. Such things as that they be protected, feel loved and accepted, maintain good family relationships, have godly friends and role models, have a desire to learn, have a sound mind, not be ruled by fear, not be addicted to anything, grow in faith, and become who God created them to be. Praying this way about your children means you don't have to be Supermom or Superdad, and that takes the pressure off your marriage. Praying *together* about your children is best, but praying alone has great benefits as well. Here are some things to pray about with regard to your marriage and raising children.

Pray to Agree on Discipline

How you discipline your children is a very important issue you have to decide together. It should not be one-sided, with one of you strict and the other lenient. If that is the case with you and your spouse, pray to find a happy meeting place somewhere between indulgent and permissive.

Seek God for wisdom and unity about how you are going to discipline your children for each offense. If *you* refuse to discipline your children, you force your *husband* (*wife*) to be the bad guy. Your husband (wife) will get very tired of being the bad guy while you look like your child's best friend. It will chip away at the foundation of your marriage until it is weakened or destroyed. Don't think for a moment that this is not a very deep issue. I have known too many marriages to break up over this serious situation.

In fact, I know a great couple who have been married nearly 25 years and their children are now teenagers. Recently the husband and wife have come into conflict over what to permit the children to do. The wife feels the husband is too permissive and the husband believes the wife is too strict. She felt that he was way too lenient when he found out that their children had experimented with drugs. She sees his permissiveness as a danger for their children, possibly jeopardizing their future. They have filed for divorce over this. Neither of them knows the Lord, but if they did, they could pray through this and come to a good solution. They could work this out so easily if humility, reliance on God, the power of prayer, and truly loving your spouse more than loving yourself were to come into play.

I can understand where she is coming from, but it would be so much better to go to Christian counseling than to break up the family. When she gets divorced, she will have completely lost control over what the children will be allowed to do when they are with the permissive spouse.

There are definitely times when you have a child endangered by the actions or inactions of a parent, but if you both are reasonable and sane people, you should be able to work this out. Especially if you pray. *Putting one another first before the children doesn't mean neglecting the children in any way.* It's just when raising them becomes an issue between you and your spouse, you have to work it out in a mutually acceptable manner. That takes prayer.

Pray to Agree on What Is Allowed

We have *two* long-haired Chihuahuas. Not by choice. Our daughter got our second grand-dog just before she went into her second year of college. Caring for her puppies was helpful to me at the time because having joint custody of these two fine examples of God's sense of humor made it easier for me when she left. It was like having a little part of her with us after she was gone, only furry. The one thing I have learned about Chihuahuas is that they are creatures of habit to the extreme. If they get to do something once, they think they have to do it all the time. Kids are a little like Chihuahuas when they are young. For example, they think that if they can come into your bed to sleep *one* night, they should be able to do it *every* night. Michael and I decided together when our first child was a baby that we did not want our children sleeping in our bed at night. We didn't want to make them feel bad about wanting to be near us, or to think that we were rejecting them, so our policy was that the one of us whose side of the bed the child came to in the middle of the night was the one who would carry or walk the child back to his or her bed and tuck them in and lay down beside them until they could get back to sleep or feel better about being in their room alone. It worked very well with each child because it only took a few times of doing that until the trip into our room didn't seem worth it to them. And then when they did come, we knew it was important.

It's not that we didn't love our children or couldn't stand to be with them. It's just that we couldn't sleep with them in bed with us. We would wake up tired and grumpy. We discovered a long time ago that not getting sleep wasn't good for our marriage. We also knew that "Chihuahua syndrome" in kids means that if you do it once, it immediately becomes a habit that is extremely hard to break.

Some people like their kids sleeping with them every night. I know some couples who have all their children and their big dogs sleeping in their bed with them and it doesn't bother them. Personally, that sounds like a nightmare, but if that works for them, great. The point is to be in agreement about it. You have to agree on the rules for your children. You have to come to some common conclusions so that there is balance in your boundaries.

Pray that you and your spouse can talk things out concerning your children. When you strongly disagree about something, pray that you both can get the mind of God on the issue. Often it's not a matter of wrong or right, but of personal preference. So if the two of you don't agree, there needs to be the working out of a compromise. And if you can't see how a compromise will ever work for you, know that God can change both of your hearts so you will do the right thing.

Communicate with your children what the rules are and why. Teach them about God's ways every day and pray with them about everything. Help them to see that prayer is a lifestyle, not something you only do in an emergency. If you are allowing your children to do things that your spouse objects to, and you continue doing it, that is putting your children before your husband (wife). What matters most is that your marriage stays strong and your intimacy doesn't get sacrificed on the altar of child obsession. You have to put each other first and come to some kind of agreement or compromise. Divorce is not good for a child, either.

Pray That You Will Have Time Alone Together

Everything you do affects your children. If you live God's way, they will benefit from that. "Oh, that they had such a heart in them that they would fear Me and always keep all My commandments, that it might be well with them and with their children forever!" (Deuteronomy 5:29). When we live God's way, our children will be kept free from the enemy's hand. "The posterity of the righteous will be delivered" (Proverbs 11:21). Likewise, if we live unrighteous lives, our children will suffer consequences for our sins.

One of the right things to do is to work on your marriage and find ways to make it better. Even though raising children takes up most of your time, you still *have* to find time to be alone together away from your children once a week, even if it's only for two hours to go to dinner. Pray that you can find someone you trust who will watch your children for a few hours once a week so that the two of you can go someplace where you are able to enjoy each other. Or take the children to someone else's house while you have a romantic time alone together at your own home.

Michael and I have two close friends, Bob and Sally, whom we met in church shortly after their first baby and ours were born. Sally and I traded babysitting favors, which was convenient for us because our children were exactly the same age and so we were set up for it. I took her daughter for three hours once a week, and she took my son for the same amount of time. Sometimes it was in the morning, sometimes in the afternoon, and sometimes it was an evening, which allowed for a date night. It was a lifesaver for all of us because none of us had any family members close by to help out the way many families do. And we all know how difficult it is to find trustworthy people who are willing and available to take care of our children.

Ask God to lead you to one or two trustworthy people who could take care of your child for a few hours once a week. Pay them so they will be more likely to say yes. Only God knows the truth about potential babysitters, so always ask Him for His peace—or lack thereof—with regard to whoever takes care of your child. Trust what the Holy Spirit whispers to your soul.

It's better to have a date night in your own home after your little darlings are in bed than it is to take a chance on a flaky babysitter.

Pray That You Can Agree on How Many Children—if Any—to Have

It's important that you come to some kind of agreement on how many children your hearts have room for—while always staying open to the plans of God and His surprises. Keep in mind that not having children can bring pressures too.

When one of you does not want to have any children, or you both want children but for one reason or another are not able to have them, this can also be a great source of stress in a marriage. I know a couple who decided not to have children because the husband had already raised a family with his first wife and didn't want to do it again. The wife in that marriage had to pray, "Lord, take away my desire for children if this is Your will. If it is not Your will, take away whatever fear my husband has that makes him not want children." In this case, the wife was able to come to terms with the fact that biological children were not in her future.

Another woman I know in the same situation devoted herself to mentoring spiritual children instead of having her own. In another case, the husband eventually changed his mind and they now have a child. Whatever your situation, and for whatever reason, pray that you and your spouse will be in unity and at peace with each other regarding this important matter.

Pray That the Two of You Will Stay Connected

Children change your marriage and your life. In the beginning you both have to accept that you are going to be too tired most days to sit down and discuss your feelings and dreams. You may be too exhausted at the end of the day to talk about much more than what the children need and how you can juggle the responsibilities of meeting those needs. Ask God to help you *both* in the midst of all that to stay connected to each other and still be good parents.

We all change through the seasons of life, and if you and your husband (wife) have not made any meaningful contact for years, then when the last child leaves home it will be especially difficult. You will feel like strangers and the house will be extremely empty. If you already have spent years totally focused on your careers, raising children, paying for a house, and keeping up with life, and you have lost contact with each other, just know that it is never too late to get that feeling of connection back. You have to talk together, spend time alone together, and reconnect.

If you're married to someone who is stubborn, stuck in his (her) ways, refusing to change, and incapable of stepping out of his (her) rut, then pray for him (her) to be set free. For his (her) own sake, as well as for yours, pray that he (she) will be delivered from stubbornness. Your future happiness together depends on it.

Pray That Both You and Your Children Will Honor Your Parents

God's commandment to honor your parents comes with a promise that says if you do, things will go well for you and you will have a long life (Ephesians 6:1-3). It is not only important to honor *your* parents, but your *husband's (wife's)* parents as well, no matter how difficult that may seem. Your graciousness to them will bring blessings upon you and your children that will be more far-reaching than you can imagine. Help your spouse to honor his (her) parents if he (she) has a hard time doing that. I have been extremely blessed in having a great mother- and father-in-law, although sadly they did not live nearly long enough. But I have heard horror stories from other people about the hurtful things that can happen in the delicate in-law relationship. Do whatever it takes to make peace with them. If they are deceased, do what you can to honor their memory to your children. If your children are married, do whatever it takes to love your daughter-in-law or son-in-law. Do whatever you need to do in order to make it easy for them to honor you. If there is any uneasiness in your relationship with them, pray that God will bring peace and love into your hearts for one another.

Even if your parents are deceased, honor them by saying positive things about them to your children. Honoring your parents has to do with having an attitude of appreciation toward them. Even if they were both the most horrible parents on earth, at least honor them for the fact that they gave you life.

While it's true you have to earn someone's respect, honor is not earned when it comes to your parents. It is commanded. Ask God to help you forgive them and to heal you from all past wounds. Honoring your parents does not mean allowing them to misbehave in a way that upsets you, your spouse, or your children. Honoring them may mean setting certain boundaries in your life that they cannot violate. If you pass down a heritage of honoring your parents to your children, it will be a legacy you will find beneficial when it comes time for them to honor you.

Honoring your parents will give you a long, good life, plus it will help you to be better parents to your children.

Pray That You Won't Blame Each Other if Something Bad Happens

Job regularly prayed for his children. "So it was, when the days of feasting had run their course, that Job would send and sanctify [*his children*], and he would rise early in the morning and offer burnt offerings according to the number of them all. For Job said, 'It may be that my sons have sinned and cursed God in their hearts.' Thus Job did regularly" (Job 1:5, emphasis added).

You may be saying to yourself, *A lot of good it did him to pray for his kids because he ended up losing all of them.* When they were all gathered together for dinner, a "great wind" hit the house and it collapsed on them, killing every one (Job 1:19). Here Job was, praying for his children and doing what he was supposed to be doing, and still something bad happened. But even so, Job's faith did not waver. He did not blame God.

If something happens to a child, too often we blame God. Or we beat ourselves up because we feel we are responsible for what happened. If a husband and wife blame each other, that will destroy the marriage, because no one can bear the blame for something happening to their children. Children are a guilt trip anyway, but especially if something goes wrong. A parent is always wondering if they have done too much or not enough. And if anything happens, such as poor grades, discipline problems at school, or they have an accident or get sick, you always blame yourself for either not being there or allowing them to be in a place or position where this could happen. And if on top of all that your spouse puts the blame on you for it, it's unbearable. When you are in the deepest pain of your life and not only is your spouse not there for you, but actually blames you, the relationship cannot bear the double-weight guilt.

God forbid that anything bad ever happen to one of your children, but if it does, don't blame your husband (wife). Don't blame God. Blame the enemy. Even if your spouse did something unwise, no one with any degree of sanity does anything to deliberately hurt their own children. Trust God in the situation and refuse to destroy your spouse and your marriage by adding a heavy load of blame on him (her). Draw close to God and He will draw near to you. He is your source of healing and restoration, and His presence will bring healing to the situation.

Pray That You Will Be a Praying Parent

We can get prideful if we devote ourselves to becoming perfect parents. We can get even *more* prideful if we buy into the belief that we have raised perfect children. In fact, this is actually dangerous ground to walk on because God blesses those who are humble and He resists those who are prideful (James 4:6).

If you feel you don't know how to be a great parent on your own, then be glad. You will have to depend on God to help you raise your children. And He will always act in response to your prayers because you have more authority over your child in prayer than you know.

It is actually healthier for your marriage if you accept that you are not a perfect parent, but God is. He is the only one who knows what is best for your children. So consult Him every day and ask Him to help you to be the best parent you can be. This is far better than trying to figure it all out on your own. The best thing you can do for your children is pray *for* them and *with* them. *Teach them* to pray. Make prayer a natural part of their lives and it will serve them well all of their days. Being a *praying parent* is the best kind of parent of all, and it will take the pressure off of you trying to be the *perfect parent*.

Turn to God whenever you become discouraged while raising your children. God understands our weaknesses and temptation to give up. He says, "You're blessed when you're at the end of your rope. With less of you there is more of God and his rule" (Matthew 5:3 MSG). He wants you to come to Him and find His grace to help you with whatever you need. The more you experience God's love and grace, the more you are able to extend His love and grace to others—especially your husband (wife) and children.

Ten Great Things to Remember When Raising Your Children

1. *Start training them as soon as they are old enough and when they are older they will know better.* "Train up a child in the way he should go, and when he is old he will not depart from it" (Proverbs 22:6).

2. *Discipline them whenever they need it.* "Foolishness is bound up in the heart of a child; the rod of correction will drive it far from him" (Proverbs 22:15).

3. *Teach your children something from God's Word every day.* "These words which I command you today shall be in your heart. You shall teach them diligently to your children, and shall talk of them when you sit in your house, when you walk by the way, when you lie down, and when you rise up" (Deuteronomy 6:6-7).

4. *Trust that your children are not destined for trouble.* "They shall not labor in vain, nor bring forth children for trouble; for they shall be the descendants of the blessed of the LORD, and their offspring with them" (Isaiah 65:23).

5. *Pray fervently day and night for your children.* "Arise, cry out in the night, at the beginning of the watches; pour out your heart like water before the face of the Lord. Lift your hands toward Him for the life of your young children, who faint from hunger at the head of every street" (Lamentations 2:19).

6. *Give them godly training, not angry commands.* "You, fathers, do not provoke your children to wrath, but bring them up in the training and admonition of the Lord" (Ephesians 6:4).

7. *When you do what's right, your children will be blessed.* "The righteous man walks in his integrity; his children are blessed after him" (Proverbs 20:7).

8. *Keep praying when things get difficult and refuse to give up.* "I would have lost heart, unless I had believed that I would see the goodness of the LORD in the land of the living. Wait on the

LORD; be of good courage, and He shall strengthen your heart; wait, I say, on the LORD!" (Psalm 27:13-14).

9. ***Know that your children are God's reward to you, no matter what it feels like sometimes.*** "Behold, children are a heritage from the LORD, the fruit of the womb is a reward" (Psalm 127:3).

10. ***Trust that the Lord hears every prayer for your children.*** "For this child I prayed, and the LORD has granted me my petition which I asked of Him" (1 Samuel 1:27).

Pray That You Can Release Your Child into God's Hands

It's important to release your children to God so that you will have the peace of knowing they are in good hands. In an excerpt from *The Power of a Praying Parent,* I described what it means to release our children to God.

> We don't want to limit what God can do in our children by clutching them to ourselves and trying to parent alone. If we are not positive that God is in control of our children's lives, we'll be ruled by fear. And the only way to be sure that God *is* in control is to surrender our hold and allow Him full access to their lives. The way to do that is to live according to His Word and His ways and pray to Him about everything. We can trust God to take care of our children even better than we can. When we release our children into the Father's hands and acknowledge that He is in control of their lives and ours, both we and our children will have greater peace (pages 35-36).

Determine together with your spouse that you are going to partner with God to raise your children. When you trust your children to God and pray for them and ask for His help in raising them, you will have more peace. That will take that feeling of pressure and burden off your shoulders. Having greater peace about your children will bring greater peace in your marriage. And that is worth praying about.

PRAYER FOR MY MARRIAGE

Prayer for Protection

LORD, I PRAY FOR PROTECTION over my children and over our marriage. Help us to learn how to pray for our children so that we never leave any aspect of their lives to chance. Your Word says that "unless the LORD builds the house, they labor in vain who build it" (Psalm 127:1). So I invite You right now to build and establish our house, our family, and our marriage. I pray that we will never be divided or torn apart. Give me and my husband (wife) great wisdom and revelation about how to raise our children. Help us to talk things through and be in complete unity, especially in the area of discipline and privileges. Your Word says that You will reveal things we need to see when we reverence You (Psalm 25:14). Show us what we need to see about ourselves and each child.

Help us to always put You first in our lives and to make each other and our marriage a priority as we are busy tending to our children. Show us any time that we sacrifice each other to a point that is detrimental to our relationship. I know You are with us to save us, and Your love in us will bring peace and joy to our family (Zephaniah 3:17). Teach us how to pray for our children and to remember Your promise that whatever we ask in Your name, You will give to us (John 16:23). In Jesus' name I pray.

Prayer for Breakthrough in Me

LORD, HELP ME TO BE balanced in my parenting. Help me to not be obsessive about my children, but rather to relinquish control over their lives to You. Help me to find the balance between focusing too much on my children and neglecting my husband (wife), and the other extreme of neglecting my children in any way. Help me to put You first and my husband (wife) second in my life, so that my focus on our children doesn't come between those two relationships. Wherever there are disagreements between me and my husband (wife) as to how to raise and discipline our children, help us to be able to communicate well with each other and resolve whatever conflict we have.

Give me Your wisdom, revelation, and discernment. Give me Your strength, patience, and love. Teach me how to truly intercede for my children without trying to impose my own will when I pray. Teach me how to pray so I can lay the burden of raising them at Your feet and partner with You in training them in the way they should go. Increase my faith to believe for all the things You put on my heart to pray about for them. Lord, I know that I don't have the ability to be the perfect parent, but *You* do. I release my children into Your hands and pray that You would protect and guide them. Help me not to live in fear about my children because of all the possible dangers, but to live in peace trusting that You are in control. In Jesus' name I pray.

Prayer for Breakthrough in My Husband (Wife)

LORD, I PRAY FOR MY husband (wife) to find the perfect balance between being overly focused on the children and the other extreme of not spending enough time with them. Help him (her) to be willing to talk with me about the raising and disciplining of each child so we can be in complete unity about everything. Let no issues of child rearing change his (her) heart toward me or undermine our relationship. Help him (her) to see the need for us to spend time together alone so that we can stay strong and connected as a married couple.

Lord, You have said in Your Word that whatever we ask we receive from You, because we keep Your commandments and do things that are pleasing in Your sight (1 John 3:22). Help my husband (wife) to obey You and do what is right in Your sight so that his (her) prayers will be answered—especially for our children. Give him (her) wisdom and revelation about all aspects of child rearing and help him (her) to be a great father (mother) to our children. In Jesus' name I pray.

Truth to Stand On

The mercy of the Lord is from everlasting to everlasting
on those who fear Him, and His righteousness to children's
children, to such as keep His covenant, and to those who
remember His commandments to do them.

Psalm 103:17-18

If you then, being evil,
know how to give good gifts to your children,
how much more will your Father who is in heaven
give good things to those who ask Him!

Matthew 7:11

He has strengthened the bars of your gates;
He has blessed your children within you.

Psalm 147:13

My grace is sufficient for you,
for My strength is made perfect in weakness…
For when I am weak, then I am strong.

2 Corinthians 12:9-10

All your children shall be taught by the Lord,
and great shall be the peace of your children.

Isaiah 54:13

6

If FINANCES GET OUT *of* CONTROL

Can there be any greater pressure in a marriage than having financial problems? And what worse financial crisis can there be than sinking heavily into debt with no way to pay your bills? The sense of being caught in a vise that is always closing in on you is a horrible feeling. Not having enough money for rent, mortgage, the electric bill, or food is unbearably frightening. Those who have been there know how important it is to do whatever it takes to stay debt free and live within your means. In order to do that in a marriage, however, you need to pray that both you and your spouse will be of one mind with regard to handling money.

Some experts say that the number one cause of divorce today has to do with financial problems. I can see why. Money is a source of life. Without it we can't have a home, food, clothing, security, or a good future. So being married to someone who is irresponsible, foolish, selfish, stupid, or careless when it comes to money can cause you to feel as though your life is being sucked away. It makes you fear that no matter how hard you work, you will never have anything to show for it. It can cause any person to feel desperate enough to do whatever is necessary to stop the bleeding—even if it means getting a divorce.

If you are married to someone who has no business sense or wisdom about finances—who can't add, subtract, or count, and has no sense of financial discipline or responsibility in handling money—then I suggest you invest in knee pads for your frequent prayer vigils.

In any marriage where one person is working hard to make a living and conserve their finances wisely and the other is foolishly spending money faster than it is coming in, there will be major problems. If one person would rather save money for the future instead of spending on luxury items, and the other wants to buy everything they want the moment they want it without any thought for the future, there will be problems. If one person tells lies and manipulates in order to hide his (her) expenditures so the other one won't find out, there will be problems. If one person doesn't care what the other wants or thinks, there will be problems. If one person is responsible and the other isn't, there will be problems. The problems mentioned above are enough to ruin any marriage.

The stress caused by spending foolishly, making unwise investments, and accumulating debt with never enough money to pay it off is beyond what any marriage can tolerate. If two people are going to live together successfully, they have to come to an agreement about how money is earned, spent, saved, given, and invested.

The Message says, "The one who stays on the job has food on the table; the witless chases whims and fancies" (Proverbs 12:11). That same verse in the New Century Version says, "Those who work their land will have plenty of food, but the one who chases empty dreams is not wise." Chasing whims, fancies, and empty dreams can ruin a person's life. When it comes to finances, some people are in dreamland. They can't put two and two together. That's why communication between a husband and wife about their finances is vital. You must have the same financial goals, the same mind about how money is handled, and be living in the same reality.

There has to be financial honesty in marriage. You and your spouse need to be upfront with one other about income and spending. You must always consider the other when buying anything. If your spouse is secretly spending money faster than either of you can earn it, then it feels as though he (she) has no consideration of your future and what you want. It puts up a wall of separation and kills love between you.

If you and your spouse have a bad habit of accumulating debt, ask God to open your eyes so you can clearly see the truth. Pray for discernment about what you don't really need and ask God to give you the strength to resist buying it. We have all bought things in our lives that were a waste of money and now wish we had the money back instead of those things. Pray that God will give you the wisdom to make sound financial decisions, and that He will help you to be wise about the things you buy. Ask Him to help you avoid getting into debt in the first place. If you are already in debt, ask God to show you how to pay it all off.

TEN THINGS TO ASK GOD FOR REGARDING YOUR FINANCES

1. To give you wisdom about your finances.
2. To help you make good decisions with regard to spending.
3. To enable you to get out of debt and stay debt free.
4. To eliminate any craving for unnecessary material possessions.
5. To help you plan ahead for future expenses.
6. To enable you to find good work that is secure.
7. To bless your employer so that you can be blessed as well.
8. To help you give to God as He has instructed.
9. To show you how to give to others according to His will.
10. To help you trust Him to meet all your needs.

Giving to God

One of the greatest keys to financial freedom is giving. The first and most important place to start is giving to God. This is a big part of getting your finances under control. Here are five things to remember about *giving to God:*

1. If you give God ten percent of what you bring in, He will pour great blessings on you. " 'Bring all the tithes into the storehouse, that there may be food in My house, and try Me now in this,' says the LORD of hosts, 'If I will not open for you the windows of heaven and pour out for you such blessing that there will not be room enough to receive it. And I will rebuke the devourer for your sakes, so that he will not destroy the fruit of your ground, nor shall the vine fail to bear fruit for you in the field,' says the LORD of hosts" (Malachi 3:10-11). God will not only bless your finances, but also He will not allow the enemy to steal from you. He will prosper the work you do.

But be sure you and your spouse are in unity on this. If your spouse is not a believer and he (she) objects to tithing, he (she) may not understand the principle of it and it won't make sense to him (her). In that case, ask what amount he (she) would feel comfortable giving and try to come to some agreement about it. Don't let this become a point of strife. Getting him (her) to come to know Jesus is more important than tithing his (her) money against his (her) will. I have seen great strife in marriages over this very thing. It's not right.

2. Don't work to build your own house and not contribute to building God's house, or it will seem as though you will never get ahead. " 'You have sown much, and bring in little; you eat, but do not have enough; you drink, but you are not filled with drink; you clothe yourselves, but no one is warm; and he who earns wages, earns wages to put into a bag with holes...You looked for much, but indeed it came to little; and when you brought it home, I blew it away. Why?' says the LORD of hosts. 'Because of My house that is in ruins, while every one of you runs to his own house' " (Haggai 1:6,9). If it ever seems as though you work hard and never get ahead, or that money is always slipping through your fingers, ask God if you are giving toward the building of His church and kingdom in the way He would have you to do.

3. You have to be faithful with what you have before God will bless you with more. In responding to a servant who wisely invested his money, the Lord said of the servant, "Well done, good and faithful servant; you were faithful over a few things, I will make you ruler over many things. Enter into the joy of your lord" (Matthew 25:21). If you are faithful to give a portion of your money to God, He will be faithful to trust you with more.

4. If you truly believe that everything you have belongs to God or came from God, you will want to be a good steward of the things He has given you. "Yours, O LORD, is the greatness, the power and the glory, the victory and the majesty; for all that is in heaven and in earth is Yours...Both riches and honor come from You, and You reign over all...For all things come from You, and of Your own we have given You" (1 Chronicles 29:11-12,14). When you believe that everything you have comes from God, it will cause you to want to give back to Him.

5. You will always receive from God far more than you give. "Give and it will be given to you: good measure, pressed down, shaken together, and running over will be put into your bosom. For with the same measure that you use, it will be measured back to you" (Luke 6:38). God's law is that you will reap a great blessing because of what you give to Him, and you can test Him on that.

Giving to Others

After giving to God, giving to others who have nothing, who can't help themselves, and who don't have enough food or clothes or a home is extremely important to God and crucial to your own financial peace and freedom. Don't give only to rich people's causes; give to those who can do nothing for you or for themselves. God sees you giving to others and considers that as something you are giving to Him. Jesus said that when He returned He would invite certain people to partake of what had been prepared for them from the foundation of the world. He will say, "I was hungry and you gave Me food; I was thirsty and you gave Me drink; I was a stranger and you took Me in; I was naked and you clothed Me." And we, the believers, will say, "When did we do that?"

And Jesus will answer, "Assuredly, I say to you, inasmuch as you did it to one of the least of these My brethren, you did it to Me" (Matthew 25:35-40). Anything we do for others, we have done it for the Lord, and that brings great rewards.

Here are some things to remember about *giving to others:*

1. Ask God to show you a person in need you can help in some way. You will be surprised at what will be revealed to you. There are always people around you who you may not even realize have great needs, and God is waiting to show you who they are. Be on the lookout for where God wants you to put your time, effort, and money.

2. Ask your husband (wife) to be a part of any giving you do, so he (she) can share in the blessing. Tell your husband (wife) what you're feeling about who you want to give to and why. If he (she) is reticent when it comes to giving, don't let that stop you from helping others. Just because your spouse doesn't understand how to open up the flow of God's blessings into his (her) life by giving doesn't mean you have to limit what God wants to do through you. There are things you can do or give that won't affect your mate.

For example, you can give food, clothes, furniture, and household items to people who can use them. Perhaps all you have to give someone at this moment is a ride, some kind of help or assistance, or an encouraging word. You can't imagine how much of a blessing doing something like these things can be to others. You never know what can bless someone else until you offer it to them.

3. Give from what you have. Even if you don't have much money to give, you may have other things that can help meet the needs of others. Do you have a talent you can use to bless someone? Ask God to show you. If you have a skill you have been using for 40 hours a week, it may be that this is the last thing you want to do when you get off work, but ask God to show you where there is a need for your skill or talent that would bless someone greatly. "Do not forget to do good and to share, for with such sacrifices God is well pleased" (Hebrews 13:16). *God doesn't require that you give money you don't have.* If you owe a debt to someone and when money comes in you give it to someone else instead of paying the person you owe, that is not right. Paying your debts is part of being a good steward. One of the greatest things about being out of debt is being able to give to others as God directs you.

4. Give to God, not to impress others. I know someone who was so into giving that he gave away practically everything at the expense of his wife and children. But his giving was not for God so much as it was to impress other people. It was giving to be admired. "Take heed that you do not do your charitable deeds before men, to be seen by them. Otherwise you have no reward from your Father in heaven" (Matthew 6:1). It's good to have a giving spirit, but when you are married you have to be considerate of your mate and come to an agreement together about giving.

5. You have to give in order to receive. If you are in need of financial blessing, give something of yourself to others today. Often, just the act of giving will break whatever has a hold on your finances. You will always have enough for what you need if you give to God and others. "This I say: He who sows sparingly will also reap sparingly, and he who sows bountifully will also reap bountifully. So let each one give as he purposes in his heart, not grudgingly or of necessity; for God loves a cheerful giver" (2 Corinthians 9:6-7). Give generously and you will receive generously from God.

Obtain Advice from Experts

If you and your spouse need financial help, seek the advice of an expert or professional. There are many good Christian financial advisers, plus excellent Christian books and seminars on the subject. If you and your husband (wife) can attend one of these seminars together, it will be greatly beneficial for you. Half the battle will be won if you can face all financial matters full force together.

One of the things financial experts advise is to not sustain credit card debt if you can avoid it. Instead, pay off your credit cards each month. I know there are times when you need to purchase something big that is a necessity and pay it off monthly, such as a new refrigerator, tires for your car, or repairs on your home. And you do need to put vacation expenses on a credit card because it is unwise to travel with large amounts of cash. But even then, be sure you can pay it all off within a few payments. Paying huge finance charges for credit card debt is like throwing your money down the drain. If buying things on credit puts you under a mountain of debt that you can't get out from under, it doesn't make you feel good about your life—or your spouse, if he (she) is the one causing the problem. A professional can help you see where you have gone wrong and how to change it.

Seven Things to Remember About Money

1. ***Keep in mind that all you have comes from God.*** "What do you have that you did not receive? Now if you did indeed receive it, why do you boast as if you had not received it?" (1 Corinthians 4:7).

2. ***Pray about every aspect of your finances.*** "Ask and it will be given to you; seek, and you will find; knock, and it will be opened to you. For everyone who asks receives, and he who seeks finds, and to him who knocks it will be opened" (Matthew 7:7-8).

3. ***Stay out of debt.*** "Owe no one anything except to love one another, for he who loves another has fulfilled the law" (Romans 13:8).

4. ***Be faithful with what God has given you.*** "He who is faithful

in what is least is faithful also in much; and he who is unjust in what is least is unjust also in much" (Luke 16:10).

5. *Spend wisely.* "Why do you spend money for what is not bread, and your wages for what does not satisfy? Listen carefully to Me, and eat what is good, and let your soul delight itself in abundance" (Isaiah 55:2).

6. *Give and you will be blessed.* "Remember the words of the Lord Jesus, that He said, 'It is more blessed to give than to receive'" (Acts 20:35).

7. *Love God, not money.* "The love of money is a root of all kinds of evil, for which some have strayed from the faith in their greediness, and pierced themselves through with many sorrows" (1 Timothy 6:10).

Learn to Simplify

Financial stress always takes a great toll on a marriage, but you can either let it tear you apart or make you stronger. One thing financial stress *can* do for you is force you to draw closer to God, to depend on Him to get you through and turn things around. It also encourages you to work more closely with your spouse so you will be on the same team financially.

Another thing a financial crunch will do is help you learn how to simplify. Learning to live more simply takes stress off your marriage and financial pressure off both of you. God will show you how to live without certain things and be wise about every purchase. I was raised extremely poor. And even after I was out on my own, I have been poor to the point that every penny, nickel, dime, and quarter counted. Sometimes it meant having food for dinner, being able to do a load of wash at the Laundromat, or paying the phone bill. This is not a good way to live, so ask God to keep you out of that kind of gut-wrenching poverty. He says He does not want His children begging bread, but He also doesn't want us to kill ourselves working for material possessions (Proverbs 23:4). We have to find that godly balance. And the way to find it, God says, is to understand that we don't have because we don't ask. He wants us to pray about the things we need.

Ask God to give you the wisdom to not purchase anything you don't need. Ask Him to help you establish an emergency savings account. Ask Him to guide you *before* you spend money on anything so you won't make a mistake you will regret. Remember that whatever you want to buy that your spouse *strongly* opposes will not be worth the toll it will take on your marriage. "Take heed and beware of covetousness, for one's life does not consist in the abundance of the things he possesses" (Luke 12:15).

You have to be able to enjoy your life, and unless you have lost all contact with reality, it is impossible to enjoy life if you are heavily burdened with debt or are struggling to just survive. You need to have money to live and also to do some things that are enjoyable, such as take a day off and go out to dinner together. Say no to things you don't absolutely have to have so that you can get out of debt and never be a slave to it again.

My husband and I try constantly to simplify our lives. We are not successful at it all the time, but when we can eliminate something we don't need—especially as we get older—our lives are richer for it. "Aspire to lead a quiet life, to mind your own business, and to work with your own hands" (1 Thessalonians 4:11). Ask God to show you ways you can work at what you love and simplify your lives together.

Gambling

There are many types of bad habits that have to do with finances, but none are as destructive as gambling. If one person is conserving and saving and denying themselves and doing all they can to stay out of debt, and their husband or wife is out gambling money away, the result is a heartbreaking sense of futility. And it is at epidemic proportions in families right now because of the easy access to gambling on the Internet and the numerous gambling places within driving distance from most cities.

If you gamble, remember you are gambling with the Lord's money. It's hard to think that God would want to bless you with riches so that they can be given to gambling casino owners. Actually, gambling casinos are betting on people losing, and they are successful because they are winning that bet. Gambling is one of the enemy's plans for your life and a pit he has prepared for you to fall into.

Some people try gambling a few times and when they win it is like an elixir, always drawing them back to experience the thrill of the win again. But the truth is they have a strong discontent with what they have, and an unwillingness to look to God to provide what they need. When God promises us that He will never leave or forsake us, He means that in the way He provides for us too. "Be content with such things as you have. For He Himself has said, 'I will never leave you nor forsake you'" (Hebrews 13:5).

Gambling may seem like the solution to a debt problem, but it never is. "There is a way that seems right to a man, but its end is the way of death" (Proverbs 14:12). Even if you win, you will eventually lose in every way. The money won't be blessed and will slip through your fingers, and you will have nothing lasting to show for it. Nothing good will come out of it.

Marriage is building a life together—a home, a family, and a future—and that cannot happen without financial security. When a husband or wife is foolishly gambling their money, a breakdown of trust happens that is extremely hard to repair. If you are trying to build a life and your spouse's out of control gambling problem is tearing down all you have built, you feel as though you have no future. No marriage can survive that.

I have seen this happen with a dear friend who started gambling to escape the emptiness in her marriage, and it became a terrible problem as she lost great amounts of money. But she has now surrendered her life completely to the Lord and is free of her gambling addiction. She has fallen back into it a couple times in the past two years and was quite discouraged each time, but I assured her that with any addiction everyone slips off the path at some point. It's to be expected that the enemy will not let you off easily. She has to remember that *falling into* the devil's trap is not sinful; *staying in it* is. Getting back up and on the right path again is where you find victory.

So don't feel discouraged if you have ever chosen a path of freedom only to find yourself slipping off of it. *There is a difference between slipping off the path you have chosen and choosing to go down the wrong path.* Declare the freedom in Christ that you have been given and get back on the path toward life and blessing.

If either you or your mate have a problem with gambling, stay in God's Word and fast and pray until you are set free. Jesus said, "If you abide in My word, you are My disciples indeed. And you shall know the truth, and the truth shall make you free" (John 8:31-32). You need a miracle from God, and when you lay all else aside and seek Him for that miracle, He will work one in your life. Determine to want God and all *He* has more than you want the fleeting and deceptive thrill of winning at gambling, and you will come to know the far greater thrill of winning in life and in your marriage.

Be Content and Work Hard While Waiting for Finances to Turn Around

Being content doesn't mean resigning yourself to thinking that this is as good as it gets and nothing will ever change. It means being content with what God has given you while you pray about your finances and wait patiently for His future blessings. "Godliness with contentment is great gain...And having food and clothing, with these we shall be content" (1 Timothy 6:6,8). Being content doesn't mean doing nothing, either. Working hard is one of the ways God blesses us.

When you work hard to provide for your family, that is not a sign of loving money. Putting the making of money *before* your family *is*.

SEVEN THINGS TO REMEMBER ABOUT THE WORK YOU DO

1. ***Begin all the work you do by seeking the Lord.*** "In every work that [Hezekiah] began in the service of the house of God, in the law and in the commandment, to seek his God, he did it with all his heart. So he prospered" (2 Chronicles 31:21).

2. ***Commit your work to God.*** "Whatever you do, do it heartily, as to the Lord and not to men" (Colossians 3:23).

3. ***Work hard and your work will be rewarded.*** "You, be strong and do not let your hands be weak, for your work shall be rewarded" (2 Chronicles 15:7).

4. ***Pray for God to establish your work.*** "Let the beauty of the LORD our God be upon us, and establish the work of our hands for us; yes, establish the work of our hands" (Psalm 90:17).

5. ***Work diligently and your wealth will increase.*** "He who has a slack hand becomes poor, but the hand of the diligent makes rich" (Proverbs 10:4-5).

6. ***Take a day to rest from your work each week.*** "Six days you shall labor and do all your work, but the seventh day is the

Sabbath of the LORD your God. In it you shall do no work"
(Exodus 20:9-10).

7. *Ask God for success in your work and He will lift you up.* "Do
   you see a man who excels in his work? He will stand before kings;
   he will not stand before unknown men" (Proverbs 22:29).

Getting Out from Under

God is the one who supplies all your needs and keeps your life from
being sucked dry with one disaster after another. Always recognize where
your provision comes from. "My God shall supply all your need according
to His riches in glory by Christ Jesus" (Philippians 4:19).

The devourer, by contrast, comes to steal and destroy all you have. The list
of ways for him to gobble up your life is endless. You can have one disaster
after another, such as the car breaks down, the house needs repair, you get
sick and have to miss work, and you have unexpected medical expenses.
But when you live God's way financially, He protects you from these things.
It's not that these things will never happen, but He blesses you in ways you
may not even realize. He hides you in the shadow of His wing and keeps
you from disaster far more than you realize (Psalm 91:1).

Jesus said, "Do not lay up for yourselves treasures on earth, where moth
and rust destroy and where thieves break in and steal; but lay up for yourselves treasures in heaven, where neither moth nor rust destroys and where
thieves do not break in and steal. For where your treasure is, there your
heart will be also" (Matthew 6:19-21). He is not saying you can never have
anything, just that your heart must be with Him and not these things.

It was said of Uzziah, one of the kings of Judah, that "as he sought the
LORD, God made him prosper" (2 Chronicles 26:5). It is the same for you
and your spouse in your marriage. Seek God's guidance in your acquiring,
giving, spending, saving, and investing. "If riches increase, do not set your
heart on them" (Psalm 62:10). Set your heart on God, be in His Word, and
live His way, and He will prosper you. "This Book of the Law shall not depart
from your mouth, but you shall meditate in it day and night, that you may
observe to do according to all that is written in it. For then you will make
your way prosperous, and then you will have good success" (Joshua 1:8).

Pray that you and your husband (wife) will be able to think *God's* way about money. If you have any bad habits with finances, ask Him for a transformed heart so you can overcome them. Ask God to renew your mind about finances so that your finances can be renewed. Don't live like the world, always trying to get out of *yesterday's* debt. Live wisely *today* and plan for your *future*. Thank God that He promises to supply everything you need. And in time when you look back over your life, you will see how He has done that.

PRAYERS FOR MY MARRIAGE

Prayer for Protection

LORD, HELP MY HUSBAND (WIFE) and me to remember that it is You who gives us the ability to produce wealth (Deuteronomy 8:18). That the earth is Yours and everything in it belongs to You (Psalm 24:1). That You, Lord, own every animal and creature and "the cattle on a thousand hills" (Psalm 50:10-11). All silver and gold and all things valuable belong to You (Haggai 2:8). Everything we have comes from You, so help us to be good stewards of our finances. Help us to be calm and wise in handling money so that we may prosper and not make hasty, rash, or impulsive decisions (Proverbs 21:5).

Help us to work diligently, to be content with what we have, and to learn to give (Proverbs 21:25-26). Help us to always discern between the dream of something more or better that is in line with Your will for our lives, and the lusting greed for material possessions that is not Your will at all. Enable us to stay out of debt and pay off any debt we have quickly. Help us to not be drawn in by the ways of the world, but instead seek after what truly satisfies our soul (Romans 12:2).

I know that having good health, a loving and supportive family, a solid marriage, great friends, good and satisfying work, and a sense of purpose in helping others is the richest life of all. Help us to always put our sights on those clear priorities. Lord, I pray that You would bless us with provision and help us to always be wise in the decisions we make regarding our spending. Give us the wisdom and the courage to resist spending foolishly. Help us to tithe and give offerings to You, and show us how you would have us to give to others. Help my husband (wife) and me to completely agree on our spending as well as our giving. In Jesus' name I pray.

Prayer for Breakthrough in Me

LORD, I PRAY THAT YOU will give me wisdom with money. Help me to generate it and spend it wisely. Help me to give according to Your will and ways. Thank You that any charitable deed I do in secret, You will reward openly (Matthew 6:1-4). Show me when I am tempted to buy something I don't need or will regret later. Show me what is a waste of money and what is not. Help me to avoid certain places that are traps for me, where I will be tempted to spend foolishly. Help me not to be drawn toward things that will not add to our lives.

I submit our finances to You and ask that You would reveal to me all that I should know or do. I don't want to look back in regret but look forward to a secure future. Reveal to me anything I need to see in myself that are bad habits with regard to spending. Help me to glorify You with the money I spend. I acknowledge You as the Lord who gives us the power to gain wealth, and I thank You that You give no burden with it (Deuteronomy 8:18). I know that I must not trust in uncertain riches but in You, for it is You "who gives us richly all things to enjoy" (1 Timothy 6:17). "Oh, how great is Your goodness, which You have laid up for those who fear You, which You have prepared for those who trust in You" (Psalm 31:19). In Jesus' name I pray.

Prayer for Breakthrough in My Husband (Wife)

I THANK YOU, JESUS, THAT You are the power and wisdom of God (1 Corinthians 1:24). I pray that You would give my husband (wife) wisdom about our finances. Help him (her) to trust You with all his (her) heart and not depend on his (her) own understanding (Proverbs 3:5). Help him (her) to not be wise in his (her) own eyes, but to fear You and stay far from evil (Proverbs 3:7). Give him (her) a good business sense and the ability to be responsible with money. Show him (her) insight into Your truth and give him (her) the power to resist temptation when it comes to needless spending. Where he (she) has made mistakes with money, I pray that You would reveal Your truth to him (her).

Where he (she) is feeling financial strain, I pray You would take the stress of that burden away. Enable him (her) to get free of all debt and understand how to avoid it in the future. Help him (her) to know that "there is nothing too hard for You" (Jeremiah 32:17). Help him (her) to know that even though there are times when he (she) is not seeing the desired fruit of his (her) labor now, that he (she) can still rejoice and say, "The LORD God is my strength; He will make my feet like deer's feet, and He will make me walk on my high hills" (Habakkuk 3:19). Help him (her) to be anxious for nothing, but to pray about everything and be thankful (Philippians 4:6). Teach him (her) to trust in You and Your promise to provide for those who love You and look to You for everything.

Help my husband (wife) to excel in his (her) work and be recognized by many for the work he (she) does (Proverbs 22:29). Help him (her) to not be lacking in diligence, but to be fervent in spirit, serving You in everything he (she) does. Establish the work of his (her) hands (Psalm 90:17). In Jesus' name I pray.

TRUTH TO STAND ON

Set your mind on things above,
not on things on the earth.

COLOSSIANS 3:2

The LORD your God will make you abound
in all the work of your hand.

DEUTERONOMY 30:9

Prepare your outside work,
make it fit for yourself in the field;
and afterward build your house.

PROVERBS 24:27

Oh, taste and see that the LORD is good;
blessed is the man who trusts in Him!

PSALM 34:8

The LORD will open to you His good treasure, the heavens,
to give the rain to your land in its season,
and to bless all the work of your hand.

DEUTERONOMY 28:12

7

If ADDICTIONS *or* OTHER DESTRUCTIVE BEHAVIORS MANIFEST

———— ✺ ————

A marriage is for two people only and exclusively. Outside of including God in your relationship, any other third party breaks the relational bond. Drugs, alcohol, and any other destructive behavior will be a third party in any marriage. It will be an intruder in your relationship together.

There is a price to pay for everything we do that is not God's will for our lives. God says, "I, the LORD, search the heart, I test the mind, even to give every man according to his ways, according to the fruit of his doings" (Jeremiah 17:10). There is also a reward for every attempt we make to do the right thing. "He will reward each according to his works" (Matthew 16:27).

Destructive behavior—or simply behavior that constantly annoys your spouse to the point of desperation—is not right, and there will always be a serious consequence for it in your marriage and personal life. But every attempt you make to rid yourself of that behavior and do what's right will bring reward.

You may not have a single bad habit and neither does your spouse, but you still must pray about this issue. There are countless couples who are now divorced because in a weak moment in their lives, one of them resorted

7

to some kind of destructive behavior that they couldn't get free of. And it became their downfall.

Why People Turn to Alcohol, Drugs, or Other Destructive Substances

Addictions and substance abuse are happening everywhere to all kinds of people—rich or poor, educated or not, young or old, and from every race. We have become a society where we can get anything we want, whenever we want it. Some destructive behaviors are not taken seriously and have even become socially acceptable. You don't have to have an addiction in order to play around with substances that have the potential to harm you. This is called risky living. This is gambling with your health, your work, your relationships, your marriage, your future, and your life.

Some people start taking drugs or drinking as a social experiment, just to follow the crowd. Some do it because they feel hopeless, insecure, or overwhelmed, and an intoxicant makes them feel better. Others want to be in *control* of their situation, and they feel as though they have control when they drink or take drugs. They let themselves get *out* of control doing something bad so that they can feel *in* control. "To a hungry soul every bitter thing is sweet" (Proverbs 27:7). People like that often say they feel something inside them compelling them to do it. I say it's the voice of the enemy of their soul luring them away from all God has for them.

People often use alcohol, drugs, or other harmful substances as a quick solution to their problems. When life becomes unbearable, this is the way they avoid facing it. They usually have a low opinion of themselves and feel inadequate. They want approval and are oversensitive to rejection. Their fear of rejection leads them to see rejection in every little thing that goes wrong, and this spurs them on to become more and more self-destructive. They develop destructive habits as a way of coping with stress, loneliness, and pain. They want to be *perfect* but feel powerless to even feel acceptable. Often the person feels as though there is an empty hole in them that needs to be filled. And actually this is true, but they are filling it with something that will destroy them instead of give them life. Using any kind of drug outside of prescriptions from a doctor is not only illegal, but there is a steep physical, mental, and emotional price to pay for every unnecessary thing a person puts into their body. This short-term pleasure always brings forth long-term misery.

The Truth About Eating Disorders and Other Compulsive Behaviors

We are not created by God to destroy ourselves. We are built to preserve our lives. We have a survival instinct in us. We don't willingly let ourselves drown, step in front of a train, jump off a high building, or put a gun to our head and pull the trigger unless we are not in our right mind or we are under the influence of something other than God.

Any kind of personality disorder involves choice. To deliberately choose something that will do damage to yourself or completely destroy your body is a disorder of the mind. People who have these kinds of disorders and practice any kind of self-destructive behavior don't fully understand who God made them to be and the purpose He has for their lives. Nor do they understand the power of God to set them free. If you or your husband (wife) struggles with any kind of personality disorder—for example, an eating disorder—pray that the *spirit* of wisdom and revelation will open your eyes to the truth. This is not just having wisdom about a few things, or having some things revealed, this is having *the Spirit* of *wisdom and revelation* so that you are able to understand *all things* needed in order to get free.

When you have a *true revelation from God* that eating disorders and any other self-destructive compulsion or behavior is a ploy of the enemy designed to keep you from realizing your purpose and becoming all God created you to be, those behaviors will fall away. Only in weak moments under enemy fire will you even consider giving place to them again. Ask God to show you what your calling is. You may not be able to understand it in full detail, but you will sense there is some great purpose God has for you, and you need to be completely available to Him in order to be in the right place at the right time.

When the Problem Is Your Spouse

Any kind of destructive behavior your spouse cannot seem to gain control over is addictive. Even if he (she) doesn't do it every day, if it is on any kind of regular basis, it is a problem that has to be addressed. When it affects the quality and success of his (her) work or physical health; when it causes him (her) to be unpleasant to others and have poor judgment or lack of control; when it does terrible things to you, your children, and other family members and friends, he (she) has a problem and needs help. If your spouse lives in denial that there *is* a problem, or thinks that what he (she) is doing is not really all that bad, ask God to reveal the truth to him (her) in the clearest way possible.

If your spouse cannot stop using drugs, alcohol, or being involved with any other addictive or destructive behavior, you have to seek *professional help* for him (her). This kind of serious addiction does not get better on its own. It is a sickness and must be treated as such. There are some people who are users but are not addicted and can stop on their own, and I have seen many success stories where reality hit and they were able to just lay it down completely and never look back. But for those who have the disease, they must have outside help.

Alcohol and drug addiction are considered diseases of the mind. Being addicted in any way is a form of mental illness. A person who drinks or does drugs and doesn't have control over the addiction cares more about himself (herself) and what *he (she)* wants than about what his (her) family's needs are. An alcoholic or drug addict may feel he (she) loves his (her) spouse and children, but actually he (she) doesn't have what it takes to *really* love them, which means getting rid of all self-destructive behavior for his (her) family's sake, as well as his (her) own. The addiction will always take priority over other people.

When you are around a spouse who is addicted to alcohol, drugs, or any other destructive behavior, their *insanity* affects your *sanity* and you can start to feel as though you are losing it. That's why you must get professional help for yourself too. Don't try to go through this alone. Your love for your troubled and sick spouse has to be strong enough to not accept what is unacceptable. You need the support and prayers of others so you can stand strong through this to complete freedom and victory for you both.

People don't change unless they want to. Pray for your spouse to *want* to change. The only changes that are lasting come when we surrender our lives completely to the Lord and give Him free rein. When we invite God to make changes in us, He makes us new.

When the Problem Is You

When I was in my twenties, before I became a believer, I used to drink and take drugs because doing so made me less timid. Drugs and alcohol seemed to release my spontaneity and sense of humor. Feeling inadequate and uncomfortable in a group of people made me afraid, and drinking took that fear away. I also wanted some relief from the pain and terrible insecurity I felt about myself and the anxiety and fear I felt about the future. Drugs and alcohol seemed to do that temporarily. And they were so readily available through the Hollywood circles I traveled in that they became like a spring that never ran dry. It's not that I felt all-powerful when I drank; I just felt *less powerless*. I did stupid and dangerous things while under the influence of those substances, and it's a miracle I lived through that period of my life. At least I had enough sense to not drink and drive. Nor did I drink when I was alone or when I was working. I was too professional and serious about my work to ever do something stupid to jeopardize it.

When I received the Lord and discovered God had a purpose for my life and a hope for my future, I did not drink like that again. That was it. I found in Jesus what I had been looking for in alcohol and drugs, and so those things instantly lost their appeal. I didn't want any part of something that was not God's will for me. I refused to find relief in the self-destructive behaviors that had nearly killed me so many times in the past. For the first time I had a sense that God had a purpose for my being born, and I wanted to stay alive and find out what that was.

It's possible to be a normal person and still fall into the trap of substance abuse and other destructive behaviors. You can even be a mature adult who has never had a problem before, and you try something once in a weak moment and find it comforting, empowering, or stress-relieving. Then every time you need comfort, relief from stress, or the feeling of empowerment, you try it again. Then you need to take more than before, because there is a tendency toward diminishing returns when it comes to this kind of behavior. Just as a gambler will place bigger and bigger bets in an attempt to regain what they've lost, an addict will take in more and more in order to gain that sense of euphoria, control, freedom, or whatever it was they experienced in the first place.

In some cases, there is an altering of chemistry in the brain, and eventually that person has a biochemical dependency. It may be that the connection between feeling good and the drugs or alcohol they consumed establishes some kind of a pattern in the brain. A person can also be predisposed to do something or inherit a tendency or a weakness from a family member.

It has been said that you can be addicted to more than one thing if you have an addictive personality. In other words, take away one addictive substance and you will find something else to be addicted to. That's why you need to pray that you will be addicted only to God's presence and His Word. That's where freedom comes from. Pray to not be a slave to this kind of behavior, but rather to be a slave to God (Romans 6:16).

People who do self-destructive things are often doing them to feel better about themselves, but the truth is, partaking in something that alters your mood and makes you think it's fulfilling you is actually luring you into a trap of delusions that keep you from experiencing the fulfillment *God* has for you. We all have a spiritual hunger. Whether we understand it as that or not, the truth is we can only be satisfied by God and nothing else.

Having a mother who is mentally ill is very similar to having a parent who is an alcoholic. My best friend in high school had an alcoholic mother, and we realized we shared the same struggles. For example, we both learned not to ever bring a friend home because we never knew what we would find. Her mother might be passed out on the floor, and mine might be having an insane rage. Our mothers were entirely unavailable to us, and we could never connect with them emotionally. We both had pacifistic fathers who worked hard to support the family, but they never rescued us from our mothers. Because of that, we felt doubtful about ourselves and fearful about the future. We felt insecure, unloved, and empty inside and didn't know how to fill that emptiness.

Our situations were swept under a rug at home. We didn't talk with our dads, families, or friends about what was happening. We only talked with each other. We felt unimportant, confused, and sad. We had little sense of purpose in life, and there was no hopeful expectation. I turned to drugs and alcohol, but she developed an eating disorder that eventually killed her. Since that time I've known countless people who had alcoholic parents, and every single one of them struggled desperately in their lives because of it.

If you have a problem stopping any kind of destructive behavior, you need to get help immediately because this will not only take its toll on you, but also on your entire family. Your bad behavior will always be an intruder in your relationships with your sons or daughters. It will make them feel abandoned because it doesn't seem as if you love them enough to quit. Next to abuse, this is the ultimate destroyer of children.

Drugs and alcohol have become your idol when it's something you love more than *God,* who has said not to do it, and more than your *husband* (*wife*), who has asked you not to do it, and more than your *children,* who are frightened by your doing it. The Bible says that those who practice drunkenness are "not wise" (Proverbs 20:1), do not "walk properly" (Romans 13:13), "will not inherit the kingdom of God" (Galatians 5:21), and will ultimately be the loser (Proverbs 23:31-32). Pray that this will not happen to you. If you can't stop this behavior by yourself, seek professional help immediately. Don't live with this problem one more day. It won't get better on its own. And don't try to handle it alone. You need all the love, support, and help from others you can get.

FIVE WAYS TO RISE ABOVE YOUR WEAKNESSES

1. *Invite the Holy Spirit to fill you afresh each day.* "[I pray] that He would grant you, according to the riches of His glory, to be strengthened with might through His Spirit in the inner man, that Christ may dwell in your hearts through faith" (Ephesians 3:16-17).

2. *Be in Christ and crucify your fleshly desires.* "Those who are Christ's have crucified the flesh with its passions and desires. If we live in the Spirit, let us also walk in the Spirit" (Galatians 5:24-25).

3. *Resist worldly temptation.* "Denying ungodliness and worldly lusts, we should live soberly, righteously, and godly in the present age" (Titus 2:12).

4. *Don't be intoxicated with anything other than the Holy Spirit.* "Do not be drunk with wine, in which is dissipation; but be filled with the Spirit" (Ephesians 5:18).

5. *Decide every day to sow to the Spirit and not the flesh.* "He who sows to his flesh will of the flesh reap corruption, but he who sows to the Spirit will of the Spirit reap everlasting life" (Galatians 6:8).

Pray for Freedom from Bad Behavior

Trying to get free of destructive habits of any kind can feel like an impossible task. The pull is so strong and your will-power seems so weak. But that is exacerbated by the enemy speaking to your mind, saying, "Do this. You deserve it after all you have been through." "You can't help it. It's just the way you are." "It's in your genes. It's in your family." "There is no power greater than this, and so you have to surrender to it." Identifying these lies and the source of them will help you see what you're facing from the proper perspective.

There is also the aspect of rebellion that can't be ignored in this. Any time *your* will is exerted over God's will, you are in rebellion against Him. You may not seem to be blatantly rebellious, but there is something that rises up within you that says, "*I* am in charge. I *will not* be told what to do. I *will* do *what* I *want* to do *when* I *want* to do it." I'm not saying you are necessarily being rebellious if you can't control your destructive habits, but I believe a rebellious spirit comes to everyone at some point as a child, and if a parent allows rebelliousness to have a place in that child's behavior instead of teaching and disciplining them away from it, this rebellious attitude or mind-set stays with them and influences their decisions and choices from then on. It causes them to say to themselves, without even consciously realizing they are doing it, "I will do what I want."

Whenever you *won't*—or *will not*—stop doing what you are doing, even though your spouse has asked you to repeatedly, you are in rebellion. You are not only in rebellion toward *him* (*her*), but most of all, you are in rebellion toward *God*. The first way to break down a stronghold of rebellion is to resist it in prayer.

If you and your husband (wife) have any uncontrollable habits, God has healing for you both. But in order to get free and move into all God has for you, you must believe that when you received Jesus as Savior, He became your Savior in *every way*. He even *saves* you from *yourself* when you ask Him to. You must believe that the Word of God has life and liberty for you. You need to believe that God hears your prayers and will answer them. You must have *faith* that the only limits to what God can do in your life are the limits *you* put on Him when you don't have *faith*. You have to understand that God has the power to set you free from whatever binds you, but you still have to *ask* for His power to manifest on your behalf.

When you realize the purpose God has for you, you won't allow any self-destructive behavior to control you. You will take whatever steps are necessary to get free of it. You will remember that Jesus is your *healer* and *deliverer* and you won't accept less than the freedom He has for you (Mark 16:17-18).

If your father or grandfather was an alcoholic, it doesn't mean *you* have to be, but it may mean there are consequences of his sins that you have had to deal with. Maybe you have struggled because those spirits were invited into your family by sins that happened before you were born. It may well be that any weakness you have was inherited. The good news is that Jesus has broken every curse in our lives, including any that came down through our family. But we still have to make an effort to stop doing anything that misses the mark God has for us.

Jesus gave His 12 disciples "power over unclean spirits, to cast them out, and to heal all kinds of sickness and all kinds of disease" (Matthew 10:1). The key words here are "all kinds." There wasn't a disease, sickness, or unclean spirit that was greater than the healing power of God. Jesus came as *your* healer and deliverer. He is the same yesterday, today, and tomorrow. Why would He bother coming as your healer or deliverer if you could be healed and delivered on your own?

What to Do When I Do the Things I Do Not Want to Do

Read these encouraging words the apostle Paul said that have been powerfully and beautifully translated by Eugene H. Peterson in The Message. See if this doesn't speak to anyone who has ever struggled with a behavior that they knew wasn't good:

> What I don't understand about myself is that I decide one way, but then I act another, doing things I absolutely despise. So if I can't be trusted to figure out what is best for myself and then do it, it becomes obvious that God's command is necessary. But I need something *more!* For if I know the law but still can't keep it, and if the power of sin within me keeps sabotaging my best intentions, I obviously need help! I realize that I don't have what it takes. I can will it, but I can't *do* it. I decide to do good, but I don't *really* do it; I decide not to do bad, but then

I do it anyway. My decisions, such as they are, don't result in actions. Something has gone wrong deep within me and gets the better of me every time. It happens so regularly that it's predictable. The moment I decide to do good, sin is there to trip me up. I truly delight in God's commands, but it's pretty obvious that not all of me joins in that delight. Parts of me covertly rebel, and just when I least expect it, they take charge. I've tried everything and nothing helps. I'm at the end of my rope. Is there no one who can do anything for me? Isn't that the real question? The answer, thank God, is that Jesus Christ can and does. He acted to set things right in this life of contradictions where I want to serve God with all my heart and mind, but am pulled by the influence of sin to do something totally different (Romans 7:15-25, emphasis added).

The point is, when you try to get free and do the right thing on your own, you can't. But with Jesus, you can do all the things you need to do because He will strengthen you and enable you to do them (Philippians 4:13). And if God is for you, who on earth can be against you? (Romans 8:31). Ask God to show you what steps to take to find all the healing, deliverance, and wholeness you and your spouse need.

PRAYERS FOR MY MARRIAGE

Prayer for Protection

LORD, I PRAY THAT YOU would protect my husband (wife) and me from any kind of self-destructive behavior. Open our eyes to see if we have allowed habits into our lives that have the potential to harm us. Bring to light all things, so that we will have nothing hidden from one another. Where we have opened ourselves up to bad or destructive habits, help us to get free. Give us the ability to cope with any frustration or anxiety we may have by taking all concerns to You and each other and not looking for relief from outside resources.

Lord, You have promised that "if we confess our sins" You are "faithful and just to forgive us our sins and to cleanse us from all unrighteousness" (1 John 1:9). Help us to confess any sin the moment we see it so that we will be cleansed from it before it can establish a hold on us. Thank You that we are "predestined to be conformed to the image" of Your Son (Romans 8:29). That's what we want. Help us to always be Your slaves and not slaves of sin (Romans 6:22). Help us to understand that the power that raised Jesus from the dead is the same power that will raise us above all that tempts us (Ephesians 1:19-20). Lift us above anything that would bring us down. In Jesus' name I pray.

Prayer for Breakthrough in Me

LORD, I PRAY THAT YOU would reveal to me any destructive habit I have embraced and help me to fully understand why I do it. Help me to truly see how it is not Your will for my life. Break any spirit of rebellion in me that causes me to feel that I can do what I want, when I want, without regard for the consequences. Enable me to see how what I do affects my husband (wife) and family. Where You or other people—especially my husband (wife) or children—have tried to warn me, give me ears to hear. Bring me to complete repentance before You and them for ever ignoring those warnings.

Help me not to hold resentment toward anyone who tries to confront me on any problem, especially my husband (wife). Enable me to remember that "open rebuke is better than love carefully concealed" and "faithful are the wounds of a friend" (Proverbs 27:5-6). I know that "You desire truth in the inward parts, and in the hidden part You will make me to know wisdom" (Psalm 51:6). Help me to become a person of truth who does not have a secret life.

Thank You, Jesus, that You are my healer. You are my refuge and strength, a very present help in times of trouble (Psalm 46:1). Thank You, God, that you are my Comforter and Helper. I cast my burden on You, Lord, knowing You will sustain me, for You have said that You will never permit the righteous to be moved (Psalm 55:22). Help me to get free of anything that influences me in a destructive way and to "stand fast therefore in the liberty by which" You have made me free, and keep me from being "entangled again with a yoke of bondage" (Galatians 5:1). I willingly present myself to You as a slave of righteousness and not uncleanness (Romans 6:19). I know that I am just flesh and I depend on the excellence of Your power to set me free (2 Corinthians 4:7).

Thank You that "I have been crucified with Christ; it is no longer I who live, but Christ lives in me; and the life which I now live in the flesh I live by faith in the Son of God, who loved me and gave Himself for me" (Galatians 2:20). So even though I may be weak in and of myself, Jesus in me is strong enough to set me free and help me to resist all temptation. Thank You that I can do what I need to do because You enable me to do it (Philippians 4:13). I pray You will restore all that has been stolen from my life by the enemy (Joel 2:25). I ask You to "build the old waste places" in me and "raise up the foundations of many generations" of my past (Isaiah 58:12). My soul waits quietly for You to save me from myself (Psalm 62:1). In Jesus' name I pray.

Prayer for Breakthrough in My Husband (Wife)

Lord, I pray that my husband (wife) will have eyes to see the truth and ears to hear Your voice speaking to him (her). May Your will be done in his (her) life. I release him (her) to You and ask You to set him (her) free from any destructive habits. I fully realize that I can't control the situation, nor do I even want to. I give up any need to try and fix things or take control of the problem. I give up any desire to make my husband (wife) change. I release him (her) into Your hands and ask You to do what it takes to make the changes You want in him (her). I pray that You, "the God of our Lord Jesus Christ, the Father of glory," will give to my husband (wife) "the spirit of wisdom and revelation" in the knowledge of You, that the eyes of his (her) understanding would be enlightened, that he (she) would "know what is the hope of His calling, what are the riches of the glory of His inheritance" and "what is the exceeding greatness" of Your power toward him (her) who believes, according to the work of Your mighty power in his (her) life (Ephesians 1:18-19).

Help him (her) face all problems and view them as something that can be overcome and not something insurmountable. Enable him (her) to take responsibility for his (her) actions and not live in denial about them. Help him (her) to be able to evaluate his (her) work or progress without beating himself (herself) up. Help him (her) to take responsibility for his (her) own life and not blame others for things that have happened. I pray that he (she) will always be completely honest with me about everything he (she) is doing. Let there be no secrets. Tear down any walls that have been erected between us.

Help him (her) to understand his (her) worth in Your sight, and to see that his (her) life is too important to waste. Help him (her) to seek You as his (her) healer and deliverer, so he (she) can find total restoration in You. To my husband (wife) I say that "sin shall not have dominion over you, for you are not under law but under grace" (Romans 6:14). I say that God has deliverance and healing for your life. I say that "the God of peace will crush Satan under your feet shortly" (Romans 16:20). I say "stand fast therefore in the liberty by which Christ has made us free, and do not be entangled again with a yoke of bondage" (Galatians 5:1). In Jesus' name I pray.

TRUTH TO STAND ON

I can do all things through Christ
who strengthens me.

PHILIPPIANS 4:13

Do not be conformed to this world,
but be transformed by the renewing of your mind,
that you may prove what is that good and
acceptable and perfect will of God.

ROMANS 12:2

All things are lawful for me, but all things are not helpful.
All things are lawful for me, but I will not be brought
under the power of any.

1 CORINTHIANS 6:12

Being confident of this very thing,
that He who has begun a good work in you
will complete it until the day of Jesus Christ.

PHILIPPIANS 1:6

My brethren, be strong in the Lord and in the power of His might.
Put on the whole armor of God,
that you may be able to stand against the wiles of the devil.

EPHESIANS 6:10-11

8

If Outside Influences Pollute *Your* Sexual Relationship

Don't think for a moment that you can skip this chapter just because your sex life with your husband (wife) is perfect and neither of you have ever had the slightest problem in that area. Don't think that because you have never viewed anything even bordering on pornography that your mind hasn't been polluted. The truth is that the enemy of your soul, your purpose, and your marriage is also the enemy of your marital intimacy. By injecting into your relationship outside influences that distract, sexual images that pollute, and worldly and self-centered attitudes that destroy, your life together sexually can easily become less than what it was intended to be.

Sex in marriage was intended by God to be more than a great way to spend an afternoon before you have kids. Or the means of escaping the tensions of a busy day. Or something you do to feel good about yourself and each other. Or a way to have children. It is also a means of unifying the two of you, joining your bodies, hearts, minds, and souls together in order to break down any strongholds erected by the enemy to destroy your marriage. Sex in marriage reaffirms the oneness, intimacy, and closeness you have as a couple. It always serves to rekindle life in the relationship, without which deadness can subtly set in.

The enemy despises your oneness with each other, and he will do all he can to undermine it. That's why everywhere you look there are sexual enticements to get you off track—if not in deed then at least in thought. Promiscuity is glorified. Temptation is justified. Casual sex is expected. Sex *outside* of marriage is exalted far above sex within marriage. You can see sexual images on something as innocuous as a billboard while you're driving down the street, or even in regular news magazines, popular TV shows, or what is supposed to be a decent film. These are all a setup by the enemy to water down the impact of your sex life with your spouse by making it less than what it should be. Or even worse, *more* than what it was ever intended to be. Sex was never intended to be an idol that we worship, but it has become that in our culture.

Sex can be exalted to the point that if you are not experiencing romantic, fulfilling, amazing sex every time you are with your husband (wife), something must be wrong with you or him (her). Because of the way our society is crazed over sex, our minds can be so completely messed up about it that we can end up with anxiety or uncertainty. Something that God meant to be meaningful and deeply enjoyable can become another added pressure, giving you doubts about yourself or your mate.

Keeping Your Eyes from Evil

What you see even innocently can affect your sexual relationship negatively. Have you ever been to a film that is supposed to have a decent rating and yet something indecent flashes suddenly in front of your eyes? And even if you close your eyes the moment you realize what it is, that scene will play over and over in your mind and infect your soul. You end up feeling shock, repulsion, stimulation, guilt, disgust, or attraction—all of which take up way too much space in your brain. You now have to spend time and energy dealing with these thoughts and feelings that you wouldn't have had to do if you had never seen those images in the first place. Now you have to seek God for cleansing so that this mental infection doesn't spread to your good sense. This kind of assault on our senses has become so widespread that we are growing increasingly used to it.

God warns us in His Word over and over that we are to flee such things. We are to turn away from it and not look at it. Change the channel the minute you see it. Get up and walk out of the theater. Close the magazine. Look away from the billboard. "A prudent man foresees evil and hides himself; the simple pass on and are punished" (Proverbs 27:12). God wants purity to reign in your sexual relationship. That means not allowing outside influences to pollute and infect it.

Any deviation from the path God has established for us—which is sex within marriage and only with your spouse—will set a snare for your soul, even if it's only happening in your own mind. Looking at any form of sex portrayed in photos and films is a snare that will have to be dealt with on a spiritual level in order to reestablish yourself on solid ground. Even if you don't realize at the time that you are in disobedience to God's laws, your soul will reap the consequences of that unintended violation.

FIVE THINGS YOU SHOULD NEVER LOOK AT

1. ***Don't look at anything that draws you away from obeying God.*** "If your eye causes you to sin, pluck it out and cast it from you. It is better for you to enter into life with one eye, rather than having two eyes, to be cast into hell fire" (Matthew 18:9).

2. ***Don't look at worthless things.*** "Turn away my eyes from looking at worthless things, and revive me in Your way" (Psalm 119:37).

3. ***Don't look at the world's attractions.*** "For all that is in the world—the lust of the flesh, the lust of the eyes, and the pride of life—is not of the Father but is of the world" (1 John 2:16).

4. ***Don't look at the dark side of life.*** "The lamp of the body is the eye. Therefore, when your eye is good, your whole body also is full of light. But when your eye is bad, your body also is full of darkness" (Luke 11:34).

5. ***Don't look away from the path God has for you.*** "Let your eyes look straight ahead, and your eyelids look right before you" (Proverbs 4:25).

There's No Comparison

One of the greatest threats to your sex life is having your mind filled with visions of perfect people having perfect sex. These images are an illusion, and they set up a dangerous trap of comparison you can fall into. When you compare your spouse or yourself to the images you see, it can make you think you either fall short of what you are supposed to be or that you are missing something great.

Let me tell you something about looking at others and feeling inadequate. When I was a teenager I used to look at pictures of beautiful people and feel ugly. But when I was in my twenties, I started working on television with some of the biggest stars at that time, and I saw how they really looked when they came in to the studio for makeup early in the morning. It was shocking. I quickly realized that anyone who has a good makeup artist, a great hair stylist and colorist, an expert to give facials, a personal trainer, a nutritionist, enough money to eat well, a great photographer who understands the necessity of good lighting, a wardrobe stylist, a good plastic surgeon (who can make you look rested and happy and not stretched and contorted), and a nanny for your children (who can watch your kids while you have all these things done) can look good. I guarantee that if you were to have all these things for a month, you would look fantastic too. How these "beautiful people" get into a position to have all these things is that they have good bone structure, charisma, and a talent of some kind.

I'm not saying there weren't any naturally beautiful people. There were. But they were far more rare than you might think. And even those people saw flaws in themselves. They, like the rest of us, always have something they don't like about their body, their face, or their abilities and talents. The point is, seeing how most people *really* look helped me to not be so hard on myself. It helped me to stop focusing on everything I saw that was wrong with me.

Don't set yourself up for negative comparisons by letting photos, films, magazines, and billboards influence your own self-image. Anything you dislike about your body, face, hair, personality, or talent can inhibit you sexually with your spouse. By all means do all you can to feel good about yourself, but don't hold yourself to a standard set forth in magazines, movies, and television. Don't put this kind of added pressure on yourself, because these images aren't real and will only undermine your sexual relationship with your husband (wife).

Consider One Another

Regarding your sexual relationship, the Bible says, "The wife does not have authority over her own body, but the husband does. And likewise the husband does not have authority over his own body, but the wife does" (1 Corinthians 7:4). That doesn't mean that you allow your husband (wife) to abuse you. Nor does it mean you can force your spouse to do something they don't want to do. And neither of you should require the other to practice abstinance far more than he (she) wants to, either. It means that if your spouse needs intimacy with you, you should provide it or have a really good reason why you can't. You have to consider your spouse's needs ahead of your own preoccupation.

Outside of the Lord's realm, sex is all about "*me* first." It's something that will make *me* feel better about *me*. But in the Lord, you always have to put one another first. So if you don't want to be intimate because you have been so hurt or disappointed by your spouse that you don't even want to be touched, then say so. Not saying anything and trying to force intimacy will surely make it go badly and do more damage than not doing anything at all. Tell him (her) you need to talk first and get things off your chest. On the other hand, just "not feeling like it" isn't a good enough excuse. Part of success in anything you do is doing what you need to do when you need to do it, whether you totally feel like it at the moment or not.

Of course, there are times when you don't feel good or you are exhausted, but that can't become the norm. The Bible says, "Do not deprive one another except with consent for a time, that you may give yourselves to fasting and prayer; and come together again so that Satan does not tempt you because of your lack of self-control" (1 Corinthians 7:5). That means when your spouse gives you signals that the time is right, you'd better be fasting and praying if you're not going to honor his (her) expressed wishes. The thing to be most concerned about with regard to abstinence is that if it goes on too long or happens too frequently in a marriage, you both are more susceptible to temptation.

Putting each other first in your sexual relationship will protect you both from temptations that arise. Whenever you refuse to have sex with your husband (wife), there is always the possibility that the enemy will place a snare right in front of him (her) the very next day. It may not be an actual person, but the sexual images that are everywhere could have a greater impact. However, if your husband (wife) has already had his (her) sexual needs fulfilled with you, he (she) won't be vulnerable to temptation when it presents itself.

The stresses of life, such as building a career, establishing a home, raising children, coping with sickness or injuries, financial struggles, disagreements, and arguments, can all affect your sex life. If a wife feels that the only time her husband is interested in her is when he wants to have sex, then she will be discouraged. If a husband feels that unless he does everything perfectly for his wife he will never have sex again, he will feel resentful. But if each of you puts the other first, an active sex life will keep your relationship alive. It will keep you feeling younger. It will clear your mind. It will balance things out between you. Forget about the bills, the disagreements, the kids, the problems at work, and concentrate on each other. If you always think in terms of *what can I do to make this good for him (her)?* instead of *what can I get out of this for me?* then your sex life will be good. You will fight off the enemy's plans for your demise every time you do.

Clear the Slate

It's important to bring any sexual encounter you had before marriage to the Lord and repent of it so that it won't affect your marriage now. Even if you never had sex before you got married, if there was anything you did with someone that you suspect was not God's will for your life, confess it before God. If it was something that was perpetrated upon you, ask God to cleanse you of the entire memory. If you don't do this, the memories of these encounters will come up like specters every time you make love to your husband (wife). They will be there with you in the bedroom. Don't allow the devil to have this stronghold. Sever those soul ties immediately. Ask God to bring them all to mind so you can confess them before Him and be free. If you were a virgin before marriage, thank God that you don't have to go through this graveyard of past memories and kick out each ghost one by one.

Pray to Resist Temptation

No matter how much you try to live a holy life, there will always come some kind of temptation. And you have to remember that when it comes, it is not God helping you to find greater fulfillment. It is the enemy trying to destroy you. But God will give you a way out. He says to *submit* to *Him* and *resist* the *devil,* and when you do, the enemy has to leave (James 4:7). If you ever find yourself being tempted, resist all inclination to act on it, humble yourself before God, and pray until the enemy is forced to exit.

The important thing in marriage is to guard your heart from any stray thoughts (Proverbs 4:23). Don't allow yourself to think of anyone else but your husband (wife) in a sexual way. The enemy will always try to capture your attention away from your spouse and then attempt to imprison you with paralyzing guilt. Don't let him get away with that. If you are ever with other people and you find a particular person attractive, force yourself to think of him or her only as your brother or sister in Christ. Ask God to help you and your spouse keep your eyes on each other and to make sexual intimacy between you a priority.

The Threat of Pornography

Of the countless people I have heard from regarding the trouble in their marriages, the two most common issues are infidelity and pornography. I have frankly been shocked at how epidemic these problems are among believers. Pornography is one of the most insidious tactics of the enemy to destroy lives and marriages today. And because it is just a few clicks away on the Internet, it is too easily accessible. A common complaint I have heard from women whose husbands are heavily into pornography is that they have watched it together as a couple hoping to enhance their sex life, but instead it destroyed their marriage.

This horrible habit starts a little at a time. Just seeing a suggestive magazine cover in an airport, gas station, or grocery store can plant a seed in the mind that grows into something insidious. The more one is exposed to it, the more seeds are planted and the deeper they grow. Then a person becomes drawn to it and starts to seek it out. They become secretive, not forthcoming, and not full-faced before the Lord. They don't have clear-eyed laughter anymore. Blindness covers their eyes so they cannot see the truth.

When I was young I received a wood-burning set. I plugged in the handheld wood burner, and whenever I pressed it to the wood it burned an image that was there permanently. Pornography is like that. It burns an image into the brain that stays there. It can cause a person to be obsessed with it to the point of insanity. It not only destroys the soul, it makes a person mentally unbalanced.

It doesn't matter how old or young you are, you can be susceptible to it at any age. When exposure to pornography happens to a young child, it plants a seed in his (her) heart that will keep growing long after the event has taken place. Somewhere down the road in adulthood it will surface. That's because behind every lustful thought is a seducing spirit that wants to draw its victim away from the things of God and toward the vile and evil that brings destruction. And it will continue silently waiting to surface in a moment of weakness. It comes straight from hell for the purpose of ensnaring you and destroying your life.

Even if you and your spouse are not tempted in the least by pornography, there are still countless sexual images everywhere that may be thrust before your eyes, and that alone can open the door to this problem. I have seen legitimate news magazines have images in an advertisement for some product that border on pornographic. There are TV shows, movies, and videos you can easily see that have suggestive material in them. I'm not talking about going to an adult bookstore and asking for the brown paper-wrapped magazines in the back room. I am not even talking about clicking on a pornographic sight on the Internet. I am talking about racy and explicit images in commercials, print ads, videos, and films. When we let our eyes see these images or hear suggestive dialogue, it pollutes our mind. When we become accustomed to it, we are susceptible to a hook of the enemy being planted in our soul. The more material like that we see, the deeper that hook will go.

Jesus said that sin happens just by looking (Matthew 5:28). But Jesus also gave the solution. "If your right eye causes you to sin, pluck it out and cast it from you; for it is more profitable for you that one of your members perish, than for your whole body to be cast into hell" (Matthew 5:29). That means if something comes on the TV that is sexual, turn it off. If it presents itself in a scene of a film, walk out. Don't even stare for a moment. Make it an instantaneous reaction. Don't let the enemy gain a stronghold in your soul. There is an evil spirit behind anything that is sexually explicit. That's why unless you have already become jaded, you will recoil whenever you see anything that even borders on pornography.

FIVE WARNINGS TO REMEMBER ABOUT LUST

1. **Lust is always against God's will.** "He no longer should live the rest of his time in the flesh for the lusts of men, but for the will of God" (1 Peter 4:2).

2. **Lust in your heart is adultery.** "I say to you that whoever looks

at a woman to lust for her has already committed adultery with her in his heart" (Matthew 5:28).

3. ***Lust always destroys peace in your soul.*** "Beloved, I beg you as sojourners and pilgrims, abstain from fleshly lusts which war against the soul" (1 Peter 2:11).

4. ***Lust wars against your spirit.*** "The flesh lusts against the Spirit, and the Spirit against the flesh; and these are contrary to one another, so that you do not do the things that you wish" (Galatians 5:17).

5. ***Lust in your heart sets a trap for your soul.*** "The righteousness of the upright will deliver them, but the unfaithful will be caught by their lust" (Proverbs 11:6).

If Your Spouse Has the Problem

It can be difficult to spot a problem with pornography in your spouse because your lives are busy and you give each other latitude and you believe for the best in each other. But if you ever sense that something is very wrong and you don't know what it is, trust the instincts God has given you and ask Him to show you what it is you are sensing. I know of situations where the wife could feel there was something wrong, even though she had no hard evidence. She only sensed the divided attentions of her husband and saw that the light had died in his eyes. Those were signs of a deeper issue.

So many times we don't see what's wrong because we don't *want* to see it. We want to see what's *right*. We want to see the *good*. We want to think the best. We don't want to see what we fear it might be because we can't bear for it to be that. We understand that everything in our life will be affected, and we can't face it. But the good news is that you are never alone when you have Jesus, who is Immanuel—the God who is with you. He has sent His Holy Spirit to come alongside of you to be your Helper and Comforter and to guide you in all things—even to face the threat of pornography in your marriage.

When a wife discovers that her husband is into pornography, it makes her feel betrayed, inadequate, unattractive, full of self-doubt, grieved, hurt, and a failure. But the truth is, it has nothing to do with her. It is not her fault in any way. No one forces someone else to become perverted. The enemy has planted a seed of lust in her husband's flesh—whether it happened to him as a child or he has allowed it as an adult—and it has trapped him.

So if your husband (wife) is into pornography, please know it is not your fault. It really has nothing to do with you. It affects you terribly, but you are not responsible. But don't desert your spouse if he (she) is willing to try to get free. The fact is, he (she) needs your support more than ever. That doesn't mean you have to suppress your feelings of anger and disappointment, but don't allow those feelings and any unforgiveness to get in the way of having your prayers answered.

You may become angry that you have to think about this problem at all, that your mind has to even be occupied with such depraved thoughts, and you will rightfully be upset about having to even wonder about whether or not the problem is really gone. There is nothing wrong with expecting human decency, and when you find a lack of it in your spouse, you grieve for the person you thought you married. Give yourself the right to grieve and be angry, but remember that it is your spouse who has the problem and you are part of the solution. Your prayers can help him (her) get free, and you can guide him (her) to get professional help. There are experts who know what to do, and your spouse has to be held accountable by someone besides you.

Once pornography has invaded your lives, you can't go back to the way you were. You have to commit to working through this and building a new life together. Seek godly counselors and prayer partners. Commit to praying through this together. No force of hell can stand against the power of God manifesting on behalf of a husband and wife who pray together.

If your husband (wife) is caught in a stronghold of the enemy, the power of your prayers for him (her) is greatly enhanced if you *fast* and pray. Even after a simple 24-hour fast where you only drink water and you pray every time you get a hunger pang, you will see God do miracles. God says that fasting is *"to loose the bonds of wickedness,* to *undo the heavy burdens,* to *let the oppressed go free,* and that you *break every yoke"* (Isaiah 58:6, emphasis added). That is exactly what you need to combat a problem of this magnitude.

If the Problem Is Yours

Every one of us has a point of weakness, a place in us where we are vulnerable, and the devil knows it. If you have an eye that wanders toward sexually charged images, every time you view one it will engrave itself deeper in your mind as well as your heart and soul. Even accidentally watching a moment of it can stay with you forever. The fantasies will one day turn to acting out in some way, and sex within your marriage will not be satisfying enough anymore.

Pornography is made up of a series of lies that a person buys into. Once planted, the seeds of pornography will spread like weeds with thorns that will choke out all other life or potential. If your mind dwells on things that are perverted, worthless, and vile, you will reap perverse, worthless, and vile things in your life.

When a spirit of lust controls you, the rest of your life begins to crumble because it destroys your soul and mind. If you look at that which is evil in the sight of God, you descend into darkness. You become a hollow person who is unable to connect in any other part of your life. "For by means of a harlot a man is reduced to a crust of bread; and an adulteress will prey upon his precious life. Can a man take fire to his bosom, and his clothes not be burned?" (Proverbs 6:26-27). It erodes the substance of who you are and who you can be. It kills healthy, fulfilling sex between a husband and wife. If you don't try to find what you need in each other, watching videos of other people having sex isn't going to make it better. In fact, it will make things worse. You can never appreciate the attractiveness of your spouse if you are seeking thrills from looking at other attractive people.

The Bible says, "I will set nothing wicked before my eyes" (Psalm 101:3). Pornography is wicked. It is an act of lust, not an act of love. Lust is all about "me" and what "I" want. It's not about sharing and building on a foundation of love. Lust is never satisfied. It always wants more.

Behind every sin is an evil spirit waiting to establish a stronghold. Every time a person gives place to that sin, the stronghold gets more established. Someone cannot be possessed by a demon if they have received Jesus as their Lord and Savior, but they can certainly invite evil into their lives by the things they do and allow, and that will keep them from realizing the good life God has for them. They can still get to heaven, but they're going to have to walk through a lot of hell here on earth before they do. God will allow the horrible condition of their soul to make them miserable because He wants them to stop worshipping at the altar of their lusts and start worshipping Him.

Any secret life of lust grieves the Holy Spirit. It makes a mockery out of a Savior who laid down His life so that we can escape sin and its consequences. It's as if He set you free in vain because you don't want what He died to give you. It offends God when His children choose to open up to that which separates them from Him.

Pornographic videos and images become branded on your mind and heart every time you see them, and they will pull you toward them like a magnet. You become stimulated more and more by pictures and images of others and less and less by your mate. There is freedom from it, but first of all you have to turn it off. You have to refuse to allow yourself to have any secret sin. The first step toward cleansing and deliverance is to recognize that this is a sin *against* God. Confession of your sin *before* God is the next step.

Jesus said, "If anyone desires to come after Me, let him deny himself, and take up his cross, and follow Me" (Matthew 16:24). Refusing to allow anything sexually explicit to come before your eyes is part of denying yourself and taking up *His* cross and following Him. Do whatever you have to do to avoid it. Whatever is tempting you, get rid of it. Throw out any videos or magazines that have any sexually explicit images and language on them. That includes the "F" word, which is sexually explicit language. This is also a snare, so do whatever you have to do in order to disconnect from it. Stop going to movies, get rid of the Internet, have your cable disconnected, disconnect your television if you are in a hotel room alone or have the "adult" channels blocked the minute you walk in the room. Get rid of anything that is not of God. Do what it takes. Cut off the source of whatever is causing you to sin.

The good news is that Jesus' death on the cross broke the power of the accuser in your life. The enemy will try to convince you otherwise and attempt to control you if you do not understand your God-given authority over him. That means you have access to the power that can set you free from anything that tries to poison your life and soul.

When you look totally to the Lord for everything, especially deliverance from things you don't even want to mention before God, you will be completely set free and no longer need to be ashamed. "They looked to Him and were radiant, and their faces were not ashamed" (Psalm 34:5). The Bible says people "should repent, turn to God, and do works befitting repentance" (Acts 26:20). Works befitting repentance means that you stop doing what you have repented of and live the way you are supposed to.

If you are in any kind of Christian leadership or place of influence, prominence, or work for the glory of God and His kingdom, you will be tempted in some way because of it. Don't try to face the temptation alone. Everyone needs two or more strong believers to stand with them ongoingly to resist the plans of the enemy for their destruction. The more the better. "Though one may be overpowered by another, two can withstand him. And a threefold cord is not quickly broken" (Ecclesiastes 4:12). Find strong believers who are in the Word, who live godly lives and who are not gossips, who will be prayer partners with you and your spouse. "Confess your trespasses to one another, and pray for one another, that you may be healed. The effective, fervent prayer of a righteous man avails much" (James 5:16).

You also need to be connected to the body of Christ through your local church (1 Corinthians 12:12). You are not fully under God's covering if you are not submitted to a godly body of believers. When you are not connected, you lose the power that comes in numbers. I am not talking about being mind-controlled; I am talking about letting your heart find a home in a church where you become part of the family there. Don't just go to church to watch what's going on. Go to be connected to what God is doing there. Make contact with the people and serve the church in some capacity. It will be a protection for you.

The Power of God's Word to Give Strength

I learned years ago that quoting Scripture, especially in your prayers, is powerful and the only thing strong enough to silence the voices of despair and desperation. The words of Scripture have power on their own, but when you speak them out loud, they increase your faith and give you strength. Scripture has the power to set us free from wherever we are stuck. Your mind can be renewed and transformed as you read God's Word because it lines your heart and mind up with God's. If you are *not* doing that, you are always drifting away from Him without even realizing it. And the drift will be subtle and almost imperceptible until one day you realize you fell and God wasn't there to catch you—because you fell far outside the parameters God has established for your life.

While outside counseling is extremely important and can make a tremendous difference, only God can fully heal the inside of us. Counseling can only help us change our behavior—which definitely needs to be changed—but it can't transform us into the people God created us to be. Only the Holy Spirit can do that. Along with counseling, you still have to establish and deepen your relationship with God. You have to stay in His Word and in communication with Him through prayer, praise, and worship. "Before I was afflicted I went astray, but now I keep Your word" (Psalm 119:67). Don't stop praying until you have the freedom you need.

PRAYERS FOR MY MARRIAGE

Prayer for Protection

LORD, I PRAY YOU WOULD BLESS our marriage in every way and specifically protect our sexual relationship. Help us to always put each other first and never sacrifice one another out of selfish disregard for the other's needs. Keep our eyes from looking at anything that would compromise our relationship. Keep our hearts from being enticed and drawn away from each other. Help us to walk properly and not in lust or strife (Romans 13:13). Enable us to always live in the Spirit so we don't fulfill the lust of the flesh (Galatians 5:16). Open our eyes to recognize ungodliness and worldliness so that we can reject those enticements and learn to live Your way.

Lord, help us to become so committed to You that nothing else matters to us more than living in obedience to Your ways. Enable us to see things from Your perspective. Help us to recognize in advance what will lead to temptation in us so that we always take steps to avoid it. Help us to stay away from anything that could tempt us to view something of an explicit nature. Expose all of our sins to Your light so that neither of us can have a secret life. Reveal everything in either of us that needs to be seen.

Where we are blind to the true nature of the things we allow ourselves to look at, open our eyes to see the truth. Where we have become imprisoned by ungodly desires, deliver us. Where we are in darkness about this, shine Your light on our attraction to disobedience (Isaiah 42:5-7). I know that "to be carnally minded is death, but to be spiritually minded is life and peace" (Romans 8:6). I know that if we live in the flesh we cannot please You (Romans 8:8). Help us to learn to live in a way that pleases You. In Jesus' name I pray.

Prayer for Breakthrough in Me

LORD, I PRAY THAT YOU would make me the wife (husband) You want me to be. Help me to fulfill my husband (wife) sexually. Teach me how to be attentive to his (her) needs and desires, and to put his (her) needs before my own. Cause us to always feel attracted to one another.

Lord, I pray that You would search my heart and reveal any evil thoughts, attractions, or fantasies I harbor so I can be free of them completely (Psalm 139:23-24). Show me the root of any kind of problem in me so that I can eliminate it absolutely. Where I have found another man (woman) attractive other than my husband (wife), I confess that as sin before You. Even if I only allowed it in my mind and never acted on it, I know it is still sin in Your eyes. Deliver me from that stronghold. Break any hold of the enemy on me (Romans 7:15-21). I love Your laws, Lord, and I don't want to have conflict in my mind that brings me into captivity to sin. Thank You, Jesus, that I can find freedom from my flesh, which serves the law of sin, so that I can serve Your laws instead (Romans 7:22-25).

Lord, I lift my eyes up to You in heaven and deliberately take them off the things of earth (Psalm 123:1). I take comfort in the fact that You are my refuge that I can go to any time I am tempted to look at anything ungodly, or see in my mind that which does not please You (Psalm 141:8). Take away all that is in me that holds the door open for sinful and lustful thoughts. Help me to be a wife (husband) who is faithful and true in thought and deed. "O LORD, You have searched me and known me...You understand my thought afar off" (Psalm 139:1-2). "Show me Your ways, O LORD...on You I wait all the day" (Psalm 25:4-5). In Jesus' name I pray.

Prayer for Breakthrough in My Husband (Wife)

LORD, I PRAY FOR MY HUSBAND's (WIFE's) mind to be protected from the lies of Satan and open to Your truth. Take all blinders completely off of him (her) so that he (she) can see every pit of lust for what it is. Help him (her) to fully understand what damage any degree of lust does to our marriage when he (she) gives place to it in any way. Open his (her) eyes to danger and give him (her) strength to avoid situations and people that could draw him (her) into it again.

Enable him (her) to see pornography and any other sexually explicit images as wrong in Your eyes. Turn his (her) eyes away from worthless things (Psalm 119:37-39). Help him (her) understand the greatness of Your power on his (her) behalf (Ephesians 1:17-19). If he (she) fails in this area, help me to trust him (her) again. Help me to still want to be intimate with him (her) and not have resentment, suspicion, or jealousy because of his (her) misplaced affections. Help me to not feel betrayed. Show me all I can do to help him (her).

Lord, I surrender my husband (wife) to You completely. Do whatever it takes to get him (her) to see the truth about all that he (she) does. Put Your love in his (her) heart for me, and keep his (her) eyes, heart, and mind from finding others attractive. Expose every lie masquerading as truth to him (her). Help him (her) to put off all conduct that is not in alignment with Your will and reject all corruption that comes from "deceitful lusts" (Ephesians 4:22). Don't let him (her) be taken down a path that leads to death and hell (Proverbs 5:3-5). Deliver him (her) and we will say, "This was the LORD's doing, and it is marvelous in our eyes" (Mark 12:11). Help him (her) to resist all temptation. Give him (her) the "spirit of wisdom and revelation" so that the eyes of his (her) understanding will be enlightened and that he (she) will know the hope of his (her) calling (Ephesians 1:17-18). In Jesus' name I pray.

TRUTH TO STAND ON

Do not be conformed to this world,
but be transformed by the renewing of your mind,
that you may prove what is that good and acceptable
and perfect will of God.

ROMANS 12:2

How can a young man cleanse his way?
By taking heed according to Your Word.
With my whole heart I have sought You;
oh, let me not wander from Your commandments!
Your word I have hidden in my heart,
that I might not sin against You.

PSALM 119:9-11

When wisdom enters your heart,
and knowledge is pleasant to your soul,
discretion will preserve you; understanding will keep you,
to deliver you from the way of evil.

PROVERBS 2:10-12

Ponder the path of your feet,
and let all your ways be established.
Do not turn to the right or the left;
remove your foot from evil.

PROVERBS 4:26-27

Those who are of a perverse heart are an abomination to the LORD,
but the blameless in their ways are His delight.

PROVERBS 11:20

9

If HARDNESS *of* HEART
CAUSES LOVE *to* DIE

I have to warn you about something. There can come a point in any marriage when you get fed up. You've lost patience with waiting to see some kind of change in your spouse. You've forgiven again and again and you're weary of the struggle. You're through with trying to make things better. You're tired of being hurt over and over and waiting for a breakthrough that never comes. Your heart begins to close a door that was once open between you. The years have taken their toll, and you subconsciously (or consciously) decide you are not going to try anymore. You no longer feel love for your husband (wife) the way you did, and you don't even care about getting it back.

This can happen in any marriage where one spouse is working to make things better and the other isn't trying at all. Your heart can grow cold and hard like a stone, and it will seem as if the love you once had has died. But the good news is that God has the power to completely turn things around. He is the God of miracles and restoration who makes all things new. Jesus—the ultimate source of resurrection power—can resurrect love that has died and soften your heart toward your spouse. He can bring your marriage to life again, and it can happen quickly.

Unlocking the Doors to the Home of Your Heart

When you get married, your heart has found a home. But your heart is also a home for whatever you allow into it. The home of your heart can be cold, uncomfortable, miserable, and barren. Or it can be full of warmth, light, love, and life. Sometimes that home is locked up because you have shut out the Lord or your spouse. But you can unlock the door if you have the right key. Jesus said, "I will give you the keys of the kingdom of heaven, and whatever you bind on earth will be bound in heaven, and whatever you loose on earth will be loosed in heaven" (Matthew 16:19). God has given us keys of authority and the power to change things—even our hearts.

It is imperative that you remind yourself often that when something goes wrong in your marriage—no matter what it is—Jesus has given you the power and authority to take charge of it in the spirit realm through prayer. That doesn't mean you attempt to dominate your spouse or get heavy-handed and make ultimatums. It means you recognize the enemy's footprint and take charge of what is happening by praying for God to break through the atmosphere of your marriage and the condition of your heart with His love and power. By praying, you open the door and welcome in His healing, deliverance, transformation, and restoration.

If there is strife, anger, anxiety, sadness, despair, hopelessness, resentment, or bitterness in your marriage relationship, you can take authority over the spirits behind those negative emotions and tell the enemy that your heart and your home are established for God's glory, and he doesn't have the right to be there because you have full authority over him. If he torments you with suggestions that your authority has been compromised because you haven't been to church lately, haven't read your Bible, or haven't obeyed all of God's laws, then declare, "Those are issues between me and my heavenly Father, and my authority comes from what *Jesus* did, not what *I* do." Then invite God's Spirit of love, joy, peace, forgiveness, and hope to be the guest of honor who is poured out in your heart and your marriage relationship.

It is up to you to do everything within your power to see that hardness does not find a way to move into your heart, because bad things are sure to happen if you don't. "Happy is the man who is always reverent, but he who hardens his heart will fall into calamity" (Proverbs 28:14). When you harden your heart toward your spouse, you have hardened it toward God as well. This is dangerous ground to be standing on.

Don't trust your heart, because it can grow hard over something you believe is completely justified. "He who trusts in his own heart is a fool, but whoever walks wisely will be delivered" (Proverbs 28:26). God sees hardness of heart as never being justified. That's because when you receive the Lord, He sends the Holy Spirit to live in your heart and soften it. "Then I will give them one heart, and I will put a new spirit within them, and take the stony heart out of their flesh, and give them a heart of flesh" (Ezekiel 11:19). Allowing your heart to become like stone means you have not given the Holy Spirit free reign in it. When you invite the Holy Spirit to flow freely through you, all others around you will be watered—especially your spouse and your children.

Repentance and Forgiveness Are Fabric-of-the-Heart Softeners

Remember the amazingly forgiving Amish people who instantly forgave the murderer who killed their children in a schoolhouse? How loving they were to even be able to say the words "I forgive you" after such a senseless and horrific tragedy. But surely there will need to be layers of forgiveness in the years to come as the extent of those violations unfold over time. Perhaps forgiveness has to be extended on every birthday that this child never celebrated, at the family gatherings this child never attended, for this child's wedding that the family never got to witness, the grandchildren that were never born, and the dreams for this child that would never be realized. Surely all that has to be forgiven over time. And I am certain with the deep faith and purity of the Amish people, they will do that.

The point is that forgiveness isn't always a onetime thing. There are layers of it that need to be recognized in any situation—especially in a marriage. Sometimes we think we have forgiven, but we don't realize how many layers there are. And if we don't deal with each layer, hardness of heart can set in and build up to monumental proportions.

King David spoke of his heart often, saying such things as, "My heart pants" (Psalm 38:10), "my heart fails me" (Psalm 40:12), "my heart is severely pained" (Psalm 55:4), "my heart is overwhelmed" (Psalm 61:2), "my heart is wounded within me" (Psalm 109:22), "my heart within me is distressed" (Psalm 143:4), and "reproach has broken my heart" (Psalm 69:20). When we have suffering in our heart like that in a prolonged and unresolved way, our heart can grow hard. But David's heart didn't grow hard, and the reason is that his heart was filled with *repentance* and *worship* of God. Those two heartfelt attitudes will always soften a heart or keep it from getting hard in the first place.

A hard heart doesn't happen overnight. It happens little by little, as layer upon layer of crustiness builds up in your heart, and then becomes covered with a seemingly impenetrable coat of armor that is designed by necessity to protect it from being shot through or broken again. Sometimes hardness of heart doesn't fully manifest until later in life. Sometimes your heart can get broken so many times that forgiveness stops flowing and there is thick scar tissue that forms around the heart, making it hard.

The good news is that no matter how long those scars have been there, they can be completely removed by being in the presence of God. "The LORD is near to those who have a broken heart, and saves such as have a contrite spirit" (Psalm 34:18). Sometimes you have to go through layers of forgiveness to strip away the layers of unforgiveness that have built up, but it can be done with a heart of repentance and forgiveness that says, "I confess where I have not had a perfect heart toward You, Lord, or my husband (wife) either, and I repent of all that. Because You have forgiven me, I can do nothing less than forgive him (her) too."

Your Heart Is Not Too Hard for God to Soften

God asked Abraham, "Is there anything too hard for the LORD?" (Genesis 18:14). He wanted to know if Abraham doubted what God could do. Our heart can get hard because we doubt that God will actually do what seems impossible to us when it comes to our marriage. When we start believing that God can't change the situation, or our spouse, or us, we lose heart and hardness sets in.

The Bible talks about Rachel laboring in childbirth, saying that she had "hard labor" (Genesis 35:16). Sometimes we have hard labor trying to bring forth new life in our marriage, and year after year it feels as though nothing ever changes. Our heart becomes hard when we have hard labor and we don't see the birth of anything. But Rachel did give birth to something great. His name was Benjamin, and he would eventually be the head of one of the 12 tribes of Israel. The bad news is that she died in the process. Often we have to die in the process of giving birth to something great. We don't have to die physically because Jesus already did that, but our selfishness and pride do have to die.

The Israelites became bitter because of the hard bondage they were under. All their work was difficult and fruitless and caused them to feel defeated. They saw no hope for the future. Perhaps you feel as though you have worked so hard in so many ways to try to make your marriage what you know it could be and what God wants it to be, and yet you feel defeated because you don't see results. Even though you may be justified in having those thoughts, God says you are not to entertain them. Your heart was not designed to carry loads of discouragement or bitterness. That will not only cause your heart to grow hard, but also it will make you sick.

If God can make heaven and earth by the power of His outstretched arm, then He can stretch His arm toward you and soften your heart in an instant. When you become discouraged, say to the Lord, "There is nothing too hard for You" and ask Him to soften your heart (Jeremiah 32:17).

How Do I Keep My Heart Soft?

1. Every day ask God to speak to you through His Word. You can become hard of hearing when it comes to God's Word, and when that happens, your heart will grow hard as well. When you shut off yourself to God's truth, you lose understanding. When you don't open your heart to hear God speak to you through His Word, you lose the opportunities He has for your blessing and healing. God's Word also reveals what is in your heart. "The word of God is living and powerful, and sharper than any two-edged sword, piercing even to the division of soul and spirit, and of joints and marrow, and is a discerner of the thoughts and intents of the heart" (Hebrews 4:12). You can be blind to what is really happening in your heart if you don't allow the Word of God to reveal it to you.

2. Prepare your heart by seeking after God each morning. The Bible says of King Rehoboam, one of the kings of Judah, that "he did evil, because he did not prepare his heart to seek the Lord" (2 Chronicles 12:14). God looks for the person who will seek Him faithfully so He can show Himself strong on their behalf. "The eyes of the Lord run to and fro throughout the whole earth, to show Himself strong on behalf of those whose heart is loyal to Him" (2 Chronicles 16:9). Prepare your heart by inviting Him to reign powerfully in you every day. When you seek after God with all that is in you, you will find Him and He will change your heart (Deuteronomy 4:29).

3. Ask God for a wise and understanding heart (1 Kings 3:12). God put wisdom in Solomon's heart because he asked for it (2 Chronicles 9:23). If you want a heart of love, compassion, wisdom, and understanding, He will give you all that when you ask Him for it. He can take away any hardness of heart and replace it with a soft heart toward your spouse. That means no matter what condition your heart is in, God can fix it (1 Chronicles 29:18).

4. Ask God to give you a repentant heart so that you are quick to see your own sin. David did some terrible things—adultery and murder being the worst. But he said, "I acknowledge my transgressions, and my sin is always before me. Against You, You only, have I sinned and done this evil in Your sight—that You may be found just when You speak, and blameless when You judge" (Psalm 51:3-4). As a result, God looked upon his heart of repentance and forgave him and blessed him. God always looks at our heart, even when we do wrong things accidentally or stupid things on purpose. "The LORD does not see as man sees; for man looks at the outward appearance, but the LORD looks at the heart" (1 Samuel 16:7). If you don't want God to see a stone when He looks at your heart, have a repentant heart that is always willing to say, "I see where I have missed the mark for the way You want me to live, and I ask You to forgive me."

5. Ask God to remove all sorrow from your heart. When your foundation is shaken and you are afraid for the future, fear melts your heart. "I am poured out like water, and all My bones are out of joint; my heart is like wax; it has melted within Me" (Psalm 22:14). But "the LORD is near to those who have a broken heart, and saves such as have a contrite spirit" (Psalm 34:18). When your heart is broken by sorrow, it breaks your very spirit. If you allow bitterness in, you become hard-hearted (Ecclesiastes 7:3-4). But if you turn to the Lord, sorrow can be taken away and your heart made purer and stronger. Pray that God will take away all sorrow from your life.

6. Ask God to instruct you even as you sleep. If you ask Him to, God will teach you in the night and you will wake up in the morning with a different heart (Psalm 16:7-9). I have seen it happen many times in my own life where I have gone to bed feeling a hardness creeping into my heart toward my husband, and I have confessed it to God and asked Him to take it away. Each time I have awakened in the morning feeling totally the opposite. Only God can change a heart that way. The Bible says that

God gave Saul another heart (1 Samuel 10:9). If you ask God, He can give you a new heart too.

7. Praise God throughout the day no matter what is happening. When you worship God, you invite His presence in greater measure into your life. In His presence your heart is changed. Always! The hardness melts away. "The sacrifices of God are a broken spirit, a broken and a contrite heart—these, O God, You will not despise" (Psalm 51:17). When we have a pure heart toward God, we can stand in His presence and receive a new heart from Him (Psalm 24:3-5).

TEN WAYS TO HAVE A CHANGE OF HEART

1. *Believe in God.* "He who believes in Me, as the Scripture has said, out of his heart will flow rivers of living water" (John 7:38).

2. *Draw near to God with your whole heart.* "These people draw near to Me with their mouth, and honor Me with their lips, but their heart is far from Me" (Matthew 15:8).

3. *Confess all sin before the Lord.* "If our heart condemns us, God is greater than our heart, and knows all things. Beloved, if our heart does not condemn us, we have confidence toward God" (1 John 3:20-21).

4. *Seek God with all your heart.* "Blessed are those who keep His testimonies, who seek Him with the whole heart!" (Psalm 119:2).

5. *Pray about everything.* "He spoke a parable to them, that men always ought to pray and not lose heart" (Luke 18:1).

6. *Trust in God more than your feelings.* "Trust in the LORD with all your heart, and lean not on your own understanding" (Proverbs 3:5).

7. *Value the Lord above all else.* "Where your treasure is, there your heart will be also" (Matthew 6:21).

8. *Pour out your heart before the Lord.* "Trust in Him at all times, you people; pour out your heart before Him; God is a refuge for us" (Psalm 62:8).

9. ***Praise God with your whole heart.*** "I will praise You, O LORD, with my whole heart; I will tell of all Your marvelous works" (Psalm 9:1).

10. ***Tell God that you love Him with all that is in you.*** "Jesus said to him, 'You shall love the LORD your God with all your heart, with all your soul, and with all your mind'" (Matthew 22:37).

Prayer Can Soften Your Heart

You know how bad you start to feel when your heart is not right toward your spouse. That's because "a sound heart is life to the body" (Proverbs 14:30). If your heart is not sound, it will harden and drain life away from you. When your heart is hard and unrepentant, you can sense that something bad will happen if you don't straighten it out (Romans 2:5).

We mistakenly believe our thoughts are harmless, but they're not. We think we can have our thoughts to ourselves and no one will know the bitterness sheltered there. But our thoughts are viable and a deep well from which we either draw life or from which we are poisoned. "Both the inward thought and the heart of man are deep" (Psalm 64:6). God knows the deep secrets of your heart (Psalm 44:21). The truth is that you will become what you think. "As he thinks in his heart, so is he" (Proverbs 23:7). If you think bitter thoughts, you will become bitter. Your thoughts affect who you are.

Whenever you want to break through any kind of hardness in your heart, fasting and prayer always does it. Fasting unleashes the power of God to break the strongholds that keep your heart captive. God says, "Turn to Me with all your heart, with fasting, with weeping, and with mourning. So rend your heart, and not your garments; return to the LORD your God, for He is gracious and merciful, slow to anger, and of great kindness; and He relents from doing harm" (Joel 2:12-13). Your heart always changes when you fast. It's amazing how something so simple can be so powerful.

When you try to make yourself stop caring about your spouse so that your heart won't hurt every time you feel rejected, you toughen up and steel yourself for the next offense. Your hard heart becomes a place of safety, an impenetrable security blanket, your coat of armor to protect you from inevitable arrows. This makes your heart harder over time until there is nothing that will soften it except a touch of the Holy Spirit.

When we become hard-hearted, we extend no grace or mercy. We become righteous in our own eyes. We think we know the truth. We not only put up an impenetrable wall between ourself and our spouse, but also between us and God. In fact, we blame God, which is a foolish and twisted way to live. "The foolishness of a man twists his way, and his heart frets against the LORD" (Proverbs 19:3). We no longer move from a place of love. You can't love God and resent your husband (wife). That's sin. If you have sin in your life that is not confessed and repented of, the Lord will not hear your prayers. "If I regard iniquity in my heart, the Lord will not hear" (Psalm 66:18). You absolutely must have your prayers heard.

When you've been hurt, it takes great courage to want to feel again, to possibly set yourself up to be hurt again. But when you let go of any hardness in your heart and confess it as sin, God can change it. We are the clay; God is the potter, and He will mold us however He wants if we fully submit to Him (Isaiah 64:8). Jesus rebuked His disciples for "their unbelief and hardness of heart" (Mark 16:14). You don't want Him to rebuke you for yours. Pray that you will never be able to hang on to a hard heart.

Ask God to show you what is in your heart that shouldn't be there, and what isn't in your heart that should be. And then ask Him to make the home of your heart a showplace for His love.

PRAYERS FOR MY MARRIAGE

Prayer for Protection

LORD, I THANK YOU THAT You are "a sun and a shield" to us and because of Your grace and glory there is no good thing that You will withhold from us when we live Your way (Psalm 84:11). I pray that You would protect my marriage from any hard-heartedness that could develop between us. I pray our hearts will never grow hard toward one another.

Help us to not be stubborn or rebellious, refusing to set our hearts right before You (Psalm 78:8). Teach us both to "number our days"—to value the time you have given us together—so that we may gain a heart of wisdom as you have promised in Your Word (Psalm 90:12). Take away any perversity in our hearts, so there is never any wrong attitude taking root in either of us (Psalm 101:4). Take away any pride or bitterness in us so that we will not displease You.

Where our hearts have become hard, soften them toward one another. I ask that rivers of Your living water will flow in and through us at all times to soften, mend, and restore our hearts (John 7:37-38). Heal any brokenness so that the damage is not irreparable, and take away any scars that form. I ask that we will always feel love for one another in our hearts. In Jesus' name I pray.

Prayer for Breakthrough in Me

LORD, I CONFESS ANY HARDNESS of my heart toward my husband (wife) as sin. Melt it like ice in the presence of the hot sun. Burn any solid, heavy, frosty lump within me until it pours out like water before You. Take my heart of stone and give me a heart of love and compassion. Break up the fallow ground where nothing good can grow and life gets choked out. I confess to any sin of anger, resentment, unforgiveness, or criticism of my husband (wife). Forgive me and cleanse my heart completely.

Lord, I pray that You would give me a pure heart toward You so that I may stand in Your holy place. Give me clean hands so that I may rise above my situation. Help me to not lift my soul toward an idol or speak words that are not true in light of Your Word so that I can receive all You have for me (Psalm 24:3-5). You know what is in my heart (Psalm 44:21). Take away all negative thoughts and feelings, and overflow my heart with good things (Psalm 45:1). May the good thoughts in my heart cause my mouth to speak wisdom and not harshness (Psalm 49:3). Create in me a clean heart, and make my spirit right before You (Psalm 51:10). I want to bring to You the sacrifice of a broken spirit and a humble heart (Psalm 51:17).

Don't let me succumb to being stubborn in my heart. I want to walk in Your counsel and not my own. Take away any disappointment in me with regard to my marriage and show me if I have blamed my husband (wife) without seeking to know what my part is in it. Remove all pride so that I can escape the consequences of sin and better hear from You. Change me by the power of Your Spirit. Cut away from my heart all that is not of You. Help me to love You and serve You with all my heart and soul (Joshua 22:5). Show me how to keep my heart with diligence (Proverbs 4:23).

Give me the wisdom to do what's right so that I will walk in my house with a perfect heart (Psalm 101:2). Break down any hardness of heart in me, and I will repent of it. Restore love in my heart for my husband (wife) if ever I don't feel it anymore. With my whole heart I seek You, and I ask that You would help me hide Your Word in my heart and keep all of Your commandments (Psalm 119:11). Help me to understand and keep Your law (Psalm 119:34). Enable me to trust You with all my heart and not depend on my own limited understanding of things.

I believe that I will see Your goodness in my life and therefore I will not lose heart. I will wait on You, Lord, and I will stand strong in all I understand of You, knowing that you will strengthen my heart (Psalm 27:13-14). Thank You that You are a God of new beginnings. Help me to take steps that signify a new beginning in me today. In Jesus' name I pray.

Prayer for Breakthrough in My Husband (Wife)

Lord, I pray that You would give my husband (wife) a heart to know You better so that his (her) heart will be soft toward both You and me. Where his (her) heart has already become hard, I pray that he (she) will turn to You with all of his (her) heart and find Your presence waiting for him (Jeremiah 29:13). Open his (her) heart to hear what You are speaking to him (her) (Acts 16:14).

Lord, I pray that You would help him (her) to have a heart filled with truth and not one that is open to the lies of the enemy. Keep him (her) from having a rebellious spirit and a stubborn heart, and make his (her) heart right before You (Psalm 81:12). Give him (her) a heart that is strong in faith so that he (she) doesn't have to be afraid of the future (Psalm 112:7). Give him (her) a heart of love for me. Resurrect it if it feels to him (her) as if it has died.

Lord, I know that pride is an abomination to You, so I pray that You would do whatever it takes to remove all pride from my husband's (wife's) heart so there is no need to suffer the punishment that comes with it (Proverbs 16:5). I know that "he who is of a proud heart stirs up strife, but he who trusts in the LORD will be prospered" (Proverbs 28:25). Don't let pride in either of us stir up strife in our marriage. Help our relationship to prosper because we look to You.

Lord, help me to be sensitive to heaviness in my husband's (wife's) heart. Show me what his (her) burdens are and how I can help ease them. Help me to encourage and support his (her) decisions. I pray that the heart of my husband (wife) will trust me so that our marriage will be blessed (Proverbs 31:11). In Jesus' name I pray.

Truth to Stand On

A good man out of the good treasure of his heart
brings forth good things, and an evil man out of the
evil treasure brings forth evil things...The heart is deceitful
above all things, and desperately wicked; who can know it?

JEREMIAH 17:9

Keep your heart with all diligence,
for out of it spring the issues of life.

PROVERBS 4:23

Wait on the LORD; be of good courage,
and He shall strengthen your heart;
wait, I say, on the LORD!

PSALM 27:14

I will give you a new heart and put a new spirit within you;
I will take the heart of stone out of your flesh
and give you a heart of flesh.

EZEKIEL 36:26

Let us not grow weary while doing good,
for in due season we shall reap if we do not lose heart.

GALATIANS 6:9

10

If You *Are* No Longer Each Other's Top Priority

———◦∞◦———

When it comes to priorities, Jesus made it crystal clear what ours should be. He said we should love God first and love others second (Matthew 22:37-40). Putting God first doesn't mean you neglect your spouse and children. It doesn't mean you abandon your family and spend all your time in church. It doesn't mean you yell at your family and tell them to fend for themselves because you're going to the mission field. Jesus said, "If you love Me, keep My commandments" (John 14:15). Putting God first means you love Him enough to always do what He says. Next to loving Him, the most important thing He says He wants you to do is to love others (1 John 3:10-18).

There have to be priorities within the "love others" command too. First of all, you have to love your husband (wife) first and your children second. The reason for that is if you don't put your spouse before your children, you may end up not having a spouse, and that is not good for your children.

You will find it amazing, however, that when you love God and put Him first in your heart, all the other priorities fall into place. Loving God doesn't mean just having occasional loving feelings for God. It means loving Him with all that is within you. It means your heart is always with Him.

Even Delilah knew it isn't really love if your heart is not in it. When Samson wouldn't tell her what she wanted to know, she said, "How can you say, 'I love you,' when your heart is not with me? You have mocked me these three times, and have not told me where your great strength lies" (Judges 16:15). Of course, he was living in sin and wasn't married to her, and he should not have even put himself in the position of being pressured to tell her in the first place. And it was his ultimate downfall that he did. But the point is, she knew that his whole heart had to be with *her* or it wasn't love. The same is true for you. Your whole heart has to be with God. And it has to be with your spouse as well. You cannot be halfhearted when it comes to your marriage being your greatest priority under God, or you will get completely off track in your life. But when you love God with all your heart, loving your spouse the way you are supposed to will be easy.

Keeping your priorities straight is not that hard until children come along, and then it becomes a lot more complex. Perhaps both of you have to work to support the family, and there is so much time needed to raise children and keep a home clean and running. Plus all the other things you need to do in order to stay healthy, be in church, and have contact with friends and family. How can you do all of this without violating what your top priorities should be? It seems you are always going to be neglecting something or someone. And most likely you will be neglecting your spouse in favor of your children. Or neglecting your family in favor of your work. But it doesn't have to be that way.

Jesus told a religious scholar who understood this principle of loving God and loving others that he was not far from the kingdom of God (Mark 12:32-34). We will be as close as possible to God's kingdom on earth when we understand this principle too.

It All Has to Flow from Love

We will feel good if we can obey some of God's "most important" laws and only neglect a few. But we are not supposed to show partiality by favoring one law over another (Malachi 2:9). We can't say, "I'll obey this law but not that one." God says He wants them all obeyed, and the only way we can do that is to love Him first and then love others.

Every law of God is fulfilled by love. Love is what leads us to obey God in the first place. The Bible says, "Love does no harm to a neighbor; therefore love is the fulfillment of the law" (Romans 13:10). We were created by *love* to *love* and be *loved*. But our love and affection must be directed toward

God first of all. We are to love nothing *more* than Him. The first of the Ten Commandments says we are to have no other God but our God. He wants us to love Him with *all* our heart, soul, and mind, and acknowledge Him as everything. That means we love Him with our whole being and not just with the words we say. That means praising Him *with all that we are* because we love Him *with all that is in us.*

Loving God will cause you to resist any kind of temptation that comes into your life to draw you away from what is most important. When God is your first priority, you are not going to allow anything to dilute or pollute your relationship with Him. You will refuse to let less important things scream for your attention.

This demand for attention is similar to when commercials come on TV that are so much louder than the regular program that you are forced to reach for the remote to adjust the sound. I don't know about you, but if I have to reach for the remote to adjust the sound because of a commercial that is too loud, then I will change the channel or turn the TV off completely. I'm amazed that some TV programmers don't yet realize we have remotes and seem to think we are going to just sit and take their volume abuse. It's the same if the program is offensive. I'm not going to allow pollution of any kind to invade my life. I will turn it off.

When you love God and you see the enemy trying to pollute your life in any way, you can grab your holy remote and turn him off completely. You don't have to listen to his abuse because you have the power to change the channel. You can turn down the volume on the voice of your flesh that screams "I want what I want." You can put God first because you love God most. If your heart is divided—in other words, you are pulled in different directions by your love for something other than God—your love for the Lord is weakened.

If you are a woman, for example, you can put God first when you go shopping. Say, "God, show me what to buy and what not to buy. I don't want to waste the money You have given me by buying something I don't need or won't wear, and I especially don't want to purchase anything that is not glorifying to You. Make me sensitive to Your will regarding this right now." Once I started praying like that, I made far fewer mistakes or unnecessary purchases. If you keep your love of God first and the love of your mate second, you can't go wrong.

If you are a man who loves sports, for example, ask God to help you not put sports' schedules before God's schedules and God's people. If you want to go to a game or watch a game on TV, don't scream at your wife, "I'm watching the game. Don't talk to me for the rest of the afternoon!" Instead, a few days earlier say, "There is a game on Sunday afternoon. Let's go to the earlier service at church and have lunch on the way home. Let me know if there is anything I can do for you before it starts." That way you make sure everything you are doing flows from love of God and the love of your spouse. This demonstrates right priorities.

I'm not saying that these simple examples I have just given you mean that you can't shop or watch sports events. I am just saying that you should ask yourself, "Do the things I am doing have a higher place in my heart than God or my spouse? Do they spring from a heart that loves God and my family?" Everything you do has to flow from your love for God.

Showing love for your husband (wife) is one of the ways you demonstrate your love for God. "If someone says, 'I love God,' and hates his brother, he is a liar; for he who does not love his brother whom he has seen, how can he love God whom he has not seen?" (1 John 4:20). Jesus said we should love others as we *love ourselves*. But there is a self-love that is selfish, prideful, and greedy, and is not born out of love for God and others. That kind of self-love is corrupt and is the root of sin. The kind of self-love Jesus is talking about appreciates your own God-given gifts, talents, uniqueness, and the wonderful way He has made you. And it motivates you to be a good steward of your body, mind, soul, and life. You will be better able to love others as yourself if you learn to love yourself the way God wants you to.

Nothing is more important than loving God and your neighbor—your brother and sister in the Lord—and your spouse is the closest neighbor you will ever have. If you love your spouse the way you love yourself, you will never do to him (her) what you would not want done to you.

Where Your Treasure Is

The way you live out those two most important commandments that fulfill all the laws of God is to seek God every day so you can be led by the Spirit. If you can't hear God guiding you, you will end up having misplaced priorities. Only God can tell you what your priorities should be in the way you live out each day. He says to seek Him and His kingdom first, and all the things you need shall be added to you (Luke 12:31). When you seek Him first, everything falls into place. Everything you need will come to you.

Our priorities can get off track when we pursue other things before God. Jesus said, "Do not worry about your life...for it is your Father's good pleasure to give you the kingdom" (Luke 12:22,32). He says to store up treasures in heaven because they don't fail. He also says that your heart will be with whatever you treasure (Luke 12:34). If your heart is with God and your spouse, you will store up treasures in heaven. If you see your marriage as being your greatest treasure next to your relationship to God—a treasure in which you will invest your whole heart—it will transform your marriage. When you put your spouse first under God, you will keep your marriage strong, free of strife, and more pleasant in every way. And that in turn will be the greatest blessing for your children.

In order to stop being prideful, selfish, and sinfully oversensitive, you have to ask God to help you be humble, selfless, and kind. That means you must be able to exhibit the fruit of the Spirit. And you can't do that unless you are walking *in* the Spirit every day. Each morning you have to wake up and say, "Fill me afresh with Your Holy Spirit, Lord, and help me to be led by Your Holy Spirit today. Help me to exhibit the fruit of Your Spirit in everything I say and do."

NINE WAYS TO DISPLAY THE FRUIT OF THE SPIRIT IN MY MARRIAGE

The Fruit of the Spirit Is:	With Regard to My Marriage:
1. Love	I will show love to my spouse every day.
2. Joy	I will invite the joy of the Lord to rise in me continually.
3. Peace	I will walk in peace and not stress.
4. Patience	I will be patient with my spouse and not lose my temper.
5. Kindness	I will show kindness to my spouse no matter what.

6. Goodness	I will do good for my spouse in every way.
7. Faithfulness	I will be faithful to my spouse in all I do.
8. Gentleness	I will be gentle and not harsh with my spouse.
9. Self-Control	I will not allow myself to get out of control.

GALATIANS 5:22-23 NCV

When You Feel You Are No Longer Your Spouse's Priority

If you feel your commitment to the marriage has remained strong but your husband's (wife's) has not, it is a terribly hurtful and disappointing situation, but don't let yourself become resentful. That only makes matters worse, and it will hurt you more than it does your spouse. It may cause you to blurt out words you will regret and further distance you from one another.

Instead, ask God to show you what the real problem is. Is your husband (wife) just too busy with work, establishing a career, raising children, or being active in the church or community? Is he (she) too preoccupied with outside interests, sports, people, or hobbies? Is it a sign of someone who is *careless* or *clueless?* Is it truly that he (she) doesn't care, or is it actually that he (she) just can't see it or figure it out on his (her) own?

Talk it out together and establish where each of you think your priorities *are right now* and where you think they *should be.* Determine what needs changing. Come to a complete understanding about the situation you're in. The most important thing is to come to an agreement. For example, there are seasons in business that are more demanding than others, and perhaps you both can agree that during this busy season a lot more time has to be put into work. Decide how you can best compensate for that loss of time together. If you are in total agreement about this, then no damage will be done.

Another example is when you have young children at home who haven't started school yet. The smaller they are, the more moment by moment attention they need. Talk to your spouse and agree that this is a season where there is not as much free time for the two of you, and so you really have to make a concentrated effort to find time for the two of you to be alone and make it count.

Still another example is when you have an important project or assignment due and you need to complete it as successfully as possible. Or when there are seasons of special interests happening, and it's either do it now or not do it at all. Talk it out and say something like, "I have to work hard on this project, but it will be completed in eight weeks and then I'll be home more." Or if you are worried about your spouse's time away from home, say something like, "Until the children start school, let's be home together as much as possible for their sake." If you can communicate and come to an understanding about these things, it will become clear that your greatest priority is still God, spouse, and children. It will set the record straight in your hearts and minds.

Another thing that will always cause us to lose track of our right priority is pride. It causes us to end up making wrong choices. Pride in either of you will always cause strife between you (Proverbs 13:10). "Pride goes before destruction, and a haughty spirit before a fall" (Proverbs 16:18). God doesn't want us to think or act as though we are better than anyone, especially our spouse. That's because pride always causes a person to think that he (she) is right, and so it's not necessary to listen to their spouse's input. This is dangerous ground to be walking on. "Be of the same mind toward one another...Do not be wise in your own opinion" (Romans 12:16).

When we get "puffed up with pride," we become like the enemy (1 Timothy 3:6). If you see pride in yourself or your spouse, pray that it will be broken. If priorities are out of order in your marriage—whether it is you, your spouse, or both of you—"come boldly to the throne of grace" that you "may obtain mercy and find grace to help in time of need" (Hebrews 4:16). Then say, "Lord, take away any pride in me so that I can see what is most important."

When the Pressure at Work Affects Your Relationship

Everyone wants to feel significant—as if what they do matters and that they can make a difference in the world in some good way. That's why the work we do is important to us. A man's work is especially important to him, in some ways more than it is for a woman. That's because a man's identity and feelings about himself are wrapped up in his work to the extreme. He throws himself into it because he continually senses the pressure to be successful. And he senses it even more when he is *not* working. A man out of work feels as though his entire life is on the brink of disaster. He feels discouraged, angry, sad, depressed, hopeless, irritable, oversensitive, and like a failure. This tremendous stress he carries can't help but spill over into his marriage.

A woman, on the other hand, seems to have a greater sense of herself as a person of value aside from her work. Her work is very important to her, and she absolutely wants to excel and succeed, but her sense of identity and personal value does not rise and fall with the success of her work.

The pressure a man feels about his work adds to the pressure in his home. If he works too long, too hard, too focused, or too obsessed, his wife feels that she is being replaced by a faceless mistress. Because the pressure a man senses about work is something he feels all the time and is such a big part of him, he may not be able to see it in himself. That's why it is crucial for a wife to pray that her husband will find fulfillment in his work. And also that he will be able to use his talents and gifts according to God's will, and that his work will be blessed. A husband should pray for his wife's work to be successful as well, and that she will find favor with the people she works with and for.

Practical Ways to Restore Your Priorities

1. Ask God to help you show love and commitment to your spouse in some tangible way every day. Be affectionate with one another in ways that aren't always about leading to sex. Showing affection to your spouse should be high on your priority list. Your spouse needs to know that he (she) is loved for who he (she) is at that moment without having to perform. Do things for him (her) that will make him (her) miss you whenever you are gone. Jesus said, "Greater love has no one than this, than to lay down one's life for his friends" (John 15:13). Ask God to show you how to lay down your life—selfish desires—for your husband (wife) in some way every day.

2. Say no to certain things whenever possible in order to spend time alone with your spouse. Try getting away together, even if it is just overnight. Drive somewhere that will take an hour or two in the car so that you can have time alone without interruption. If you are married to a workaholic, try to convince him (her) that time away alone would be the best thing for *him (her)*. Time alone together can make a major difference in your relationship.

Michael and I have been to a number of marriage retreats, and during a particular one not long ago we found that even after 34 years of marriage we were still learning new things. Not that we had never heard these things before, but this time there was actual breakthrough. My husband likes to stay home, so we used to have two semiannual dates a year outside of birthdays. What my husband took away from this retreat was that he needed to take me out on a date night once a week. I had stopped hoping for that years ago, but something clicked with him, and now we go to dinner and sometimes to a film almost every week—although it is a lot harder to find a decent film than it is to find a good restaurant. Doing this has made all the difference in our relationship. We try to make time for that, and it's something we look forward to. It seems like such a simple thing, but it is an impactful way to put each other first. So no matter how busy we are during the rest of the week, we know we will have that time alone for a few hours.

3. Have a devotional time together with your spouse as often as you can. If you can't do it every day, then try for at least once a week. If your husband (wife) is resistant to that, ask if you can just read a verse or two of Scripture to him (her) periodically and see if he (she) will let you pray for him (her). Praying together is one of the most life-changing things you can do for each other—even if only one of you does the praying.

Priority equals time. We all have to put aside some things to make time for what is most important. If something comes up that takes up all of your time—a sick child, an injured elderly parent, the finishing of a big project—communicate with your spouse that this is just temporary and you will be back spending quality time together as soon as the situation is under control.

Don't Drink the Enemy's Kool-Aid

"Drinking the Kool-Aid" is a phrase that comes from the 1978 Jonestown massacre in Guyana, in which some members of the Peoples Temple cult committed suicide by drinking cyanide-laced Kool-Aid. For those of you too young to remember this incident, in the 1970s there rose up a guru named Jim Jones. I was aware of him early on because of my housekeeper, Rosetta, who worked for me every Saturday for about five years. She was a Christian, but somehow she and her church got into following Jim Jones. She started talking about him frequently and how great he was, and I sensed right away that she had an unhealthy esteem for this "spiritual leader." When she started wearing a long necklace attached to a 2"x4" plastic photo holder with a photo of Jim Jones encased in it, I told her in detail about my reservations regarding her allegiance to him. In our conversation she told me that Jim Jones had acquired land in Guyana and was asking his followers to go there and work the land, and he would take care of their needs. She was seriously considering going.

I had a terrible feeling about that for her sake, and so I prayed fervently for her to come to her senses. The more I prayed, the more strongly I felt that this was the enemy's doing. Thanks be to God, the next time I talked to her about it I succeeded in convincing her not to go. I persuaded her on the grounds that it was a big mistake for her to leave her son. I knew she'd had a hard life, and she wanted someone to take care of her and allow her to serve the Lord at the same time. And she thought that her son at age 19 was old enough to be on his own.

"But he still needs you," I said. "You can't just leave him. Besides, I don't believe this is what God wants you to do."

She finally decided not to go, and it wasn't many months after that when Jim Jones gave his followers in Guyana the poisoned Kool-Aid. Except for a very few who escaped, Jim Jones' followers died. It was sad beyond belief.

The point is, the devil always has some kind of poison waiting for us that he hopes we will drink. Don't partake of the enemy's drink of death and destruction—especially with regard to your priorities and your marriage. Remember that the devil "is a liar and the father of it" (John 8:44). The enemy will tell you that everything in your life is more important than your marriage—your work is more important, and so are your dreams, your children, your friends, your relatives, your recreation, your interests, your career, or even what you do with your own time. Don't drink in those lies. They are poison to you and will prove to be your downfall. Instead, drink the "same spiritual drink" from "that spiritual Rock" which is Christ (1 Corinthians 10:4). Overcome the enemy's lies with God's truth, because God "who is in you is greater than [the enemy] who is in the world" (1 John 4:4).

After the incident happened, my housekeeper grieved terribly for all of her friends who died in Guyana. It was an unbearable disaster that shook her life tremendously, but she might have been one of them. Had I not taken a strong stand against her going, I would have regretted that for the rest of my life. I am taking a strong stand against the devil's plans for you too. I don't want you to buy into the trap he has set for you and your marriage by enticing you to let your priorities get out of order. Love God and love your husband (wife), and all else will fall into place.

PRAYERS FOR MY MARRIAGE

Prayer for Protection

LORD, I PRAY YOU WOULD HELP my husband (wife) and me to always make You our top priority, and to make each other our priority under You. Enable us to live in Your love so that we can learn to love each other the way You want us to. Make us to be vessels through which Your love flows. Show us how to establish right priorities in our marriage and in our family.

I pray that we will not do anything "through selfish ambition or conceit, but in lowliness of mind" may we esteem each other better than ourselves (Philippians 2:3). Help us to always find time for one another to be a help, support, encourager, uplifter, lover, companion, and sharer of good things. Enable us to always bear the burden of the other concerning the difficult things that happen in life. Help us to choose each other over the other seemingly important things that vie for our attention. Teach us to set aside time to be together alone and to reaffirm each other as our top priority under You. In our seasons of necessary busyness, help us to be understanding of one another and in agreement as to how to handle those times successfully. Thank You that You have chosen us to be people for Yourself, "a special treasure" for Your glory (Deuteronomy 7:6). Help us to always find our treasure in You above all else. In Jesus' name I pray.

Prayer for Breakthrough in Me

LORD, HELP ME TO ALWAYS put You first in my life and to put my husband (wife) next above everything else. Show me how to do that and how to let him (her) clearly know that this is what I am doing. I look to You to teach me the way I should walk and what I should do (Psalm 143:8). Reveal to me any place where my priorities are off. Show me where I have put other things, people, or activities before You or my husband (wife). If I have made my husband (wife) feel as though he (she) is less than a top priority in my life, help me to apologize to him (her) and make amends for it. Where damage has been done to our relationship because of it, I pray You would heal those wounds. Restore us to the place where we should be. Help me to put our children in highest priority, just under You, Lord, and my husband (wife), for I know that the greatest blessing for them is that we stay together.

Thank You that Your love for me is everlasting, and that in Your lovingkindness You are always drawing me closer to You (Jeremiah 31:3). Help me to seek You first in all things, to keep Your commandments, and to abide in Your love (John 15:9-10). Thank You that before I chose You, You chose me that I "should be holy and without blame" before You in love (Ephesians 1:3-6). I know my holiness and blamelessness comes from all that Jesus *is,* being attributed to me. I am forever grateful, and I long to please You in every way—especially in the way I prioritize my life. In Jesus' name I pray.

Prayer for Breakthrough in My Husband (Wife)

LORD, I PRAY THAT YOU would penetrate my husband's (wife's) heart with Your love. Help him (her) to understand the greatness of it. Deliver him (her) from any lies of the enemy that have caused him (her) to doubt Your love for him (her). Jesus, You have said, "God is love, and he who abides in love abides in God, and God in him" (1 John 4:16). Help my husband (wife) learn to love You above all else. Let everything he (she) does be done in love (1 Corinthians 16:14).

Where his (her) priorities are out of order, I pray You would help him (her) to realize he (she) needs to put You first, me second, and our children next before everything else. Help him (her) to see where he (she) must make necessary changes in the way he (she) spends time. Help him (her) to not feel so pressured by his (her) work that it overtakes his (her) life and our family suffers. Bless his (her) work so that he (she) can accomplish more in less time. Enable him (her) to say no to the things which do not please You and are not to be high on the priority list. Don't let him (her) be led astray by delusion, and don't let his (her) fears come upon him (her) (Isaiah 66:4). Help him (her) to clearly see what is most important in life and what is not. Help him (her) to choose the path of humility and righteousness. Thank You that whatever we ask in Your name, You will give us (John 15:16). In Jesus' name I pray.

Truth to Stand On

Seek first the kingdom of God and His righteousness,
and all these things shall be added to you.

Matthew 6:33

Humble yourselves under the mighty hand of God,
that He may exalt you in due time,
casting all your care upon Him, for He cares for you.

1 Peter 5:6-7

I call heaven and earth as witnesses today against you,
that I have set before you life and death, blessing and cursing; therefore
choose life, that both you and your descendants may live.

Deuteronomy 30:19

If it seems evil to you to serve the Lord,
choose for yourselves this day whom you will serve...
But as for me and my house, we will serve the Lord.

Joshua 24:15

Cause me to hear Your lovingkindness in the morning,
for in You do I trust; cause me to know the way in which I should walk,
for I lift up my soul to You.

Psalm 143:8

11

IF *the* "D" WORD
BECOMES *an* OPTION

———— ∽ ————

A marriage—just like the people in it—is either growing deeper and more solid, or it is breaking down and becoming more vulnerable. It never stays in just one place, although it may feel as though it does sometimes. Marriage actually has a life of its own and can move forward or backward. It can breathe deeply when given fresh air, or it can suffocate if it is deprived of spiritual oxygen. Each spouse has a great influence on which direction their marriage will go by the words they speak, the way they act, and the fervency of their prayers. Fresh air or suffocation. It's their choice.

The good news in all this is that even when you have made mistakes in your marriage and should have done things differently, God is a God of second chances. That's something not all couples are willing to give each other, but God always gives us another opportunity to make things right. That means if your marriage is headed in the wrong direction, it's never too late to turn things around.

Most people get married with the intention of staying married in a wonderful relationship for the rest of their lives. You're in love with each other, and you both have an idea of what you think life together is going to be like. But it is impossible to know exactly what you are getting into before you're married, no matter how long you have dated or known each other. We don't even know *ourselves* completely before we're married, let alone the person we are marrying.

Marriage reveals everything we are because there is no place to hide—not even from ourselves. The marriage contract changes things. The relationship is now *really* up close and personal, and the ways we formerly disguised ourselves no longer work. The truth comes out. That's why a marriage requires commitment and work. A 50-50 partnership doesn't cut it. Each person has to give 100 percent of themselves to the other. And that's not easy to do when we are all selfish enough to want to hold back.

One person can be so wrapped up in themselves or their work that they are completely unaware that their spouse is feeling neglected and lonely. They believe that everything is great, but their spouse is miserable. Because there is no communication, it's going to come as a surprise when the lonely spouse leaves or has an affair. The point is, if *one* person in a marriage doesn't think everything is great, then the marriage is not great.

Marriage has to be worked on all the time so it can grow stronger and deeper. If it doesn't grow, it is deteriorating. It may feel as though it is maintaining, but in unseen places it is breaking down. It's like putting a pin in an egg and letting the contents inside slowly drain out. You don't see that happening. The egg looks the same. But then one day pressure is put on the egg and it cracks to the point of destruction. When everything cracks in a marriage, divorce can seem like the only way to save your own life in an impossible situation. Didn't we all learn that Humpty Dumpty could never be put back together again?

A Violent Sin

God hates divorce, "for it covers one's garment with violence" (Malachi 2:16). He uses the words "hate" and "violence" to describe His feelings about divorce. After He said this to His people at the end of the Old Testament, He didn't speak to them again for about 400 years. That's an even longer silence than what happens between warring couples. I think He means it.

God says "a husband is not to divorce his wife" (1 Corinthians 7:11). That "what God has joined together, let not man separate" (Mark 10:9). It was because of our hard-heartedness that divorce came about, but God never intended for it to be that way (Matthew 19:7-8). Divorce was never supposed to happen. But our hard hearts made room for it, even knowing that God hates it.

The reason the divorce rate is so high is because divorce is considered an *option* in the minds of at least half of the people getting divorced. It is spoken of as the *solution*. It appears to be the *only way out* of a miserable situation. If you have the mind-set that you don't want that option, that solution, or that way out, it forces you to have to find *another* option, a better solution, and a way *through* your seemingly impossible situation.

God is a witness to your marriage, viewing it as a covenant, which means *enduring commitment and faithfulness to one another.* When two people get divorced, it is a violent shattering of that covenant and of God's order for their lives. But when you keep your marriage vows, God stands behind your marriage. That's why your prayers for the preservation and strengthening of your relationship have such power. They are already God's will before you even speak them. Praying puts God's will into action. It means God's power will stand against any enemy you face—whether the enemy comes from the outside or it is actually one or both of you.

Refuse to Use the "D" Word

As I mentioned earlier, I was married before I became a believer to someone who also was not a believer. That marriage was doomed from the start because I went into it knowing it wouldn't last. I just wanted to have a home and some kind of companionship, even if those things were only temporary. Divorce was always at the back of my mind. I didn't expect my marriage to last two years, and we never even made it to the second anniversary. As miserable as that marriage was—and *I* was the one who left *him*—the divorce was awful. It felt as though my life were ripping apart. I didn't know about covenants and God's ways, but even so I felt the violence God speaks of with regard to divorce. I can't imagine how painful a divorce is when you don't want it and your spouse does.

Ideally, this issue of divorce is best decided once and for all *before* you get married. But whether you are recently married or you've been married a long time, you can decide today to not let the word "divorce" become an option in your thoughts or words. Even if you and your spouse have talked about divorce in the past, agree to not think of it as an option and to never speak of it as a threat to each other again. Instead, agree to talk things out and listen to each other's feelings and thoughts. Agree that you will do whatever it takes to get beyond every impasse or problem that arises, because above all you don't want this relationship to fail. You don't want to divide up the property, the children, the income, and start all over again. You definitely don't want the things that have been bothering you for a long time to continue, but you do want to find a way to make some changes and work it out.

You have to remember that your words always have power. When you say the word "divorce" as a solution or a threat, there is a spirit of divorce that gets into your mind and heart—or your husband's (wife's) mind and heart—and the enemy waits at the door you have just opened to use it against you. You may have merely used the word as an idle threat, perhaps to bring about an awakening as to the seriousness of the situation, but not meaning to actually follow through on it, but now you have planted that thought in your husband's (wife's) mind. You have put it out there in your relationship, and the enemy will feed the idea so it can grow like a cancer.

God thinks of divorce as treachery. "The LORD has been witness between you and the wife of your youth, with whom you have dealt treacherously; yet she is your companion and your wife by covenant. But did He not make them one, having a remnant of the Spirit? And why one? He seeks godly offspring. Therefore take heed to your spirit, and let none deal treacherously with the wife of his youth" (Malachi 2:14-15). God wants us to have a strong commitment to love and take care of each other. He likes unconditional love because He invented it. That's who *He is*. God has joined you together in a covenant, not only with each other but with Him as well. If you deal treacherously with each other by divorcing, it grieves His Holy Spirit.

Don't Offend God by the Way You Treat Each Other

Marriage is supposed to be a manifestation of the relationship between Christ and the church. Christ doesn't walk out on, get fed up with, leave, desert, or divorce the church. He also doesn't get rude, abusive, mean, inconsiderate, selfish, unaffectionate, arrogant, or angry with the church, either. All problems in a marriage could be solved if each person were to become more Christlike, especially with one another. A relationship disintegrates slowly with each careless word or insensitive action and every opportunity missed to comfort and support the other. It breaks down gradually with every criticism or complaint voiced to the other without any affirmation and love. If one of you treats the other with disregard, abuse, or dishonor, you are shutting off blessings God has for your life.

God says He wants you to have the kind of love for one another that is patient, not arrogant or prideful, not rude or selfish, and not easily provoked. He wants you to be the kind of people who don't think about evil things, don't enjoy lawlessness, are willing to put up with imperfection, and who believe for the best in each other. He wants you to have the kind of love that never loses hope and believes that with God, everything will turn out right. He wants you to have the kind of love that embraces the truth and is willing to endure whatever is necessary in order to do the right thing (1 Corinthians 13:4-7). God says that kind of love never fails, even though all else will (1 Corinthians 13:8). This kind of love comes from God and can only be developed by spending time with God. That's because being in the presence of God changes us.

Transformation is found in the presence of God.

God can transform us from someone who doesn't know how to love into someone who loves the way that He does. All we have to do is ask Him to work that in us and then do what He says.

Of course, it's impossible to be perfect for each other. There are no two people who can live up to one another's expectations all the time. At some point there are going to be disagreements. The things that one person does are going to get on the other's nerves. Each one is going to disappoint the other sometime. But it's what happens during those times that sets the marriage on one path or the other. One path with the fresh air leads to growing deeper and better together; the other path of suffocation leads to a breaking down of the bond of love and commitment.

When offenses happen—and they will in even the best of circumstances because of the differences in male and female perspectives—these things have to be talked out. When you try to come to a mutual understanding and you never can because one of you *refuses* to work it out, you can become so discouraged and hopeless that you withdraw and stop trying. But when you invite God to help you communicate and be of one mind and one spirit, things work out. You can grow through the difficult times when you walk through them together with God.

Emotional Divorce

You become divorced in your heart first. That's why even though a couple may be committed to staying married, their hearts can still be divorced from one another. That sucks the oxygen out of a marriage, and it becomes lifeless. The Lord does not like that. And neither do we. Living in a dead and miserable marriage is hell on earth. And it doesn't glorify God in the least.

Whenever one spouse starts to feel *unloved,* and the other spouse is *unloving,* they are in dangerous territory. They can then become strangers living in the same house but never making contact. And this is far more common than most people care to admit. At that point, the relationship is dying. If one or both of them then become involved in the activities of life and never include the other, they are headed for emotional divorce. They will grow completely apart if they don't take immediate steps to stop it. They have to start saying no to everything and everyone else and yes to each other. They have to decide if those activities and people are going to be that important to them if their marriage fails. Don't settle for an emotional divorce. Don't settle for less than what God has for you in your marriage. And what He has for you cannot come about if you have a big "D" branded on your heart that represents the divorce you are always considering and leaving open as an option. Once that gets into your heart, it will start to burn an imprint. If you let it stay there long enough, it gives you a way out and keeps your relationship from growing deeper and more committed.

The more you give place to divorce as an option, the deeper the imprint burns, the greater the distance that grows between you, and the more disconnected you will feel from one another until you have a spirit of divorce. Then it becomes a tearing of the heart. It becomes not about *if* you will divorce, but *when.* Once the "D" word takes hold in your mind, it almost has a life of its own. The spirit of divorce takes over and gets the process rolling. It's as though a divorce demon says, "I'll take it from here." Then you stop making plans for a future together and you only make plans for a future alone. Things will get worse between you, and one day when you have constant strife, arguments, and discord, divorce will seem like a pleasant relief.

If you are in a dead marriage relationship where there is no joy, no pleasure, no communication, no common interests or goals, nothing to look forward to, and no hope for the future—in other words, no fresh air—then you must do something immediately. Get before the Lord and confess every thought you have had of divorce so the spirit of divorce won't establish a stronghold in your heart. Pray for God to renew a right spirit in you and in your spouse. If your husband (wife) won't sit down and work things out, then find a good Christian marriage counselor. Counseling is much cheaper than a divorce. And often it takes a wise third party who knows what they're doing to wake up people who are drifting apart.

TWELVE REASONS WHY DIVORCE IS BAD FOR YOU

1. It's something God hates.
2. It destroys what was once your dream.
3. You have to divide up your children between you.
4. Your children will suffer more than you know.
5. Many friends will desert you.
6. You won't feel as comfortable in church.
7. You may lose your home.
8. There will be loss of income.
9. Family gatherings will never be the same.
10. It takes a big toll on your health.
11. You will have to divide up all your belongings.
12. You will always have a sense of failure about it.

Leaving a Legacy of Divorce

Children always suffer in a divorce. If that isn't true, then why are there so many books for the hurting adult children of divorced parents? And why are they selling so well? It's because these people struggle terribly. They know what it's like to have their worst fears come upon them. They have seen their prayers that Mom and Dad won't get divorced not be answered by God. (That is, if they were not made to understand that their prayers weren't answered because of the strong will of one or both of their parents.) They blame themselves for the divorce. They have trouble in school because they are hurt, depressed, anxious, confused, and unable to concentrate. They frequently seek alcohol, drugs, and promiscuity as a way out of their pain.

For your children, divorce is like experiencing a death, only without the sympathy one receives from others when there is a real death. In a physical death there is a mourning period, a period of recovery, and then you eventually grieve less. With a divorce, however, they are not afforded a mourning period with sympathy cards. There is no period of recovery. And they never seem to grieve less. They may *appear* as though they do, but they carry the ramifications of the divorce into their own relationships. They have fear and insecurity in their own marriage later on. I know there are exceptions to that, but they are not the majority. The majority are hurting. Keeping your children from all that pain is worth whatever effort it takes to stay married.

If you have children and you are already divorced, pray they won't blame themselves. Ask God to heal them of any guilt they carry for thinking that if they had been a better kid, this divorce wouldn't have happened. And pray they won't blame you or your spouse, either. Everything that goes wrong in their life after the divorce might be seen as their parents' fault. They will have a harder time honoring you if they are blaming you for their miserable life. Pray that they will forgive you and be free of anger so they won't get into trouble and grow up to take their anger out on the person they marry.

Twelve Good Reasons to Stay Married

1. It pleases God.
2. Married people live longer.
3. You will be healthier.
4. You don't have to divide up your income.
5. You don't have to divide up your children.
6. You will be more protected.
7. You don't have to live alone.
8. You can build something together.
9. You won't leave a legacy of divorce for your family.
10. You don't have to move into a smaller place.
11. You will be able to lift up one another when you fall.
12. Your prayers together are more powerful.

How to Avoid a Divorce

Pray often that you and your spouse will always take a strong stand against divorce. Declare that you are building your marriage on the Word of God, and therefore you will not allow the enemy to break apart what God has joined together. Declare that your marriage is God's plan, and you will not leave a legacy of divorce and brokenness for your children.

Every marriage is vulnerable. Every husband-and-wife relationship takes work. In the best of situations the marriage can still deteriorate and fall apart. I have seen what appears to be the greatest relationships disintegrate. Nothing surprises me in that regard anymore. No one knows what really goes on in a marriage except the two people who are in it. But you have to do whatever it takes to turn your marriage in the right direction and away from divorce. And that means not letting divorce stay in your heart. You have to guard your heart and not allow into it what God says is evil (Proverbs 4:23). You have to say, "I will not let divorce be an option for me. I will not seek divorce as the solution to my marriage problems."

Pray that you will not put other things or people before God or your spouse. Ask God to help you see where work or activities have taken over your life. Be brave and ask your spouse to share how *he (she)* feels. He (she) will be more than happy to tell you. But the thing is, you have to *listen* to what he (she) says and *not ignore* it. You have to *show interest* in his (her) *perspective.* Get rid of all anger, resentment, unforgiveness, and bitterness *before* you come together to talk. These emotions have absolutely no place in a marriage that lasts.

No marriage is too far gone to save if both partners want to save it. But if you are married to someone who is determined to divorce, there are still things you can do and ways you can pray that can also save it. I've seen marriages that have gone through divorce court be saved when the wife or husband started to pray fervently. However, if you have done all that you can do and your spouse is still determined to leave, release him (her) into God's hands. Let God deal with him (her), and you get on with doing what God has called you to do.

I am not saying there are no grounds for divorce. Some marriages are a disaster from the beginning, and allowing yourself to be destroyed in a marriage is not glorifying to God, either. When I was married the first time, I told someone I would rather be dead than stay married and I meant it. I didn't want to live another day in the hell I was in. I know many people have that same feeling, and my heart goes out to them. The person they are married to may be too mean, abusive, angry, godless, or evil to ever be able to work things out, and they need to save their own lives. People have to do what they have to do in order to survive, and God won't strike them with lightning. Marriage was never designed by God to destroy you. He has a better life for you than that.

I by no means want to bring condemnation on anyone who has been divorced in the past. I myself am a member of that group, but there is healing from the effects of it: restoration of your heart and a new beginning given to you by the Lord. God either makes all things new or He doesn't. If you choose to believe the Bible, then you are a candidate for complete renewal. But it is a mistake to remarry until you have found that place of restoration and wholeness God has for you. You also need an understanding and knowledge of why your marriage didn't work the first time and why you think it will this time. Seek good counsel and much prayer through this process.

There has to be something to look forward to in your marriage. If you're married to someone who is getting meaner and more inconsiderate with each passing year and seems to enjoy being that way, all you will see for your future is being alone with someone like that. You can either become resigned to that joyless life or choose to not lose the dream in your heart for the future. Ask God for a miracle. I have seen Him do a miracle for me in our marriage. It took years of praying, but I am glad I didn't give up.

We sometimes believe our heart is a private domain and we can think whatever we want, but it's not true. Whenever you entertain a thought that isn't of the Lord, you are inviting trouble. If you are struggling with thoughts of divorce, draw near to God and let Him fight the battle for you. "Do not be afraid. Stand still, and see the salvation of the LORD, which He will accomplish for you today...The LORD will fight for you, and you shall hold your peace" (Exodus 14:13-14). Put a protective guard over your heart, and don't let the "D" word in. You will be glad you stood your ground in the battle and won.

PRAYERS FOR MY MARRIAGE

Prayer for Protection

LORD, I PRAY YOU WOULD HELP my husband (wife) and me to rise far above any thoughts of divorce as a solution to our problems or a way out of our marriage. Take away any desire in our hearts for it. Keep our hearts so close to You and each other that we never even speak the word "divorce" in regard to each other and never harbor the idea of divorce in our minds. God, help us to always be affectionate to one another, "in honor giving preference to one another" (Romans 12:10). Show us where we are doing things that are breaking our marriage down instead of building it up. Help us both to grow stronger in You and learn to treat each other in a way that pleases You.

Help us to stand strong together through every problem and to not be afraid to seek outside help when we need it. Keep us from ever falling into denial about what is going on in our relationship so that we are blinded to what the enemy is doing. Help us to confess as sin before You any time we think about divorce as a solution to the problems in our marriage. In Jesus' name I pray.

Prayer for Breakthrough in Me

LORD, I CONFESS ANY TIME that I have ever considered divorce in my mind or have uttered that word to my husband (wife), friends, or family members in regard to my marriage. Whenever I have thought of divorce as an option or a way out of our problems, I ask You to forgive me, for I know it displeases You. I know You hate divorce and it grieves Your Spirit, so I pray that You would help me to never do that again from this day forward.

I reject any spirit of divorce that I have invited into my heart and our marriage by the careless words I have spoken or thoughts I have had. I repent of any time I have even thought about what it would be like to be married to someone else. I recognize these thoughts as evil and adulterous, and I repent of them before You. I turn to You to find solutions to any problems in my marriage. Give me wisdom to do things Your way. In Jesus' name I pray.

Prayer for Breakthrough in My Husband (Wife)

LORD, I ASK THAT YOU would take any thoughts of divorce out of my husband's (wife's) mind and heart. Where he (she) has entertained those kinds of thoughts, I ask that You open his (her) eyes to see how far away that is from Your best for his (her) life and our lives together. For any time we have discussed divorce or he (she) has used the word "divorce" as a way out of our problems, I come before You on my husband's (wife's) behalf and ask for Your forgiveness. Forgive him (her) for that sin so that a spirit of divorce cannot find a home in his (her) heart. If it already has, I ask that You would break that stronghold by the power of Your Spirit. Destroy that lie of the enemy so that it can never rise up again. Show him (her) a better way, which is Your way for our lives. Let there be no divorce in our future. In Jesus' name I pray.

TRUTH TO STAND ON

The Lord God of Israel says that He hates divorce,
for it covers one's garment with violence.

MALACHI 2:16

I say to you that whoever divorces his wife for any reason
except sexual immorality causes her to commit adultery;
and whoever marries a woman who is divorced commits adultery.

MATTHEW 5:32

If any brother has a wife who does not believe,
and she is willing to live with him, let him not divorce her.
And a woman who has a husband who does not believe,
if he is willing to live with her, let her not divorce him.

1 CORINTHIANS 7:12-13

Therefore, what God has joined together,
let not man separate.

MATTHEW 19:6

If two lie down together,
they will keep warm;
but how can one be warm alone?

ECCLESIASTES 4:11

12

If INFIDELITY
SHAKES *Your*
FOUNDATION

God is so grieved by infidelity in marriage that, as much as He hates divorce, He allows infidelity to be grounds enough to justify it. If your husband (wife) committed adultery, you could get a divorce if you wanted to because God understands the devastation of infidelity in our souls. Sex was God's idea, and He had a specific plan for the way it should be so that the greatest fulfillment could happen in our lives. Adultery violates that plan, and the consequences for it are severe.

Sexual sin does the greatest damage of all sins, besides murder, because its consequences are so far-reaching. One of the reasons for that is because you become one with whomever you have sex. Your soul is tied to them. "Do you not know that your bodies are members of Christ? Shall I then take the members of Christ and make them members of a harlot? Certainly not! Or do you not know that he who is joined to a harlot is one body with her? For 'the two,' He says, 'shall become one flesh'" (1 Corinthians 6:15-16).

Sexual sin not only violates a trust and a covenant made before God, but it hurts your soul and body. Every other sin a person does is outside the body, but sexual immorality is a sin against your own body (1 Corinthians 6:18). Our bodies belong to God and His Spirit dwells in them. Whatever you do with your body you are doing with the temple of the Holy Spirit (1 Corinthians 3:16-17).

If we commit one sin, we are guilty of all sins in God's eyes (James 2:10). But some sins do more damage in our lives than others. Pastor Jack Hayford says, "Sex sins are not harder for God to forgive, but they are more *damaging* at a personal and social dimension than other sins. Sexual sin assaults the fountainhead of every great thing that God intended for our lives on this earth, and it leaves in its wake a destructive fallout that can permeate generations."*

Adultery begins with the eyes and in the heart long before the physical act actually happens. Jesus said that "whoever looks at a woman to lust for her has already committed adultery with her in his heart" (Matthew 5:28). Adultery, even in the heart, destroys the soul (Proverbs 6:32).

What Do I Do if It Happens to Me?

I have talked with more people whose marriages were devastated by infidelity than for any other reason. It is epidemic because of our culture. You may not realize how prevalent it is because few people let it be known to others. It's embarrassing for everyone involved, and not many want to disclose it. The way I see it, if your spouse commits adultery, you have two choices:

1. Stay and do whatever it takes to find healing and restoration for both of you and your marriage.
2. Leave and move on with your life.

There is a third possibility, which is to stay and make his (her) life as miserable as he (she) has made yours by letting your anger, unforgiveness, and bitterness make him (her) pay for what happened for the rest of your lives. But that's not really a choice; it's a cop out.

As far as the "stay and do whatever it takes" choice, there is one particular couple who recovered from infidelity better than any couple I have ever known. They were both believers who were faithful in their church. They were excellent parents who volunteered in the schools their children attended. They seemed to have a wonderful marriage and family. However, the husband discovered that his wife had been having an affair with another man. When he confronted her, she admitted it was true.

---

* Jack Hayford, *Fatal Attractions* (Ventura, CA: Regal Books, 2004), p.11.

The husband came to our house to tell us that he had discovered this affair and to share how angry and devastated he felt. He asked us for our prayer support as he dealt with the aftermath of it all. However, as he sought the Lord, he realized that he wanted to save his marriage more than he wanted revenge. So he took time off from work and spent uninterrupted quality time with his wife, listening to her tell him everything that had been going on inside of her through the years that led up to the affair. I also went to his wife and talked with her and prayed for her, and I gained some understanding of how this had happened. It appeared that neither one of them wanted a divorce, so Michael and I both prayed that they could survive this.

Just a few weeks later, the husband brought his wife to our house on a Saturday morning saying he wanted to tell us something. The four of us sat together in a private room where no one else in the house could hear and he said he wanted to take the blame for what happened. He told us that God had opened his eyes to how insensitive he had been to his wife's needs and requests for years, and he wanted to apologize in front of us for his part in this and for his anger and disappointment in her when he came to our house the first time.

I have never heard anything so amazing as this tender and heartfelt apology by this husband. He knew he had set up a condition in his marriage that led to his wife's downfall and he took *full* responsibility. His wife was so touched by his declaration of unconditional love, and his commitment to do whatever it took to save their marriage, that she was completely broken and repentant.

After that, he took time off from his business and traveled with her to places she had longed to go, and he did things with her that she had asked him to do for years and years. They went to counseling together as well as separately. They stayed in the church, and they stayed with each other. Their marriage survived this terrible disaster, and it is still strong today. Their children are now grown and married with children of their own, and there has been no legacy of divorce for their family to inherit.

They survived what would have destroyed most people. And in the years since this began, the husband's business has been thriving beyond anyone's wildest dreams. I believe it was due to his willingness to examine himself and let God show him where he could have been a better husband. And he was humble enough to not only receive what God showed him, but also he was willing to expose his failings in front of his wife and his friends so that she could be healed and their marriage restored. He is the perfect example of what it means to have a repentant heart.

I will never forget the amazing generosity of spirit of that husband or the beauty of his wife's restoration. He wasn't living in denial or letting his wife off the hook. He was placing himself *on* the hook the way Jesus did. And I think only someone completely sold out to the Lord could do what that husband did. He certainly had the heart of the Lord, and he refused to receive any accolades for it. He admitted that God had to deal with him to get him to that point because that was not his initial reaction. But I applaud him for listening to what God was saying, and I applaud her for truly repenting, and I applaud them both for turning what could have been their greatest disaster into God's greatest blessing for their marriage and family.

On the other hand, I know another couple where the wife had an affair, but the husband was insistent on her paying retribution for what she had done. There was no recognition on his part that he was in any way responsible. His young wife had been emotionally damaged in her childhood and had grown up insecure and hurting. Not long after they married, they moved to a city a thousand miles away from all friends and family so he could go to a particular school. The problem was he also worked full-time as well as went to school full-time, so he was never home. She was extremely lonely and felt abandoned and was insecure enough to fall into an affair with someone at her workplace.

Of course, she was wrong to do it, and there were great consequences for it, but she was completely repentant and wanted to keep her marriage together. He, on the other hand, left her immediately and moved back home to his family. He refused to see her except with a counselor he had chosen, and she had to drive hundreds of miles alone to get there and back. He did not let her forget that this was her failure and he had every right to make these demands on her. He refused to handle the situation any other way, and he had nothing remotely resembling a repentant heart. This couple, as you might suspect, are divorced now.

They might have had a different outcome if that husband would have said to his unfaithful wife, "What you have done has devastated me, but I love you no matter what. I have sought the Lord, and I see how I have been complicit in this. He showed me how I abandoned you to work and go to school when you needed me most. Even though I was doing that for us and I thought you understood that, as the head of the house I did not serve you well. I want us to stay together and work this out. Let's go to counseling and let's seek God together, and let Him change us both so that our marriage will last."

I know this is extremely hard to do. And it's easy for me to say because I have never had anything at all like that happen to me. And I'm sure it takes more forgiveness and courage than I have on my own. But I have seen the results of laying down all pride and selfishness to save your marriage, and I know that the outcome is good.

God gives us a *way out* because this kind of betrayal is so devastating. But He also gives us a way to *rise above* and find His total restoration. Some people are willing to give up their God-given option of divorce in order to save their marriage and see it become all that God wants it to be. Those people are the heroes among us.

If Your Spouse Has Already Committed Adultery

If infidelity has already happened with your spouse, God has given you a way out. No questions asked. You are free to go. God understands that the pain of your husband's (wife's) adultery can be too hard to bear. He doesn't require you to endure it. However, if you choose to stay and work it out, and are willing to humble yourself before Him and hear what He is saying to you about how to proceed, God can work a miracle. You, as the violated spouse, have two choices:

1. *Forgive* and move on.
2. *Forgive* and stay.

Either way forgiveness is a must, because the alternative will kill you. Don't even think of trying to pay your spouse back for all the pain he (she) has caused you. That never works, and it will always hurt you more than it hurts him (her). Plus, it makes you look bad, and then he (she) feels justified in finding someone else. Instead, let him (her) fully know your pain and get to a counselor immediately—either on your own or with him (her). Preferably both. Write him (her) a nasty letter putting the worst of all your feelings down on paper, but don't send it. Shred it instead. Then write a letter to God telling Him what you're feeling and what you want Him to do in you and your spouse. Keep that one in a special place where you can read it again and perhaps show it to your husband (wife) if the time seems right. Above all, ask God to work complete forgiveness in your heart, because He is the only one who can. God knows you can't do it fully on your own.

There are, however, people who are adulterers without repentance. There is a difference between someone who commits an act of infidelity and feels remorse and repents and does whatever is necessary to make things right with God and their spouse, and the other extreme of a person who commits acts of infidelity over and over again without repentance. You can only take so much. That's the way God feels too. That's why He gives you a way out.

One woman I know forgave her husband at least three times that I'm aware of for his adulterous affairs with three different women. She mistakenly thought each time that her love and forgiveness would be enough. But it wasn't, because he continued to be entirely selfish and unrepentant. His next affair was with her best friend, for whom he left his wife so they could marry. About a year after he had married this second wife, he called his first wife and begged her to take him back. She said simply, "It's too late." She had forgiven him, but she knew he had not changed and it would happen again.

I advise anyone who has a spouse who commits sexual infidelity over and over and you cannot live with it anymore to release him (her) and let God deal with him (her) while you recover and move on. Don't torture yourself another minute. God has a better life for you than that.

Adulterers who refuse to change their ways will not inherit the kingdom of God or anything the Lord has for them (1 Corinthians 6:9-10). That particular adulterous husband I just mentioned had an extremely successful career, but his star stopped rising soon after all this occurred. In fact, a major tragedy happened to him and his star completely fell from the sky. I have seen more up-and-coming people with great futures ahead of them lose it all because they couldn't keep themselves from adultery. They didn't see that this was the enemy's plan to destroy the great future God had for them, and so they went with their flesh instead of submitting themselves to the Spirit of God.

Don't be afraid to let an adulterous spouse come to the end of himself (herself). "Blows that hurt cleanse away evil, as do stripes the inner depths of the heart" (Proverbs 20:30). Be strong enough to let him (her) suffer the natural consequences for what was done, because it can wake a person up to their own sin and cleanse their heart of evil. That being said, you also have to examine yourself to see where you are complicit in any way.

The Bible says that a wise person builds their house, but a foolish person pulls it down with their hands (Proverbs 14:1). You have to ask God, *Have I done anything to pull down my house? Is there something more I could have done to build it up?* We can all think of things we should have done differently in our marriages. I'm not saying this to make you feel guilty, especially if your spouse has committed adultery. Adultery is always wrong. It is never justified under any circumstances. And the adulterer is always guilty. But remember what I said earlier about having a repentant heart? In order for healing to come in a marriage for any reason, there always has to be an examining of your own heart, soul, and mind before the Lord. You always have to tell God that you are willing to see any place in you where you have fallen short of His will for your life.

Did you treat your spouse with disrespect? Were you inconsiderate of his (her) needs? Did you deny him (her) sexual gratification? These things are not justification for him (her) to commit adultery, but sometimes we set the stage for those things to happen because we weren't careful to guard the marriage in thought, word, deed, and prayer.

When a husband or wife feels lonely, disconnected, distanced, disappointed, or abandoned emotionally by their spouse, all it takes is being around someone who gives them a strong sense of being understood, acknowledged, or cared about. They are vulnerable, and this can establish a connection with that person. Even if it doesn't turn into physical infidelity, there is an infidelity of the heart that occurs, and that is not pleasing to God, either (Matthew 15:19).

Do you realize, *husbands,* that every time you are rude, critical, demeaning, verbally abusive, cruel, neglectful, or abandoning of your wife that you create in her a fertile ground into which seeds of unfaithfulness can be planted? Unless she is extremely strong in the Lord, deep longings and thoughts will come to her heart and mind, and she can become ripe for an affair of the heart, if not the body. It's amazing how attractive someone else can look to you when the person who is supposed to love you no longer acts as though he (she) does (2 Timothy 2:22). If you have set your wife up for that kind of fall, then you are partly to blame for what happens.

Do you realize, *wives,* that every time you criticize your husband in a demeaning way, put him down in front of others, neglect to compliment him and let him know that he is valuable to you, or refuse to have sex with him that you make it much more difficult for him to resist the temptations that are everywhere around him? You set him up for infidelity. He is more susceptible to flattery and unholy attention than he would have been otherwise.

Of course, there are certain husbands and wives who have already determined in their heart that they are open to the slightest advance from someone and will welcome any opportunity to commit adultery. There is nothing you can do with these people because they have a "self-sickness" and are wired for sin. They will not change without a professional counselor in their face confronting them, and even then that may not work. So don't blame yourself if you feel you have done your best to be a good husband or wife and your spouse still cheats. It is not your fault, and there is nothing you could have done to stop it. Tell him (her) "Goodbye and good luck!" and move on to better things.

Seven Things That Are True About Adultery

1. ***God told us not to do it in His Ten Commandments.*** "You shall not commit adultery" (Exodus 20:14).

2. ***Jesus said don't do it.*** "Jesus said, 'you shall not murder,' 'you shall not commit adultery,' 'you shall not steal' " (Matthew 19:18).

3. ***Adultery brings judgment upon you.*** "Marriage is honorable among all, and the bed undefiled; but fornicators and adulterers God will judge" (Hebrews 13:4).

4. ***Adultery happens in the heart as well as the body.*** "I say to you that whoever looks at a woman to lust for her has already committed adultery with her in his heart" (Matthew 5:28).

5. ***Adultery will cause you to lose out on all God has for you.*** "Do you not know that the unrighteous will not inherit the kingdom of God? Do not be deceived. Neither fornicators, nor idolaters, nor adulterers, nor homosexuals, nor sodomites" (1 Corinthians 6:9).

6. ***Adultery is entirely a work of the flesh, and as such it will reap death in your life.*** "The works of the flesh are evident, which are: adultery, fornication, uncleanness, lewdness" (Galatians 5:19).

7. ***Adultery will destroy you.*** "Whoever commits adultery with a woman lacks understanding; he who does so destroys his own soul" (Proverbs 6:32).

The Devil's Favorite Target

The devil's most prized target, as far as tempting someone toward infidelity, are the leaders in the body of Christ—and especially pastors and their wives. That's because these people are on the front lines and are doing the most to lead people in the kingdom of God. The enemy will come in like a tsunami to their hearts and emotions, especially after he has bombarded them with discouragement on one end of the spectrum and pride on the other. It is such an all-out spiritual assault on them that we in the body of Christ have to surround our pastors and spiritual leaders and their families with prayer. If we don't, they will suffer. When *they* suffer, so do *we* (1 Corinthians 12:14,26).

We must pray that they are able to be honest with the people closest to them, whom they trust, about the temptations they face. And we must pray against the rising up of a spirit of gossip. One of the sorriest sins is gossip. When someone confides a struggle to another in confidence asking for prayer, and the person who was told the confidence then goes and tells others, their sin of gossiping is as great as the sin they are gossiping about. Gossip in the church is a sin that keeps leaders and their families from sharing what needs to be shared in order for healing and renewal to come. It keeps them from seeking the prayer support they need. Do all you can to stop gossip.

If You Are Ever Attracted to Someone Else

Infidelity begins in the mind before any action ever takes place. And that is where it has to stop as well. "From within, out of the heart of men, proceed evil thoughts, adulteries, fornications...all these evil things come from within and defile a man" (Mark 7:21,23). You have to carefully monitor your thoughts. If you ever find yourself thinking about someone else besides your husband (wife), and wondering if they might be the perfect mate for you, this is adultery of the mind. And the consequences will be serious.

If you ever find you can't stop thinking about a certain person in that way, go before God immediately and confess it and pray for deliverance from those thoughts. Stay before the Lord until this obsession is gone. There is no good that will come out of it and the consequences for pursuing it, or allowing it to overtake you, could ruin your life. Ask someone to pray with you about this. It's possible that you could tell your husband (wife), but then after your attraction is gone—which it will be if you stay before the Lord long enough—then your poor husband (wife) is left having to sort through all the rejection and hurt feelings. It's not worth it. I say, go to the Lord and prostrate yourself on the ground. Fast and pray. Stay there before Him until this thing is broken. Every time the feeling comes back, humble yourself before God. If all that doesn't work, and this attraction becomes an obsession, call in a close friend who doesn't gossip to stand with you in prayer and break this stronghold of the enemy. If even that fails, then tell your husband (wife) and go to counseling together. You're going to need it.

If you are attracted to someone, by all means don't tell that person. It only opens up feelings in him (her) of being appreciated in the wrong way. It inspires an intimacy between the two of you because of a secret you now share. At the first sign of an attraction, don't fool yourself with fancy words like "attraction" and "affair" that make it sound like flowers in spring. Call it what it is—adultery of the heart and fornication of the mind. Don't create a sexual tension or inspire an attraction in the other person, or force that person to have to fight one off. Leave them out of it. This is between you and God. Tell God, a counselor, or your spouse, or all three.

An adulterous spirit is a strong spirit. It's heady and will try to make you think you have finally found the one you have been waiting for and the fulfillment of a perfect life is ahead. But it is all an illusion. The one you have been waiting for is actually at home waiting for *you*. And you need to go back and give your marriage all your efforts to make it work. You need to give God a chance to do a miracle.

I know a young pastor's wife who was having a strong attraction toward someone other than her husband in her church. She had come to the point where she felt her marriage was not anything like what she thought it would be. She came to me for help, and I suggested she call two other women she trusted to pray with her as well. Between the three of us we stood by her, talking with her and praying with and for her, until we saw that thing completely broken.

We are all vulnerable to being attracted in our mind to people around us, but I was convinced beyond any doubt that for her this was a ploy of the enemy to destroy the great ministry she and her husband would one day have. We prayed that this work of hell in her life be broken completely. It took months to finally break through this, but we did. And she and her husband went on to have a great marriage and many years together in a highly successful ministry. They raised a wonderful family with children and grandchildren. No one else ever knew about it, not even her husband, and definitely not the person she was attracted to. This was entirely a battle in the spirit, and the enemy lost.

If you find yourself attracted to another person other than your husband (wife), ask God to break that attraction like severing the head off of a snake so that there is no way it can ever regenerate. Ask Him to put a guard over your heart to protect it from any further sinful intrusion. You have authority over evil in your life. "Sin lies at the door. And its desire is for you, but you should rule over it" (Genesis 4:7). The enemy wants to entice you away from the life God has for you, but God has given you the power to put a stop to it.

You will be able to tell if there is still a residue in your heart with regard to any ungodly attraction if you are sad when you don't see that person. Or if you have excitement when you do. You will know you are free when you see that person one day and you thank God with all your heart that you didn't act on your attraction. That you didn't sacrifice your marriage, your children, or your life for it. You will wonder, *What in the world was I thinking?* And you will thank God that He rescued you from your own foolishness.

It Can Happen to Anyone, but It Doesn't Have To

Don't think for a moment that you could never fall into an adulterous trap. It is a strong, heady thing that can wrap around you like an invisible python, and when the time is right it will constrict your good sense until you can't breathe. And it can happen with someone you never dreamed it could. Or it might happen suddenly with someone you just met. It's insidious, treacherous, and devious, a deceitful entrapment that can sweep you away and entice you to do things you will regret. That's why you can never entertain any infatuation, or any soul connection, or even a flirtation with another person of the opposite sex. (Or of the same sex, for that matter.)

There were two important things I prayed for in a marriage partner. One was that he must have a strong personal relationship with God through Jesus Christ. It was out of the question for me to think of sharing my life with someone who didn't share my love for the Lord. I couldn't imagine how to make a marriage work without it. The other important thing I prayed for in a husband was that he would be faithful to me. I knew I could never tolerate sexual sin in marriage. I wouldn't be able to live with it. God answered my prayers and gave me a husband who loves Him and has always been faithful. Michael's faithfulness to me and to the Lord is his most admirable quality in my mind, and he has never given me any reason to doubt it. Even so, I have prayed throughout all of our 34 years of marriage that the enemy would never be able to destroy us with any kind of temptation to sexual sin. I believe that has not only kept us strong but also away from danger.

Seduction is subtle and opportunities are everywhere, and you may be approached by someone somewhere, sometime. We've all heard of people who get themselves into an adulterous situation and say, "I wasn't looking to fall in love or have an affair; it just happened." It just happened because they let thoughts of an adulterous affair get into their mind. They didn't have to look *for* it. They needed to stop looking *at* it when it presented itself. We all have enough insecurity in us to be attracted to flattery or admiration. We all have enough pride that we can be puffed up from someone's attention. We all are vulnerable to inappropriate feelings. We can be strong, humble, and secure 99.99 percent of the time, but in a moment of weakness or overconfidence, we can fall.

It can happen to anyone, but it won't happen to everyone. It won't happen to those who have learned to keep their heart with all diligence, who understand the ploy of the enemy, and who know how to stand against it.

In *The Anatomy of Seduction*, Jack Hayford lists four "steps of an advancing seduction." These are danger signs that should sound a major alarm in each of us if any one of them ever occurs:

1. Mental preoccupation about the other person
2. An unusual desire to be near or around the person

3. A growing desire to give frequent compliments

4. The supposition that an "innocent" fling or flirtation can be indulged*

If you sense any of these four warnings happening in you, run as fast as you can to God, get on your face before Him, confess your unholy attraction as sin, ask Him to take it away completely, and stay there until it is gone. If even for the briefest of moments there is a temptation that you give in to, a hook will lodge itself in your heart and bring you pain one way or another. It's not worth sacrificing your marriage and the future God has for you.

You know how it is when you entertain someone in your home. You *invite* them *in*. You give them a *place* to sit. You provide something of sustenance to *sustain* them. It is the same with lustful images or thoughts. They come across your mind, but you are the one who *invites them in*. You are the one who gives them a *place to reside* in your heart. You are the one who *sustains them with unholy longings*.

What you must do is command these thoughts to leave. That might seem rude to a guest in your home, yet if your guest was doing something that would destroy your life or close the door to God's best for you, you would demand that this person leave immediately. And so you must do with adulterous thoughts that try to stay in your mind. Throw them out, close the door to your heart, and lock it behind them. The Bible warns us about being enraptured by immorality, saying that the adulterer "did not know it would cost him his life" (Proverbs 7:20,22-23). Lust seduces us away from the life God has for us and into the pit the enemy has set as a snare.

An adulterous spirit is everywhere. It's in the workplace, in the neighborhood, sadly in some churches—nearly every place you go. It is impossible to avoid contact with it completely. You have to be clear in your understanding of what it is—which is a trap to ensnare and destroy you and your marriage. And what it is *not*—a means of achieving true happiness and fulfillment.

Remember that no matter how strong the temptation is, God will not allow you to be tempted beyond what you are able to resist. He will give you a way out and give you the strength and the ability to successfully resist it (1 Corinthians 10:13). Cling to God and embrace Him as your way out of all temptation, especially infidelity.

---

* Jack Hayford, *Fatal Attractions* (Ventura, CA: Regal Books, 2004), pp. 42-44.

Prayers for My Marriage

Prayer for Protection

LORD, I PRAY YOU WOULD protect my marriage from any kind of infidelity. May adultery be far from us and never find a place in either of our minds or hearts. Pour Your wisdom and knowledge into us so that we are too wise and too smart to allow the enemy to sneak up on our blind side and throw temptation in our path. I pray You would not allow temptation to even come near us. Keep us far from anyone who would try to lead us into anything evil. Remove anyone from our lives who would ever tempt us with adulterous thoughts.

Lord, I know that in You "are hidden all the treasures of wisdom and knowledge" (Colossians 2:3). Give us the ability to see danger in advance and the wisdom to not do anything stupid. "Let us walk properly" (Romans 13:13). Keep us from ever "having eyes full of adultery and that cannot cease from sin" (2 Peter 2:14). Help us to live in integrity before You and each other so that we will walk securely (Proverbs 10:9). Establish us in our faith. Keep us from being deceived by the world and the enemy (Colossians 2:6-8). Thank You, Lord, that we are complete in You and need not seek anything outside of what You have given us in each other and in You (Colossians 2:10). In Jesus' name I pray.

Prayer for Breakthrough in Me

LORD, HELP ME TO LOVE You with all my heart, soul, mind, and strength, and help me to love my husband (wife) the same way (Mark 12:30). Keep me far from the broad way that leads to destruction, and help me to always choose the narrow gate that leads to life (Matthew 7:13-14). Thank You for my husband (wife) and for the marriage You have given us. I smash down any dream I have entertained of being loved by someone else. Help me to see this as a false god I have set up to worship in place of You.

Lord, show me anything in me that has given place to infidelity in my heart. Wherever I have thought of another man (woman) and how it would be to be married to him (her) instead of my husband (wife), I confess that as sin. Where I have found myself attracted to someone of the opposite sex who is not my spouse, I also confess that before You as sin. Take all sinful and lustful thoughts out of my heart. I refuse to listen to the lies of the enemy telling me that anything would be better for me than what I have in my husband (wife).

I rebuke the devourer, who would come to destroy me with temptation, and say that I will serve only You, Lord. Thank You, Jesus, that You understand temptation and are able to help me when I am tempted (Hebrews 2:18). Lord, I ask that my desire would always be only for my husband (wife) and no one else. Help me to be so sold out to You that nothing and no one can buy my affections away from my husband (wife). In Jesus' name I pray.

Prayer for Breakthrough in My Husband (Wife)

Lord, I pray You would fill my husband's (wife's) heart with Your Spirit so that it does not wander from me and our marriage to anyone else. Remove from him (her) all opportunities for anything inappropriate or anything that crosses the line of decency. Take away all lust and attraction from his (her) heart and replace it with Your love. Show me all I can do to build him (her) up and be the wife (husband) he (she) needs me to be. Help him (her) to flee all adulterous thoughts and be able to glorify You in his (her) body, soul, and spirit (1 Corinthians 6:18-20).

Where he (she) has crossed that line and succumbed to temptation in his (her) thoughts or deeds, restore him (her) to You. Help him (her) confess every transgression because his (her) sin will always be with him (her) until that happens (Psalm 51:1-3). Wash him (her) thoroughly from his (her) iniquity. I pray that if he (she) sins against You or me in any way, that his (her) sins will find him (her) out (Numbers 32:23). Deliver him (her) from all immorality. Do what it takes to bring him (her) to his (her) knees before You in repentance so that he (she) can be restored and cleansed to become "a vessel for honor" for Your glory prepared for every good work (2 Timothy 2:20-22). In Jesus' name I pray.

Truth to Stand On

Each one is tempted when he is drawn away by his own desires and
enticed. Then, when desire has conceived, it gives birth to sin;
and sin, when it is full-grown, brings forth death.

James 1:14-15

No temptation has overtaken you except such as is common to man;
but God is faithful, who will not allow you to be tempted
beyond what you are able, but with the temptation will also make the
way of escape, that you may be able to bear it.

1 Corinthians 10:13

This is the will of God, your sanctification:
that you should abstain from sexual immorality; that each of you should
know how to possess his own vessel in sanctification and honor.

1 Thessalonians 4:3-4

Nevertheless, because of sexual immorality, let each man have his own
wife, and let each woman have her own husband.

1 Corinthians 7:2

Watch and pray, lest you enter into temptation.
The spirit indeed is willing, but the flesh is weak.

Matthew 26:41

13

If ONE *of* YOU DECIDES *to* LEAVE HOME

———— ⟳ ————

Separation begins in the heart long before anyone ever decides to move out of their home. It first starts when communication breaks down and the husband or wife no longer understands what the other is thinking, feeling, going through, or planning. It is reinforced by anger, rudeness, abuse, unforgiveness, or negative emotions. It intensifies when arguments happen over such things as the children, financial problems, one person's destructive behavior, or an unsatisfying to nonexistent sex life. The separation of heart grows wider if either the husband or the wife develops a hardness of heart, or it becomes obvious that they are no longer each other's top priority. Not long after that, divorce begins to be thought of as a way out of the marriage, and the separation process is nearly complete. All it will take is an act of infidelity or some other action that brings great hurt, and an overwhelming sense of hopelessness will push it all over the edge. At that point, leaving the marriage will seem like a relief.

The good news is that this process can be *stopped* at any point and totally *reversed* if there is *repentance* of heart and *forgiveness* flowing from *both* husband and wife to one another. All it takes is one person saying, "I don't want to go on like this. I want to make some changes. I want to seek the Lord and have Him make changes in you and me and in us together. Let's talk about the things that are bothering each of us and get counseling if we need to. I am willing to confess before you and before God anything I have done or not done that was wrong. I want to ask for your forgiveness. I am willing to do what it takes to turn things around and renew our marriage so it will last."

I guarantee that if a man or woman would say those words to their spouse and mean them, and if their spouse would receive them and agree to say the same thing in return, they could not only save their marriage, but they would make it better than they ever thought it could be. Sadly, too many people don't recognize the signs until it's too late. They are clueless to what is happening in themselves, and blind to all that is going on in their spouse.

How many stories have we heard about a husband who comes home to find that his wife has suddenly moved out? He is shocked and baffled, but this was not a quick decision for her. She had been contemplating this for a very long time. No woman decides to leave her home and marriage on a whim. And a woman with children will not leave her home without thinking long and hard about it. It is way too traumatic and difficult to uproot children, deprive them of their parent, and start all over while trying to support them and find child care. There has to be an emotional separation happening long before any physical separation occurs. If the husband was surprised, it's probably because he had not been listening for a very long time. Once a woman finally makes that decision, she is not going to come back unless there are some major changes made.

We've also heard countless stories of a wife who was suddenly left by her husband. Again, there were surely signs of emotional separation long before the physical separation occurred. There had to have been communication problems, sexual problems, or just plain compatibility problems. And she may not have been really listening to him for a long time, either. Of course, there are men who can be easily seduced by another woman and way too many women who will go after a married man. But the wife always has home field advantage if she makes herself and their home a place he doesn't want to leave. The reason a man can "suddenly" leave a marriage and do something impulsive, as in go off with his secretary, is because at that point he doubts if things will ever get any better at home.

Is There Ever a Right Time to Leave?

In regard to having a separation with the intent of working things out, you need to be led by the Holy Spirit. The case for a husband or wife leaving and separating from their spouse has to be made on the grounds that they care enough about the person they are leaving—as well as themselves and their children—to do what's best. The motivation must be to save and not to punish. They do it because staying would be worse. Sometimes extreme measures are needed in extreme situations.

There are some believers who think that separation is the best thing you can do for someone who needs a wake-up call. Sometimes it takes a major shock to force a person to face the truth about themselves and what they are doing. It is definitely a wake-up call when your spouse moves out of the home, but I have seen this tactic completely backfire and have the opposite effect. In one case, a husband moved out and separated from his wife over something relatively trivial, and this drove her into the arms and comfort of another man because of her tremendous fear of abandonment and rejection. That's why much prayer has to go into a decision like this. You have to have the mind of God. It is not a "one size fits all." There are no guarantees. "A man's heart plans his way, but the LORD directs his steps" (Proverbs 16:9). Make plans for your life, but not without the leading of the Holy Spirit.

One wife moved out and said she wouldn't come back if her husband didn't make major changes. But after much time passed and a great deal of effort had gone into counseling that did not prove productive, it was easy to just go ahead and file the divorce papers. If you are separated too long, it can seem more convenient to just stay separated. Of course, the best reason to separate is if there is abuse in the home directed at either a spouse or a child. You have to get away from a violent spouse and a volatile home situation until you both are calm enough to work things out. Also, if there is adultery, separation may be necessary before there can be restoration.

One young woman I know had just been married a couple years to a young man she had met in church. They had an adorable baby who was about a year old when she found out that her husband had been having an affair with someone at work. The young wife was devastated and immediately took the baby and moved in with her parents. She went for counseling at her church, and she, her parents, the counselor, and her pastor agreed that she should stay separated from him until he was willing to come in for counseling on a regular basis and do whatever it took to turn his life around.

The husband was so devastated that his wife and child were gone, and so disgusted with himself for what he had done, that he agreed to do whatever it took to restore his family. He started going regularly to counseling and to church, and he became so completely broken and repentant that he was able to experience a major deliverance from a longtime problem with sexual addiction. He had never faced his problem before, and his wife was unaware of it. His life was completely transformed, and his wife was totally forgiving. Only God can do that. She and the baby eventually moved back home with him, and the two of them started a business together that is thriving today. This was one of the greatest success stories I have heard with regard to separation as a solution. It is a perfect example of how a devastating situation can be turned around for the glory of God.

God says a woman is not to leave her husband, but if she does she is to remain unmarried or try to be reconciled to him (1 Corinthians 7:10-11). That means you don't just leave because you get a better offer. It means leaving is done with the intention of reconciling, if possible, or of protecting yourself or your children from a situation that is destroying you—whether physically, mentally, or emotionally.

If Separation Has Already Happened

If your spouse left you, or you have left him (her), there has to be a very good reason why there is so much unhappiness in your marriage. No one in a great marriage leaves their home and family. Ask God to show you what the true reasons are. Along with that, find a counselor and mature believers who can help you sort through your past, present, and future, and pray with you. Don't try to go through this alone. You need the support of others. You need to be candid about what is happening in your life and be able to ask for prayer concerning it.

Whenever you get a chance to meet your spouse face-to-face, if even for a moment, look your best. Don't wear the same thing he (she) has seen you in every day for the past five years. Be clean, fresh smelling, and put together well. Do something to enhance your attractiveness. Your competition for his (her) affection is out there doing all that and more. Give your spouse every reason to want to be with you again. Make yourself desirable, like you were when he (she) fell in love with you. When you have the opportunity to speak to your husband (wife), say words that are kind, loving, and appreciative. Ask God to flow His love through you to your husband (wife).

Ask God to bring your husband (wife) home and give you patience to wait for His timing. Praise God that in this waiting time you will have an opportunity to become more like the Lord. Thank Him that He has joy waiting for both of you in the midst of this trial.

Without sidestepping or minimizing what sins your spouse has committed that led to this separation, be willing to admit anything you have done or not done that has contributed as well. Tell your spouse that you want to work with him (her) to build a good life, and you are willing to do whatever it takes. Listen to his (her) complaints about whatever you've done wrong with an open and receptive heart. Even if your spouse says it's over and you are through, continue to pray. Many a heart has been changed because a husband and wife refused to stop praying.

While you are waiting for God to restore your marriage, go on a self-improvement marathon. Do whatever you need to do to improve yourself both spiritually, physically, emotionally, or mentally. Become appealing and magnetic. Grow your soul and your mind. Become interesting and interested.

Wives, a husband needs a wife, not a mother. Even if he has needed a mother that he didn't have at one time in his life, you are not the one to fill that role. So first of all, don't look like his mother. Fix yourself up so that you don't make him feel old because you look unatractive and dowdy. And don't act like his mother by nagging him about picking up his socks.

Husbands, a wife doesn't need a son; she needs a husband. So don't try to make her into your mother. You are the husband, so take charge of things that need to be done around the house and don't make her have to ask you over and over to do them. Treat her with honor, and she will honor you. Treat her like the best thing that ever happened to you, and she will be. And pick up your socks so she doesn't have to trip over them every day and be annoyed.

Remember that separation is not divorce. And it doesn't have to end in divorce. Not if you pray that it won't. With God, things can change. People can change. But they have to at least *want* to. They have to at least have some degree of love and appreciation for their spouse and want to see that fire rekindled and the marriage restored.

Deepening your relationship with God is one of the best things you can do for your marriage. Get close to God and ask Him to show you the truth about yourself, about your spouse, about your marriage, and about His ways.

God asks you to come to Him in your struggle and lay your problems at His feet, and He will give you a place of rest from them. Do that and you will have peace in your heart, no matter what is going on in your marriage.

TEN THINGS GOD SAYS
ABOUT FINDING A PLACE OF REST

1. *God has promised you rest.* "Therefore, since a promise remains of entering His rest, let us fear lest any of you seem to have come short of it" (Hebrews 4:1).

2. *You will find rest in God's presence.* "He said, 'My Presence will go with you, and I will give you rest'" (Exodus 33:14).

3. *God is with you to give you rest in every situation.* "Is not the LORD your God with you? And has He not given you rest on every side?" (1 Chronicles 22:18).

4. *God has rest and refreshing for you if you will listen to Him.* "He said, 'This is the rest with which You may cause the weary to rest,' and, 'This is the refreshing;' yet they would not hear" (Isaiah 28:12).

5. *God's rest is complete and all-encompassing.* "Now the LORD my God has given me rest on every side; there is neither adversary nor evil occurrence" (1 Kings 5:4).

6. *Because you are God's child, He has rest for your soul.* "There remains therefore a rest for the people of God" (Hebrews 4:9).

7. *When you are burdened, God will give you rest.* "Come to Me, all you who labor and are heavy laden, and I will give you rest" (Matthew 11:28).

8. *When you turn to God, you will find rest.* "In returning and rest you shall be saved; in quietness and confidence shall be your strength" (Isaiah 30:15).

9. *When you yoke up with God, He will give your soul rest.* "Take My yoke upon you and learn from Me, for I am gentle and lowly in heart, and you will find rest for your souls" (Matthew 11:29).

10. *When you obey God, you will find rest.* "To whom did He swear that they would not enter His rest, but to those who did not obey?" (Hebrews 3:18).

Time to Let Go

With all that being said about learning to find God's rest and not giving up hope when you are separated, there is a time when you need to let go. Of course, you need to release your spouse into God's hands right from the beginning of the separation, but I am talking about *really* letting go.

One lady I know tried to get her husband back for years after he left her. She was still trying to get him back even after he was married to someone else and had two children with his new wife. During her marriage to him, she never made any effort to look nice, smell nice, or keep the house clean. She never wore makeup or perfume, never fixed her hair to be in any way attractive, never wore clothes that had the least bit of flattering style to them, and never used a breath mint. A husband (wife) has to feel somewhat attracted to the person they are married to.

Her husband complained often about these things, but she paid no attention. She was child-obsessed, and that's where all her efforts went. Everything was for their children, and no attempt was made to please him. She was determined to homeschool all four of their children full-time, over the strong objections of her husband. He wanted to have some kind of companion in his wife, but she would not take any time away from her children, not even for a couple hours to go out to dinner with him. I'm all for homeschooling; I did it myself for a while. But if it becomes an issue in a marriage to the point of destroying the relationship, I don't see how that is ultimately benefiting the children.

When he first left her, she still made no effort whatsoever to clean up the house or fix herself up when he came to pick up their children for the day. She had a great opportunity right then to win him back, but she didn't use it to any advantage whatsoever. They ended up divorced, and she had to put the children in school full-time anyway and go to work. It would have taken so little effort to listen to her husband and see how strongly he felt and take the necessary steps to do what he needed. He needed a companion, a wife, and a sex partner, but she was so devoted to her children that she didn't have time to be any of the above. She never saw that if she really cared about her children, she would have made sure they had a happy father. Her children would have had an easier time in school than they did living through the divorce of their parents.

That's why it is important to listen carefully to your spouse. What are the comments, observations, or opinions he (she) has made in the past? Think back. Have any of them been repeated, even subtly? Try to understand the signs. Do you remember the example of Wrigley and the praying paws in the communication chapter? His wants were expressed so subtly, and we knew that if we didn't read him right, there might be an unpleasant mess to clean up. Do you get my analogy here? Ask God to show you what is really going on in your mate's heart and life. You may *think* you know, but no one really knows the heart of another without being told. Only God sees the inner workings of the heart. Ask Him to show you what your spouse won't reveal.

I used to wonder why people could be married for 35 years and then get a divorce. I thought if you stuck it out that long, why wouldn't you stay with it the rest of the way? But I realize that the older you get, the harder it is to take abuse of any kind. You come to a point where you realize you don't have that many years left, and you absolutely cannot spend them being miserable the way you have been. Don't let that happen to you. If you are miserable now, do something about it. It is not going to get better on its own. Talk to your spouse and make him (her) listen to how you feel. Ask him (her) to talk to you about what is going on inside of him (her). Go to counseling if you need to.

If you and your spouse have never even considered moving out, thank God and ask Him what each of you can do to make sure that neither of you would ever want to. Pray that God will help you do whatever it takes to see that you never become separated in your hearts. Pray for wisdom so you can be the best wife (husband) possible. "If any of you lacks wisdom, let him ask of God, who gives to all liberally and without reproach, and it will be given to him" (James 1:5). Ask God to make you both so wise that you will have enough sense to never get separated in your hearts in the first place.

PRAYERS FOR MY MARRIAGE

Prayer for Protection

Lord, I pray You would protect my marriage from the separation of heart that can happen when two people stop communicating. Help us to always be in close contact and emotionally current with one another. Help us to learn to do what pleases the other and not be neglectful of each other's needs. Teach us to be kind when we could be stern, merciful when we could be judgmental, and forgiving when we could take offense. Open our eyes whenever either of us is blind to what is going on inside the other. Show us where we have been preoccupied with other things and other people. Give us revelation so that we can see the truth and stay on the path You have for us (Proverbs 29:18).

Lord, Your Word says that You allow calamity because of sin when people forsake You and worship other gods (Jeremiah 1:16). I pray that my husband (wife) and I will never depart from Your ways and get so wrapped up in other things that we begin to serve those things instead of You. Keep us on track and on the path You have for us so that calamity never comes near us. One of the greatest calamities would be to separate from one another. I pray that it would never happen to us in any way. Help us to always pray and be watchful about this. If You are *for* us, who can be *against* us? (Romans 8:31). In Jesus' name I pray.

Prayer for Breakthrough in Me

Lord, I confess any place where I have separated myself in my heart from my husband (wife). I break that hardness in me that has kept me distanced—whether as a self-protective measure or just by being preoccupied with other things. I know any kind of distance between two people, especially whom You have made to be one, goes against Your will. I recognize this state of mind as an offense against You. Thank You that because of Your love for me, I am more than a conqueror, and I can conquer this. Thank You that nothing can ever separate me from Your love (Romans 8:37-39).

I refuse to let myself become anxious about any sense of distance I feel between my husband (wife) and me. Instead, I come to You with thanksgiving for who You are and all that You have done for us, and I let my requests be made known to You. Thank You that Your peace which passes all understanding will keep my heart and mind in Christ Jesus (Philippians 4:6-7). I will not let my heart be troubled, but I will trust in You instead (John 14:1). I know that Your grace is sufficient for me and Your strength is made perfect in my weakness. I can trust that when I am weak You will make me strong, because I depend on You (2 Corinthians 12:9-10). Even if I am deserted, You are still here for me and will be to me what my husband (wife) can't or doesn't want to be (Isaiah 54:4-5). If it ever does come to a separation between us, I pray that You would help us to be reconciled to one another again. Bring forth any changes in both of us that are needed. In Jesus' name I pray.

Prayer for Breakthrough in My Husband (Wife)

LORD, WHERE MY HUSBAND (WIFE) has separated from me in any way—whether physically, emotionally, or mentally—I pray You would bring him (her) back. Thank You, Lord, that even though he (she) may leave me, You have promised that You never will (Deuteronomy 31:6). Lord, I pray for restoration of any emotional and physical separation between us. Change our hearts and help me to be everything he (she) needs me to be. Restore us emotionally together again. Give me courage and strength to fight for our relationship until it is the way You want it to be.

I pray that he (she) will not be lured into any trap or enticement by the enemy. Open his (her) eyes to see that if You are for us, no one can be against us and succeed (Romans 8:31). Help him (her) to understand that separation, except for the purpose of working things out, is not Your perfect will for our lives. I trust that anything we go through will be for Your glory (Romans 8:18). Enable him (her) to "taste and see that" You are a good God and that he (she) will find the greatest blessings by following You and trusting in Your ways. (Psalm 34:8).

Help him (her) to hear Your voice and follow You (John 10:27). Draw us both closer to You and closer to each other. Where our love for one another has failed, help us to fall in love all over again in even greater measure than ever before. Just as no one can "separate us from the love of Christ," I pray that nothing will be able to separate us from our love for each other (Romans 8:35). In Jesus' name I pray.

TRUTH TO STAND ON

I consider that the sufferings of this present time
are not worthy to be compared with the glory
which shall be revealed in us.

ROMANS 8:18

Count it all joy when you fall into various trials,
knowing that the testing of your faith produces patience.
But let patience have its perfect work,
that you may be perfect and complete, lacking nothing.

JAMES 1:3-4

Two are better than one, because they have a good
reward for their labor. For if they fall,
one will lift up his companion.
But woe to him who is alone when he falls,
for he has no one to help him up.

ECCLESIASTES 4:9-10

The LORD will perfect that which concerns me;
Your mercy, O LORD, endures forever;
do not forsake the works of Your hands.

PSALM 138:8

He Himself has said, "I will never leave you nor forsake you."
So we may boldly say: "The LORD is my helper;
I will not fear. What can man do to me?"

HEBREWS 13:5-6

14

If HOPE SEEMS LOST *and* YOU NEED *a* MIRACLE

There are seasons in every marriage. First there is the romantic-in-love-exciting-passionate-fun-getting-to-know-each-other period. This is when love is so heady you can't see clearly, which means you can't clearly see what you've gotten into. The intensity of that period will fade no matter how you try to keep it from happening, and although that feeling is great, it is entirely exhausting. The next stage is the busy-making-a-home-establishing-a-career time. When the children come there is the too-little-sleep-never-a-moment-when-something-doesn't-need-to-be-done-and-there-is-not-enough-time-in-a-day period. Later comes the children-are-gone-and-you-have-to-remember-why-you-got-married-and-get-to-know-each-other-and-fall-in-love-all-over-again period. Then it's the I'm-too-old-to-put-up-with-this-anymore-and-I-don't-want-to-spend-what-little-time-I-have-left-with-this-kind-of-misery-so-there-have-to-be-some-changes-made season. And that's where a lot of marriages end. But if you can work hard and both be willing to make changes and get past that, you will have the I-hope-we-grow-old-together-because-I-don't-want-to-be-with-anyone-else-and-I-know-we-will-take-care-of-each-other-until-the-end period to look forward to.

Things can go wrong in a marriage in any one of these seasons, but if you know these times are coming, and you know they will end, it makes getting through them a lot easier. It gives you hope in each season.

You may feel full of hope about your marriage today, and if so, I pray that it will always be that way for you. May you both be prisoners of hope no matter what happens in your lives together (Zechariah 9:12). However, if you ever do start to feel hopeless about any particular aspect of your marriage, let this chapter be an encouragement to you. And if you ever get to the point where you feel that all hope is lost for your marriage and it would take nothing less than a miracle to save it, then I have good news for you. God is in the miracle business. That means even if it got so bad that you were in divorce proceedings, and the divorce papers had already been signed and the ink is completely dry, there is still hope.

Over the years I have heard from countless couples who had come to that point in the divorce proceedings and one of them started to pray for the other and things turned around to the point of total reconciliation. They canceled all plans to be divorced and got completely back together. Some had to get remarried because the divorce was final.

One particular couple is precious to me because their story is so touching and miraculous. They waited for more than two hours while I signed books, and they came up to me at the end of the line. They told me they had experienced great strife in their marriage and had separated. While they were separated, he was put in prison for a year, and she eventually filed for divorce. He received the Lord while in prison, and the day before he was to be released, someone gave him a copy of *The Power of a Praying Husband*. He read the entire book the day and night before he was to be freed from prison, and he said he knew in those moments as he was reading that his life would never be the same. He called his wife when he got out and told her what had happened and that God had revealed to him what kind of husband he was supposed to be and how he needed to be praying for her every day. He asked her to take him back, and he promised to do whatever it took to be the husband she needed.

His part of the story was amazing enough, but then his wife continued, saying that she too had been given a book just a few days before he was to be released called *The Power of a Praying Wife*. When she read it, she said her eyes were opened as to how she needed to be praying for her husband.

As they were relating this story to me, their eyes filled with tears and they struggled to get out the words without choking up. They told me that they had driven hundreds of miles just to tell me their story and to thank me in person for writing the books and saving their marriage. They had canceled their divorce and were back together, and their marriage was strong and their lives had been set on a totally different path than they had ever been on before. They showed me their worn books and asked if I would sign a special message to them. I told them that meeting them and hearing their story was one of the best gifts I have ever received, and I will always remember them and keep them in my prayers. They were in a hopeless situation, but when they started to pray for one another, God did a miracle.

Our God is a God of hope. He is the all-powerful God of the universe, and nothing is too hard for Him. What He did for them, He can do for you if you will commit to pray for your husband (wife). He will be with you to guide and help you every step of the way. God's will is to save, restore, and preserve your marriage, and if you seek Him for that, He will give you everything you need to do it.

Waiting for Your Miracle

You may not feel hopeless about your entire marriage, but perhaps just one aspect of it. Maybe your spouse has a habit that drives you crazy. Or maybe you have a problem your spouse has no patience with, and without his (her) support you feel you cannot overcome it. You may feel hopeless because you can't see how your situation can ever be any different. But take comfort in knowing that as long as you walk close to God, your sorrow will end. "Weeping may endure for a night, but joy comes in the morning" (Psalm 30:5). There are no guarantees that your spouse will change, but it is certain that *you* will. And if *you* do, it's a good possibility that *he (she)* will eventually too. Your trouble will be gone one way or another.

Because God is a God of miracles, He can bring back what has been lost or resurrect what has died. When you turn to God as your only hope for a miracle, you are in the best position to receive one. But you must come to the point where you give up—not on the marriage, but on trying to make a miracle happen yourself. Humble yourself before God like a child and tell Him you can't do this without Him (Matthew 18:4). Tell Him you have to come to the point where your hope is entirely in Him, and you trust that because of His great love for you, you will never be disappointed by the hope that is in you. The hope that is in you reflects your faith in God. And all things are possible to him who believes (Romans 5:5).

Hope in the Lord means that anything can happen because God is in charge, and He is the God of the impossible. He can turn anything around in an instant. You can be in despair one moment, and suddenly there can be a change of heart and you are headed in the direction of joy. The greatest thing you can do while waiting for your miracle is to let the joy of the Lord rise in your heart.

Hope allows you to keep making plans for your future. Hopelessness keeps you from seeing a future at all.

Jesus said, "By your patience possess your souls" (Luke 21:19). At first glance this verse seems as if you almost have to be passive and wait around for things to happen and someday maybe they will get under control. But Jack Hayford says, "In this verse, the Greek word for 'patience' *(hupomone)* means 'to bear up under pressure.' That is the call of the hour as the pressure of seducing spirits linked to the last days are loose and at work" (*The Anatomy of Seduction,* p. 45).

With this perspective and dimension of understanding, the word "patience" becomes very active. Being patient—or bearing up under pressure—is how we win. Sometimes victory comes simply because we are not giving up—even if we have to fight one battle after another. Too many people give up way too early. I could have given up in my marriage a long time before I started to see changes in my husband—and in me. But both of us have truly changed. And I believe these changes are lasting because God did a miracle in our lives. I feel Michael and I communicate far better, and he doesn't let anger control him as before. It took a lot of prayer, and bearing up under pressure (patience), but it happened. We made it, and we are in that last stage now where we know we will always be together, and whatever happens we will work it out. There is great peace in that.

That's why you can't view losing hope as the end of the world. It is actually a setup for God to do a miracle. We win by standing strong to the end. We say, "God, help me to be at peace where I am right now in the situation I am in, knowing You won't leave me there forever. Help me to say as Paul did that, " 'I have learned in whatever state I am, to be content' " (Philippians 4:11).

As long as you are walking with God, and you have not turned your back on the Holy Spirit, then you are going from glory to glory and strength to strength, whether it feels like it or not. "We all, with unveiled face, beholding as in a mirror the glory of the Lord, are being transformed into the same image from glory to glory, just as by the Spirit of the Lord" (2 Corinthians 3:18). You are becoming more like Him. So once you pray, believe that God has heard and move into the peace that He has for you while you bear up under pressure. It's not the kind of peace you can get from anything in the world, because there is no earthly reason for it (John 14:27).

TEN THINGS TO REMEMBER ABOUT GOD'S PEACE

1. ***Knowing God brings peace and strength.*** "The LORD will give strength to His people; the LORD will bless His people with peace" (Psalm 29:11).

2. ***Seeing that the Lord fights for you brings peace.*** "The LORD will fight for you, and you shall hold your peace" (Exodus 14:14).

3. ***Humility brings peace.*** "The meek shall inherit the earth, and shall delight themselves in the abundance of peace" (Psalm 37:11).

4. ***Obedience brings peace.*** "Oh, that you had heeded My commandments! Then your peace would have been like a river" (Isaiah 48:18).

5. ***Faith brings peace.*** "Your faith has saved you. Go in peace" (Luke 7:50).

6. ***Knowing Jesus brings us His peace.*** "Peace I leave with you, My peace I give to you; not as the world gives do I give to you. Let not your heart be troubled, neither let it be afraid" (John 14:27).

7. ***Life in the Spirit brings peace.*** "To be carnally minded is death, but to be spiritually minded is life and peace" (Romans 8:6).

8. ***Living God's way brings peace.*** "The work of righteousness will be peace, and the effect of righteousness, quietness and assurance forever" (Isaiah 32:17).

9. ***Loving God's laws brings peace and protection.*** "Great peace

> have those who love Your law, and nothing causes them to
> stumble" (Psalm 119:165).
>
> 10. ***Pursuing peace with others brings the peace of God.*** "Pursue
>   peace with all people, and holiness, without which no one will
>   see the Lord" (Hebrews 12:14).

If You Have Lost All Hope

Even if you or your husband (wife) has given up hope on the marriage, if just *one of you* wants your marriage transformed, and *God* wants your marriage transformed, that's two out of three. And that is a powerful enough majority to sway the last third of the equation. Pray that God will give you and your husband (wife) the ability to see the situation from the Lord's perspective. Pray that you both will be able to lift your eyes up to the hills where your help comes from (Psalm 121:1).

If you are truly wanting to see your marriage restored to wholeness or made to be all it is supposed to be, don't be around people who tell you you are crazy to even consider being together. (Unless, of course, you are in an abusive situation and they are trying to tell you something for your own good.) Pray that any pain, disappointment, or discouragement you or your spouse experience will drive you closer to God and not further away. Find people who are supportive of what you are trying to do and believe for in your marriage.

If you've been married long enough to experience more than a few trials, know that prayer to the almighty God of the universe, who invented marriage in the first place, unleashes His power to restore it. God says, "When you pass through the waters, I will be with you; and through the rivers, they shall not overflow you. When you walk through the fire, you shall not be burned, nor shall the flame scorch you. For I am the LORD your God, the Holy One of Israel, your Savior" (Isaiah 43:2-3).

Remember that hopelessness doesn't happen overnight, although things can happen suddenly that thrust you into a hopeless state. Hopelessness usually happens little by little, as each offense, each disappointment, each hurt builds up until discouragement sets in and covers those things like cement, solidifying the wall that has been built. Hopelessness usually happens when your prayers have not yet been answered and you don't believe they ever will be.

You may feel as though you and your marriage are in a free fall and only the hand of God can reach out and save you before you crash at the bottom, but your prayers can influence the hand of God at any moment. That's why you always have hope. When you have given up hope that *anything* will ever be any different, know that God's will is to change *everything* in your life. Know that you can reject hopelessness and put your hope in a miracle-working God.

When you put your hope in God, you will not be disappointed (Isaiah 49:23), good things will happen to you (Lamentations 3:25), you will please God (Psalm 147:11), you won't need to be sad (Psalm 42:11), and you will find rest (Psalm 62:5).

TEN GOOD REASONS TO NOT LOSE HOPE

1. ***You have hope because of Jesus.*** "Blessed be the God and Father of our Lord Jesus Christ, who according to His abundant mercy has begotten us again to a living hope through the resurrection of Jesus Christ from the dead" (1 Peter 1:3).

2. ***God's plan is to give you hope.*** " 'I know the thoughts that I think toward you,' says the LORD, 'thoughts of peace and not of evil, to give you a future and a hope' " (Jeremiah 29:11).

3. ***God's Word gives you hope.*** "For whatever things were written before were written for our learning, that we through the patience and comfort of the Scriptures might have hope" (Romans 15:4).

4. ***God is pleased when you put your hope in Him.*** "The Lord takes pleasure in those who fear Him, in those who hope in His mercy" (Psalm 147:11).

5. ***When you put your hope in God, He keeps His eye on you.*** "But the eyes of the LORD are on those who fear him, on those whose hope is in his unfailing love" (Psalm 33:18 NIV).

6. ***There is always hope for your future.*** "There is surely a future hope for you, and your hope will not be cut off" (Proverbs 23:18 NIV).

7. ***God fills you with hope as you put your trust in Him.*** "May the God of hope fill you with all joy and peace as you trust in him, so that you may overflow with hope by the power of the Holy Spirit" (Romans 15:13 NIV).

8. ***You always have hope that God will deliver you.*** "He has delivered us from such a deadly peril, and he will deliver us. On him we have set our hope that He will continue to deliver us" (2 Corinthians 1:10 NIV).

9. ***We have hope because God is faithful to keep His promise.*** "Let us hold fast the confession of our hope without wavering, for He who promised is faithful" (Hebrews 10:23).

10. ***True hope is when you don't give up, even when you see every reason to.*** "We were saved in this hope, but hope that is seen is not hope; for why does one still hope for what he sees?" (Romans 8:24).

The love and respect that is commanded in the Bible between husband and wife is not based on "if you feel like it" or "if your spouse deserves it." It's based on doing what God says to do because He has poured love into your heart. God loves us even when we do something wrong and disappoint Him. He loves us even when we forget to love Him back and neglect to spend time with Him. He says we are to love others even when they don't seem to love us. "If you love those who love you, what reward have you?" (Matthew 5:46). The reason we can love at all times is because of the unconditional love of God poured into our hearts.

That's why you have to keep loving your spouse, even when hope seems lost. Don't allow negative thoughts about yourself, your spouse, or your marriage to dominate your mind. Demand of your thoughts that they be positive and good. Cast down every argument that "exalts itself against the knowledge of God, bringing every thought into captivity to the obedience of Christ" (2 Corinthians 10:5). Require of yourself to be loving to others the way the Lord is toward you. Set your heart as Daniel did to understand the Lord and His ways, and humble yourself before Him. The angel said to Daniel, "Do not fear, Daniel, for from the first day that you set your heart to understand, and to humble yourself before your God, your words were heard; and I have come because of your words" (Daniel 10:12). When you do that, you can trust that your prayers are being heard. And because your hope is in the Lord, you will not be disappointed.

PRAYERS FOR MY MARRIAGE

Prayer for Protection

LORD, I COMMIT MY MARRIAGE to You. May it become all You want it to be. Even in times where we may suffer hurt or misunderstanding, I believe You are able to keep all I have committed to You (2 Timothy 1:12). I pray You would help my husband (wife) and me to never fall into hopelessness, especially with regard to our relationship and marriage. Help us to grow strong in faith—faith in You and in each other. Help us to put our hope in You, for You are our helper and protector (Psalm 33:20). May Your unfailing love and favor rest on us (Psalm 33:22). Enable us to inherit all You have for us because we have hope in our hearts (Psalm 37:9).

Lord, I pray we will always have patience to wait for You to work in our lives and our marriage. Thank You that because You were crucified and resurrected from the dead, we can have hope that You will resurrect anything in our lives no matter how dead and hopeless it may seem (1 Peter 1:3). Help us to not give up on each other, but rather to "let patience have its perfect work" in us so that we "may be perfect and complete, lacking nothing" (James 1:4). Help us to "lay aside every weight, and the sin which so easily ensnares us, and let us run with endurance the race that is set before us, looking unto Jesus, the author and finisher of our faith, who for the joy that was set before Him endured the cross" (Hebrews 12:1-2). Help us to keep our eyes on You. In Jesus' name I pray.

Prayer for Breakthrough in Me

LORD, I COME BEFORE YOU and cast all my cares at Your feet, knowing that You care for me (1 Peter 5:7). I thank You that Your plans for me are for a good future filled with peace and hope (Jeremiah 29:11). Help me to remember that no matter what is happening in my life and in my marriage, You will never leave me or forsake me.

Lord, I confess as sin any time I have felt hopeless about my situation and especially about important aspects of my marriage. Your Word says that "hope deferred makes the heart sick, but when desire comes, it is a tree of life" (Proverbs 13:12). When time passes for so long and I see no change, I feel heartsick and hopeless. But I confess any hopelessness I have to You, for You have said that whatever doesn't come from faith is sin (Romans 14:23). It reveals that my faith in Your power to change things is weak. I pray that You would help me to not hesitate to hope again out of fear that I will be disappointed. I commit to trusting in You at all times. I pour out my heart before You, knowing You are my God of refuge (Psalm 62:8).

Help me to become like a child—entirely dependent upon You, for I know that this is the safest place I can be. I pray that You would "search me, O God, and know my heart; try me, and know my anxieties; and see if there is any wicked way in me, and lead me in the way everlasting" (Psalm 139:23-24). Enable me to become all I need to be. In the midst of challenges in my marriage I say, "Be merciful to me, O God, be merciful to me! For my soul trusts in You; and in the shadow of Your wings I will make my refuge, until these calamities have passed by" (Psalm 57:1).

Even though we may suffer at times in this marriage because of things one of us has done or not done, I know that You are "able to do exceedingly abundantly above all that we ask or think, according to the power that works in us" (Ephesians 3:20-21). I will be strong and take heart because my hope is in You (Psalm 31:24). Thank You that You put my tears in Your bottle (Psalm 56:8). I pray that You, Holy Spirit, would give me "beauty for ashes, the oil of joy for mourning, and the garment of praise for the spirit of heaviness" (Isaiah 61:1-3). Make me to be a pillar of righteousness for Your glory. Help me to not cease my "work of faith, labor of love, and patience of hope in our Lord Jesus Christ" for I know You can change everything in my life (1 Thessalonians 1:3). In Jesus' name I pray.

Prayer for Breakthrough in My Husband (Wife)

Lord, I commit my husband (wife) into Your hands. I pray that any hopelessness he (she) has felt about himself (herself) will be taken out of his (her) heart. Make him (her) all You created him (her) to be. Break down any strongholds in his (her) mind where hopelessness has been allowed to reign. Help him (her) to put his (her) hope in You and understand that it is not by our might or power, but by Your Spirit that our relationship can be transformed to become all it was made to be. Take away any hopelessness he (she) feels about me, our marriage, and our life together. Thank You that You are the God of hope, and You are "the same yesterday, today, and forever" (Hebrews 13:8).

Holy Spirit, help my husband (wife) to understand that because of You our situation is never hopeless (John 14:26). Even though we may have difficulties, we are not crushed because You sustain us. We don't have to live with despair because our hope is in You. "We are hard pressed on every side, yet not crushed; we are perplexed, but not in despair" (2 Corinthians 4:8). I pray that the eyes of his (her) understanding will be opened so that he (she) may know the hope of Your calling on his (her) life, and come to understand "what is the exceeding greatness" of Your power toward those who believe (Ephesians 1:18-19). Give him (her) unfailing hope and faith in You. In Jesus' name I pray.

Truth to Stand On

Those who wait on the Lord shall renew their strength;
they shall mount up with wings like eagles,
they shall run and not be weary,
they shall walk and not faint.

Isaiah 40:31

For everyone who asks receives, and he who seeks finds,
and to him who knocks it will be opened.

Matthew 7:8

The righteous cry out, and the Lord hears,
and delivers them out of all their troubles.

Psalm 34:17 niv

O Israel, put your hope in the Lord,
for with the Lord is unfailing love and
with him is full redemption.

Psalm 130:7 niv

Being confident of this very thing,
that He who has begun a good work in you
will complete it until the day of Jesus Christ.

Philippians 1:6

PLAN *to* BE *a*
SUCCESS STORY

———⟨∞⟩———

Just last week I heard of another couple close to us who are getting a divorce. They are Christian parents of two and are well known in our community. They always seemed like the perfect family, so talented and funny. Everyone loves them. Their family is being *ripped apart* now, and all the people around them are *deeply saddened.*

Today I talked with a single mom who was married for 25 years but has been divorced for five, and she is still hurting over the divorce. She works very hard to support herself and her two children, and she always struggles with guilt over the time she has to be away from them in order to do that. Her entire extended family has been *negatively impacted* by this.

Recently a well-respected pastor divorced his wife because she resumed an unholy relationship with an old boyfriend. There had been tremendous loneliness in their marriage for some time. The congregation and the community are *shaken*, as well as their children.

Days ago a wonderful young couple severed their relationship completely because of a terrible misunderstanding on both their parts. Their families are *devastated and grieved,* and the *fallout* seems to be without end.

I know all of these fine people personally, and it breaks my heart to see their *sadness and pain*—especially when I know that it all could have been avoided because God has a better way. I don't judge them. I know how hard it is to make a marriage work. But I also know that it is worth every effort to rise above the problems and hurt and see that your marriage not only survives, but becomes good and solid. That's what happened in my marriage, and it was worth the years it took of praying and learning to live God's way, even in the face of hopelessness. It was worth having my heart reconstructed by God until repentance, forgiveness, and love flowed through it every day no matter what. This is something God did because I was willing to do what it takes. That's why my prayer for you is that you too will find the strength, faith, and courage to do whatever it takes to see your marriage become one of the success stories. And I will be pulling for you all the way.

Michael & Stormie

have been married for more than three decades
and have three grown children.

OTHER BOOKS
BY STORMIE OMARTIAN

THE POWER OF A PRAYING® WOMAN
Stormie Omartian's bestselling books have helped hundreds of thousands of individuals pray more effectively for their spouses, their children, and their nation. Now she has written a book on a subject she knows intimately: being a praying woman. Stormie's deep knowledge of Scripture and candid examples from her own prayer life provide guidance for women who seek to trust God with deep longings and cover every area of life with prayer.

THE POWER OF A PRAYING® WIFE
Stormie shares how wives can develop a deeper relationship with their husbands by praying for them. With this practical advice on praying for specific areas, including decision making, fears, spiritual strength, and sexuality, women will discover the fulfilling marriage God intended.

THE POWER OF A PRAYING® HUSBAND
Building on the success of *The Power of a Praying® Wife,* Stormie offers this guide to help husbands pray more effectively for their wives. Each chapter features comments from well-known Christian men, biblical wisdom, and prayer ideas.

THE POWER OF A PRAYING® PARENT
This powerful book for parents offers 30 easy-to-read chapters that focus on specific areas of prayers for children. This personal, practical guide leads the way to enriched, strong prayer lives for both moms and dads.

THE POWER OF A PRAYING WOMAN® BIBLE
This devotional study Bible with NIV text contains brief introductions for each book of the Bible, inspiring and informative articles and sidebars, and all-new prayers Stormie uses to apply verses to her prayer life.

JUST ENOUGH LIGHT FOR THE STEP I'M ON
New Christians and those experiencing life changes or difficult times will appreciate Stormie's honesty, candor, and advice based on experience and the Word of God in this collection of devotional readings perfect for the pressures of today's world.